Praise for *Recovering the Sacred*

2005 Gustavus Myers Book Award Honorable Mention

Written in an accessible style, *Recovering the Sacred* documents the remarkable stories of indigenous communities whose tenacity and resilience has enabled them to reclaim their lands, resources, and life ways after enduring centuries of incalculable loss.
—Wilma Mankiller, author, *Every Day is a Good Day*

Thoughtful, tough, impressively informed, *Recovering the Sacred* tells a profound story. To survive, we need to listen.
—Louise Erdrich, author, *Love Medicine*

A fascinating read that puts Native American communities' struggles for justice into historical and environmental context. Winona's fierce dedication to the indigenous environmental and women's movements infuses her analysis with a first-person understanding—deep and powerful on many levels.
—Bonnie Raitt, musician/activist

Recovering the Sacred is a brilliant study of cases dealing with rights to land, resources, culture, religion, and genetic information. LaDuke offers a much-needed challenge to the existing ethical constructs that govern these rights claims. This book will be a valuable resource for attorneys, scholars, and community members alike.
—Rebecca Tsosie, author, *American Indian Law: Native Nations and the Federal System*

With precision and eloquence, LaDuke makes clear not only that the theft of all things indigenous continues to this day but that resistance to this theft is becoming ever stronger. She makes equally clear that if we are to survive we must stop stealing from and begin listening to those whose land we have stolen, whose land we live on.
—Derrick Jensen, author, *A Language Older than Words*

A river of tears fell down my cheeks as I read *Recovering the Sacred*. This is a must read for anyone who wants to know the truth about Federal Indian Policy, past and present.

— Charon Asetoyer, editor, *Indigenous Women's Health Book: Within the Sacred Circle*

Fierce in her convictions, forceful in her analysis, and engaging in her writing, LaDuke connects the dots between indigenous struggles, the toxic and sacrilegious practices of multinational corporations, and the wellness of all of us who must share our fragile planet.

—Robert Warrior, author, *The People and the Word: Reading Native Nonfiction*

In this powerful book, LaDuke explores issues that go way beyond the desecration of the environment and into the heart of insidious crimes against the very DNA of Native peoples.

—Amy Ray, musician/activist

LaDuke skillfully demonstrates why the protection of Native spiritual practices is critical to social justice struggles and to the survival of the planet. She weaves together a broad range of issues that all point to the impact of European cultural and spiritual genocide on indigenous peoples. LaDuke demonstrates again why she is one of the leading Native thinkers and activists today.

—Andrea Smith, author, *Conquest: Sexual Violence and American Indian Genocide*

Through the voices of ordinary Native Americans, writer and full-time activist Winona LaDuke is able to transform highly complex issues into stories that touch the heart.

—Roxanne Dunbar-Ortiz, author, *Outlaw Woman*

Winona LaDuke's "activist scholarship" captures the essence of politicized spirituality that [combines] "ecological integrity" with our cultural identity for "spiritual health." It is books such as this one that will insure the passing of history and knowledge from one generation to the next.

—M.A. Jaimes Guerrero, editor, *The State of Native America*

Recovering the Sacred

The Power of Naming and Claiming

Winona LaDuke

Haymarket Books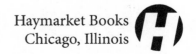
Chicago, Illinois

© 2005 Winona LaDuke
First published 1999 by South End Press, Cambridge, Massachusetts.

Cover art, "Earth Hunters," (detail) by Rabbett Strickland, reproduced courtesy of the artist.

This edition published in 2016 by
Haymarket Books
P.O. Box 180165
Chicago, IL 60618
773-583-7884
www.haymarketbooks.org
info@haymarketbooks.org

ISBN: 978-1-60846-627-6

Distributed to the trade in the US through Consortium Book Sales and Distribution (www.cbsd.com) and internationally through Ingram Publisher Services International (www.ingramcontent.com).

This book was published with the generous support of Lannan Foundation and Wallace Action Fund.

Special discounts are available for bulk purchases by organizations and institutions. Please call 773-583-7884 or email info@haymarketbooks.org for more information.

Printed in the United States.

Library of Congress Cataloging-in-Publication data is available.

Entered into digital printing January 2020.

Contents

Acknowledgements

It is a great privilege for me to write, to try and tell these stories, retelling dreams of this recovering. In the writing of this book, I have been supported, loved, and nurtured by many. First and foremost, my family—Waseyabin, Ashleigh, Jon, Ajuawak, Gwekaanimad, Faye and Sasha Brown, Leslie Walking Elk, John Livingstone, Bob Shimek, Audrey Thayer, Lori Pourier, Sheyhela, Chris Eyre, Jason Westigard, Justin Dimmel, and my loving parents, Betty LaDuke and Peter Westigard, who along with my grandmother, Helen Bernstein, have loved me and supported me through trying times, heated discussions, and endless cups of coffee.

I have immense gratitude and respect for my colleagues at White Earth Land Recovery Project and Honor the Earth – Ron and Diane Chilton, who make all things possible; Margaret Smith, whose leadership and example I can only hope to follow in a *gitimaagis* way; Joe LaGarde, Paul Schultz, Sarah Alexander, Donna Cahill, Becky Niemi, Pat Wichern, Janice Chilton, and all our staff who hold our life, organizations, and the work of a community and all its pieces together. I also would like to express my immense gratitude to Natalie Marker, Becky Bodonyi, Marissa Woltman, Flora Brown, Okaadaak (Carolyn Fuqua), and Margaret Olmos, who searched through the depths of footnote hell for the footnote spirits. These women make our work at Honor real (along with an amazing board and Emily Saliers and Amy Ray, who have been the greatest of friends and allies in my life).

Also this would not be possible without Loie Hayes who waited patiently through a Vice-Presidential run, changing diapers, wild rice processing, injured horses, wind turbines, Honor the Earth concert tours, litigation, and lobbying to get text and notes. Finally, above all, *chi-miigwech* to all those who allowed me to write their stories and dreams in this book.

Dedication

Mii sa
Gi-mishoomisinaabaniig
gaye
Ayaanike bimaadizijig

This America
has been a burden
of steel and mad
death,
but, look now,
there are flowers
and new grass
and a spring wind
rising
from Sand Creek.

—Simon Ortiz, *from Sand Creek*

What is Sacred?

How does a community heal itself from the ravages of the past? That is the question I asked in writing this book. I found an answer in the multifaceted process of recovering that which is "sacred." This complex and intergenerational process is essential to our vitality as Indigenous peoples and ultimately as individuals. This book documents some of our community's work to recover the sacred and to heal.

What qualifies something as sacred? That is a question asked in courtrooms and city council meetings across the country. Under consideration is the preservation or destruction of places like the Valley of the Chiefs in what is now eastern Montana and Medicine Lake in northern California, as well as the fate of skeletons and other artifacts mummified by collectors and held in museums against the will of their rightful inheritors. Debates on how the past is understood and what the future might bring have bearing on genetic research, reclamation of mining sites, reparations for broken treaties, and reconciliation between descendants of murderers and their victims. At stake is nothing less than the ecological integrity of the land base and the physical and social health of Native Americans throughout the continent. In the end there is no absence of irony: the integrity of what is sacred to Native Americans will be determined by the government that has been responsible for doing everything in its power to destroy Native American cultures.

Xenophobia and a deep fear of Native spiritual practices came to the Americas with the first Europeans. Papal law was the foundation of colonialism; the Church served as handmaiden to military, economic, and spiritual genocide and domination. Centuries of papal bulls posited the supremacy of Christendom over all other beliefs, sanctified manifest destiny, and authorized even the most brutal practices of colonialism. Some of the most virulent and disgraceful manifestations of Christian dominance found expression in the conquest and colonization of the Americas.

Religious dominance became the centerpiece of early reservation policy as Native religious expression was outlawed in this country. To practice a traditional form of worship was to risk a death sentence for many peoples. The Wounded Knee Massacre of 1890 occurred in large part because of the fear of the Ghost Dance Religion, which had spread throughout the American West. Hundreds of Native spiritual leaders were sent to the Hiawatha Asylum for Insane Indians for their spiritual beliefs.[1]

The history of religious colonialism, including the genocide perpetrated by the Catholic Church (particularly in Latin America), is a wound from which Native communities have not yet healed. The notion that non-Christian spiritual practices could have validity was entirely ignored or actively suppressed for centuries. So it was by necessity that Native spiritual practitioners went deep into the woods or into the heartland of their territory to keep up their traditions, always knowing that their job was to keep alive their teachers' instructions, and, hence, their way of life.

Native spiritual practices and Judeo-Christian traditions are based on very different paradigms. Native American rituals are frequently based on the reaffirmation of the relationship of humans to the Creation. Many of our oral traditions tell of the place of the "little brother" (the humans) in the larger Creation. Our gratitude for our part in Creation and for the gifts given to us by the Creator is continuously reinforced in Midewiwin lodges, Sundance ceremonies, world renewal ceremonies, and many others. Understanding the complexity of these belief systems is central to understanding the societies built on those spiritual foundations—the relationship of peoples to their sacred lands, to relatives with fins or hooves, to the plant and animal foods that anchor a way of life.[2]

Chris Peters, a Pohik-la from northern California and president of the Seventh Generation Fund, broadly defines Native spiritual practices as affirmation-based and characterizes Judeo-Christian faiths as commemorative.[3] Judeo-Christian teachings and events frequently commemorate a set of historical events: Easter, Christmas, Passover, and Hannukah are examples. Vine Deloria, Jr., echoes this distinction:

> Unlike the Mass or the Passover which both commemorate past historical religious events and which believers understand as also occurring in a timeless setting beyond the reach of the corruption of temporal processes, Native American religious practitioners are seeking to introduce a sense of order into the chaotic physical present as a prelude to experiencing the universal moment of complete fulfillment.[4]

The difference in the paradigms of these spiritual practices has, over time, become a source of great conflict in the Americas. Some 200 years after the U. S. Constitution guaranteed freedom of religion for most Americans, Congress passed the American Indian Religious Freedom Act in 1978 and President Carter signed it into law. Although the act contains worthy language that seems to reflect the founders' concepts of religious liberty, it has but a few teeth. The act states:

> It shall be the policy of the United States to protect and preserve for American Indians their inherent right of freedom to believe, express, and exercise the traditional religions of the American Indian, Eskimo, Aleut and native Hawaiians, including but not limited to access to sites, use and possession of sacred objects, and the freedom to worship through ceremonial and traditional rites.[5]

While the law ensured that Native people could hold many of their ceremonies, it did not protect the places where many of these rituals take place or the relatives and elements central to these ceremonies, such as salt from the sacred Salt Mother for the Zuni or salmon for the Nez Perce. The Religious Freedom Act was amplified by President Clinton's 1996 Executive Order 13007, for preservation of sacred sites: "In managing Federal lands, each executive branch agency with statutory or administrative responsibility for the management of Federal lands shall...avoid adversely affecting the physical integrity of such sacred sites."[6]

Those protections were applied to lands held by the federal government, not by private interests, although many sacred sites advocates have urged compliance by other landholders to the spirit and intent of the law. The Bush administration, however, has by and large ignored that executive order.[7] Today, increasing numbers of sacred sites and all that embodies the sacred are threatened.

While Judeo-Christian sacred sites such as "the Holy Land" are recognized, the existence of other holy lands has been denied. There is a place on the shore of Lake Superior, or Gichi Gummi, where the Giant laid down to sleep. There is a place in Zuni's alpine prairie to which the Salt Woman moved and hoped to rest. There is a place in the heart of Lakota territory where the people go to vision quest and remember the children who ascended from there to the sky to become the Pleiades. There is a place known as the Falls of a Woman's Hair that is the epicenter of a salmon culture. And there is a mountain upon which the Anishinaabeg rested during their migration and from where they looked back to find their prophesized destination. The concept of "holy land" cannot be exclusive in a multi-cultural and multi-spiritual society, yet indeed it has been treated as such.

We have a problem of two separate spiritual paradigms and one dominant culture—make that a dominant culture with an immense appetite for natural resources. The animals, the trees and other plants, even the minerals under the ground and the water from the lakes and streams, all have been expropriated from Native American territories. Land taken from Native peoples either by force or the colonists' law was the basis for an industrial infrastructure and now a standard of living that consumes a third of the world's resources.

By the 1930s, Native territories had been reduced to about 4% of our original land base. More than 75% of our sacred sites have been removed from our care and jurisdiction.[8] Native people must now request permission to use their own sacred sites and, more often than not, find that those sites are in danger of being desecrated or obliterated.

The challenge of attempting to maintain your spiritual practice in a new millennium is complicated by the destruction of that which you need for your ceremonial practice. The annihilation of 50 million buffalo in the Great Plains region by the beginning of the 20th century caused immense hardship for traditional spiritual practices of the region, especially since the *Pte Oyate*, the buffalo nation, is considered the older brother of the Lakota nation and of many other Indigenous cultures of the region. Similarly, the decimation of the salmon in northwest rivers like the Columbia and the Klamath, caused by dam projects, over-fishing, and water diversion, has resulted in great emotional, social, and spiritual devastation to the Yakama, Wasco, Umatilla, Nez Perce, and other peoples of the region. New efforts to domesticate, patent, and genetically modify wild rice similarly concern the Anishinaabeg people of the Great Lakes.

It is more than 500 years since the European invasion of North America and more than 200 years since the formation of the United States. Despite these centuries of spiritual challenges, Native people continue, as we have for centuries, to always express our thankfulness to Creation—in our prayers, our songs, and our understanding of the sacredness of the land.

Dr. Henrietta Mann is a Northern Cheyenne woman and chair of the Native American Studies Department at Montana State University. She reiterates the significance of the natural world to Native spiritual teaching:

> Over the time we have been here, we have built cultural ways on and about this land. We have our own respected versions of how we came to be. These origin stories—that we emerged or fell from the sky or were brought forth—connect us to this land and establish our realities, our belief systems. We have spiritual responsibilities to renew the Earth and we do this through our ceremonies so that our Mother, the Earth, can continue to support us. Mutuality and respect are part of our tradition—give and take. Somewhere along the way, I hope people will learn that you can't just take, that you have to give back to the land.[9]

Part I

Sacred Lands and Sacred Places

Traditional *lele* (a shrine at which offerings are made) on the highest point of
the mountain volcano, Mauna Kea, Hawaii, with a few of the 13 observato-
ries in the background.
(Photo from *Mauna Kea—Temple Under Siege* by Na Maka o ka "Aina;
www.namaka.com.

God, Squirrels, and the Universe

The Mt. Graham International Observatory and the University of Arizona

They stole our Mountain from us and now they want to take away our spiritual way of life....

—Ola Cassadore Davis, Apache Survival Coalition[1]

At dawn, the young Apache women begin to dance in the Sunrise Ceremonial, a series of rites that is months in preparation and that takes many days and much love to actualize. The Sunrise Ceremonial is a gift to a young girl from her family, recognizing her passage into womanhood. This ceremony, like many other aspects of Apache life, connects young women, and indeed a people, to an ancient history. In a new millennium filled with Dodge trucks, iPods, computers, and hip-hop, that history is still alive and in the making. Apache culture is always changing, but essential elements—language, spiritual practice, food, ceremony—all remain, as does the mountain *Dzil nchaa si an,* to which much of Apache life is connected. Not unlike the challenge of becoming a woman, this and other Apache ceremonies are faced with the crushing jackhammer of industrial society and a project that strikes at the center of the Apache world.

When he wanted to pray for his daughter's impending womanhood ceremony, Wendsler Nosie, an Apache man, traveled from his home on the San Carlos Reservation to *Dzil nchaa si an,* or Mt. Graham. It was 1998, and his prayers would take him across land now claimed by the University of Arizona's Astronomy Department. On the mountain, Wendsler Nosie was arrested for trespassing, an unsavory incident that prompted the University of Arizona to develop a permit system. Under the policy, "American Indian requests for religious use of the telescope site must be submitted in writing at least two business days before the planned visit. The request should include specific description of the area to be visited, and should be submitted by enrolled members of federally recognized tribes."[2] A permit to pray.

Religious freedom is a fundamental part of the U.S. Bill of Rights, and one would think, especially with the passage of the American Indian Religious Freedom Act, that religious freedom would be protected for Native people. That is so, as long as your religious practice does not involve access to a sacred site coveted by others or if your religious practice does not involve the use of natural resources made scarce by the profit motive. This act amounts to no guarantee of freedom of religion for Native people, and the discussion of Native spiritual practice in the new millennium inevitably turns toward conflicts of worldviews, and the relativity of political and economic power in our society.

In this case, it is the question of a set of telescopes: a project called the Mt. Graham International Observatory, situated in the center of the Apache universe. At the center of the controversy are three distinct worldviews: those of the Catholic Church, the scientific community, and the Apache people. Lining up on the different sides are various interests: millions of dollars, hundreds of public interest groups and Native communities, and the voice of the Vatican. In short, it's not pretty.

Despite more than a decade of opposition by the Apaches and 30 or more national and international environmental groups, Congress approved three telescopes, with four additional ones contingent upon completion of full environmental and cultural studies relevant to National Forest land. Environmentalists, including the Arizona Fish and Game Commission and pretty much every group from Greenpeace to the Humane Society, have opposed the telescopes.

Two telescopes have been built already on Mt. Graham, one by the Vatican, and the second by the Germany-based Max Planck Institute. The push behind the projects, however, comes from a third set of white men: those at the University of Arizona's Department of Astronomy. Each subsequent telescope proposal has been increasingly controversial. It is the University of Arizona's proposed Columbus Scope that most threatens Mt. Graham.

The Columbus Scope is a Large Binocular Telescope (LBT). The LBT is expected to be the world's third most powerful telescope, behind Mauna Kea and Chile, and the largest telescope on a single mount. The University of Arizona has cultivated a consortium of investors to share the projected expense of more than $100 million. In the words of a local newspaper, the project has turned the University of Arizona into a "star-whore."[3]

The proposed host of the project, Mt. Graham, rises 10,700 feet up from the Sonoran Desert, home to clouds at the top, 18 perennial streams, and hot springs at its base. It is an oasis in the midst of a desert. It is also one of the state's largest mountains, a part of the Pinaleño Range. As a consequence of both its location and height, Mt. Graham possesses more life zones and vegetative communities than any other solitary mountain in North America. Within those vegetative zones live small and unusual animals and plants that are not found anywhere else in the world. They have evolved there since Pleistocene times and the glacial recession, cached away in the solitary and pristine refuge that has been Mt. Graham—until now. One of those critters, the Mount Graham Red Squirrel, has been the most threatened by the project and should have been protected under the Endangered Species Act, since there are fewer than 300 of them in the world. The Columbus project, added to the two existing telescopes, would destroy some 25% of a unique 472-acre virgin spruce fir forest.

Mt. Graham is also central to Apache religion. "Mt. Graham is the chief, the most important sacred mountain," explains Franklin Stanley, Sr., San Carlos Apache spiritual leader. "The Mountain is home of the Mountain spirit and other sacred beings which gave creation, guidance, strength, knowledge and direction to the Apache people by way of *Dzil nchaa si an*. He comes to teach the Apache men and women to sing special spiritual words that help them to acquire the power to become medicine men and women." In addition to this, many of the herbs and waters essential for Apache ceremonies come from *Dzil nchaa si an*. "This is our religion, these are our traditions. The Apache relationship with the mountain includes showing respect to the things we have discovered in revelations, or that the mountain has given to us. We Apache must retain Mt. Graham as a sacred mountain in order to follow our religion," Stanley explains.[4]

The Apache and the Wars

> I want a good, strong, and lasting peace. When God made the world, he gave one part to the white man and another to the Apache. What was it? Why did they come together? Now that I am to speak, the sun, the moon, the earth, the air, the waters, the birds and beasts, even the children unborn shall rejoice at my words....
> When I was young I walked all over this country, east and west, and saw no other people than the Apaches. After many summers I walked again and found another race of people had come to take it. How is it? Why is it that the Apaches wait to die—that they carry their lives on their fingernails? They roam over the hills and plains and want the heavens to fall on them. The Apaches were once a great nation; they are now but few, and because of this they want to die and so carry their lives on their fingernails. Many have been killed in battle. You must speak straight so that your words may go as sunlight to our heart. Tell me, if the Virgin Mary has walked throughout all of the land, why has she never entered the wickiups of the Apaches?
> Why have we never seen or heard her?
>
> —Cochise[5]

Mt. Graham is the heart of the Apache homeland. Although the Apache traversed the entire region spanning northern Mexico and the states of Arizona and New Mexico, their farmlands, crops, and harvesting sites were often in areas near the mountain, where the ecosystem would support their agricultural life and where the water drainage supported an immense diversity of plant and animal life. It is this same land they had to defend, first from their neighbors, and then from the encroaching Spaniards and Americans.

In the 1540s, Coronado was the first European to pass through the region looking for his City of Gold. There was no such city, but there were, as we now know, plenty of other riches to exploit. So it was that the Spaniards moved in from the South, establishing a reign that brought with it the Catholic Church, the friars, slavery, and horses, the last of which proved to be of most interest to the Apaches.[6]

The Spaniards' tenure was spotty. Spain had many lands to capture and Indigenous resistance kept its northern colonial frontier unstable. The Apaches were renowned guerilla fighters and, with their superior knowledge of the terrain, they outflanked the Spaniards on many occasions. It was the Pueblo Revolt of 1680, however, led by Pope, a leader of San Juan Pueblo, that would send the Spaniards retreating to the south. Four hundred soldiers were killed, and 2,500 settlers were sent packing. Unfortunately for the Apache and other southwestern tribes, the Spaniards would return with more priests and more soldiers, and the Americans would follow them. By 1848, the Treaty of Guadalupe Hidalgo secured American access to Apache territory, and the California gold rush the following year cemented a need for safe passage across the land.

With the economic interest came the return of the military, and with that came more Apache resistance. An incident with a rancher by the name of John Ward in 1861 provided the spark for 35 years of Apache wars. Ward wrongly suspected Chiricahua Apache chief Cochise of kidnapping his children and stealing his cattle. When Ward reported his allegation to the army garrison at Fort Buchanan, about 40 miles south of Tucson, Lieutenant Bascom took a force of 54 men into the heart of Chiricahua territory at Apache Pass. Cochise spoke with Bascom, claimed his innocence, and even offered to aid the rancher in recovering the children. Bascom informed the chief he was to be arrested, and when Cochise escaped, Bascom took the remaining Apaches as hostages. Negotiation attempts failed, and killings escalated on both sides.

On one side, the great Apache chiefs Cochise, Eskiminzin (Aravaipa or Western Apache), Nachise, Delshay (Tonto Apache), and others lined up; on the other, the Americans brought in the renowned Indian fighters Kit Carson and the generals Carlton, Howard, and Crook, all fresh from other Indian wars to the north. Local citizens joined the fight. Such was the story of the so-called Camp Grant massacre of mostly Aravaipa Apaches:

> Citizens of Tucson, who feared and hated all Apaches, whether peaceful or not, organized a vigilante force of close to 150 Anglos, Mexicans and Papago Indian mercenaries. On the morning of April 30, 1871, they moved on the Aravaipas and, sweeping through the sleeping camp, massacred from 86 to 150 of the innocents, mostly women and children. Of the survivors, women were raped and children carried to slavery.[7]

The brutality was immense. Many of those massacred were killed almost as sport: raped first and then mutilated, their heads bashed in and their limbs hacked off. The bodies were all stripped. Although President Ulysses Grant had devised his post–Civil War Peace Policy to avoid such massacres and sent a peace commissioner to Arizona, justice was never rendered. The five-day trial ended with a 19-minute jury deliberation and the release of the Tucson killers.[8] It was this massacre that sparked interest from Washington in securing reservations for the Apaches. By 1873, 6,000 Apaches and other tribes were enrolled on reservations in Arizona and New Mexico.

Reservation life was tenuous at best. The Apache, like other Native people, saw their best lands taken by encroachers and their people sink into a deep poverty. While Mt. Graham was included initially in the San Carlos Reservation, the reservation area was soon reduced. The Apache were squeezed into arid barrens and jurisdiction over the mountain transferred from the tribe to the U.S. Forest Service.[9] It was not long before the Apache began to resist. On the San Carlos Reservation two leaders became prominent: Geronimo, who had fought with Cochise, and Victorio, who came from the Mimbreño Apaches and had been reared under the leadership of Mangas Coloradas. From 1881 to 1886, these two launched reservation rebellions and prison breakouts. In what would become one of the most pitched battles in the history of the Indian Wars, these Apaches took on a succession of generals, ending with General Nelson Miles. At one point, Miles took 5,000 soldiers into Mexico to track down 24 Apaches.

It was on September 4, 1886, at Skeleton Canyon, just 65 miles south of Apache Pass, that a weary Geronimo and his followers finally gave themselves up. Geronimo and 50 other Apaches were sent in shackles to Fort Pickens in Pensacola, Florida. A year later they were moved to Alabama. Some of the Eskiminzin's Aravaipas were finally allowed to return to San Carlos, but the fine citizens of Arizona refused to allow Geronimo and the Chiricahua Apaches to return to their homeland. In 1894, the Apaches were finally sent to Fort Sill, Oklahoma, where Geronimo died a prisoner of war in 1909.[10]

Raising Arizona

A century after Geronimo and his followers gave themselves up to the military at Skeleton Canyon—a long time in the history of a state born so recently, but a short time in the lifespan of the Apache people—the expanding settler community turned a deaf ear and blind eye to the sacredness of Mt. Graham. The University of Arizona hoped to use the mountain to showcase its cutting-edge Mirror Laboratory, a centerpiece of both military and telescope technologies. The proposed Mt. Graham International Observatory with its tens of millions of dollars in mirror contract orders would mean more money for the university and jobs to boost the local economy.[11]

It's not that the University of Arizona was unaware of Apache interests in the area. Both the published and unpublished works of the foremost ethnographer of the Western Apache, Grenville Goodwin, were housed in its own collections. Despite this, explains anthropologist Elizabeth Brandt, telescope investors hired "an expert—who had never worked with the Apache and who never spoke to a living Apache—to downplay the evidence," which included religious paraphernalia and shrines documented by Goodwin, and oral histories from Apache elders conducted in the early 1930s. "The elders mentioned that Mt. Graham was sacred, and they recounted military engagements and other activities taking place there.... Telescope proponents have been biased toward the 'built' environment, wanting to see extensive ruins, a temple or a church, or perhaps a burning bush as evidence of 'sacredness,'" according to Brandt. Noting that Apache traditions favored less impact on the physical environment rather than more, Brandt points out, "It is worth recalling, also, that Apaches have had to spend much of the last three centuries hiding from people who wanted to kill them."[12]

The traditional spiritual leaders of the Apache have repeatedly spoken out, supported by four separate tribal council resolutions from the San Carlos Tribal Council. Those have been buttressed by resolutions from most major Native organizations, including the National Congress of American Indians and the International Indian Treaty Council. The Native position has been pretty clear on this. This opposition has been key in the loss of over two dozen potential academic and financial partners of the University of Arizona. Past partners have included the Smithsonian Institute, Harvard, Michigan State, and the University of Pittsburgh. To their credit, these and other partners have abandoned the Mt. Graham development and publicly criticized the proposal.

"Basically the University [of Arizona] is a pariah," explains Peter Warshall, a Fulbright scholar who also happens to be the University of Arizona biologist who conducted the 1985 environmental impact study of the project on Mt. Graham. "It has done everything possible to avoid the law, rather than following it. There is no controversy to that. Rather than...trying to embrace the law, they have, you might say, taken the low road."[13]

Over the years, the university has spent well over a million dollars lobbying to secure the first peacetime exemption from all U.S. cultural, religious, and environmental protection laws, including the Endangered Species Act, the National Historic Preservation Act, the National Forest Management Act, the National Environmental Policy Act, and the American Indian Religious Freedom Act. The university, with then-partner the Smithsonian Institute, was able to secure an exclusion of 3,500 acres of the summit of Mt. Graham from a congressional wilderness designation. In short, it illustrated the might that goes with money and found, not surprisingly, that few adversaries could muster the same amount of resources.

The university's aspirations are not modest. Starting in the late 1970s, university leaders have worked to "expand the U of A into one of the top research institutions in America. [Then university president John Schaefer's] sales pitch to legislators and Arizonans: Together they would build 'The Harvard of the West.' "[14]

The University of Arizona had some powerful allies on its side, including Senators John McCain and Dennis DeConcini.[15] The governments of Germany and Italy, and, most significantly, the Vatican have also supported the university. It was the pope himself who wanted the first telescope built on Mt. Graham, the Vatican Advanced Technology Telescope (VATT). Why, one might wonder, would the Vatican want a telescope?

One could say that the Church has been grappling with the universe ever since it had to "eat crow" on that little problem with Galileo. Coming to terms with the fact that the Earth revolved around the sun, and not the other way around, was a pretty difficult cross to bear. Ever since 1891, the Vatican has tried to demonstrate that the Church was neither "the friend of obscurantism,...[nor] the enemy of science and progress," in the words of Pope Leo XIII.[16] The Church built several telescopes in and near Rome and sponsored its own collection of astronomers, but in 1980 the light pollution from urbanizing Rome forced the Vatican to find a new place for its viewing of the universe.[17] Casting its eyes abroad, it found Mt. Graham in southern Arizona. One wonders what would happen if the VATT discovers new planets orbiting other stars and maybe some intelligent life elsewhere? In the opinion of Vatican astronomer George Coyne, "Should intelligent life be found, the church would be obliged to address the question of whether extraterrestrials might be brought within the fold and baptized."[18]

You've got to give the Church credit for tenacity in the face of resistance. With only some success in its missionizing of Apaches during the past 400 years, the Church has remained insistent, in some ways, on shoving Christianity down Apache throats. From the Apache perspective, the telescope, seeing God through the eyes of the Catholic Church and the mirrors, is a continuation of colonization. Or in the words of Brad Allison, one Apache traditionalist, "This is where we pray. This is where our ancestors are. It's like looking into the womb of a woman. We don't do that. Why don't you go somewhere else and do it? This is our home."[19]

In Search of the Authentic Apaches

> We are not convinced by any of the arguments thus far presented that Mt. Graham possesses a sacred character which precludes responsible and legitimate use of the land.... In fact, we believe that responsible and legitimate use of the land enhances its sacred character.... The Vatican Observatory would like to learn about any such genuine concerns of authentic Apaches.... Since no credible argument has been presented, the Vatican will continue with the construction and operation of the advanced Technology Telescope on Mt. Graham.
>
> —George Coyne, Vatican Observatory[20]

Ah, the problem of finding "authentic" Indians. Not that anyone looked very hard. No formal attempts were made to meet with the Apache until four years after the project had been proposed.[21] Only years after VATT was built did the Vatican directly address the Indigenous community: "We invite our Apache brothers and sisters to join in finding the Spirit of the Mountains reflected in the brilliance of the night skies."[22]

The Vatican maintained that no sincere Apaches found the proposed Columbus Scope offensive, even going so far as to say that the "Vatican Observatory is extremely sensitive to criticism that accuses it of religious indifference." Instead, the Vatican is more concerned that some Apaches are being used to make a point, alleging that these people are being "exploited by outsiders who are radically opposed to the observatory." These individuals have, according to the Vatican, "manipulated the Endangered Species Act.... These idealogues now seek to manipulate American Indians. No mountain is as sacred as a human being, and there is no desecration more despicable than the use of a human person for self-serving purposes."[23] Apparently, the Vatican had not noted the numerous resolutions by the San Carlos Apache Tribal Council, including a 2001 resolution stating:

> The American Indian Religious Freedom Act guarantees Indian people unimpeded access to such sacred sites and locations.... The proposed destruction of this mountain will contribute directly to the destruction of fundamental aspects of the spiritual and cultural life of the Apaches.[24]

In the meantime, the Church has had some problems with mere mortals, sticking its foot in its mouth in regard to the telescope project. At one point, Reverend Charles Polzer, a Jesuit priest and spokesperson for the Vatican observatory, called the opposition to the telescope a conspiracy that "comes out of the Jewish lawyers of the ACLU to undermine and destroy the Catholic Church."[25] The Roman Catholic Diocese of Tucson later reported that Father Polzer expressed his "total sadness and regret at having made that remark."[26] The Church, however, has not recanted its remarks about the Apaches. Referring to Apache religious beliefs, Polzer asserted:

> Rarely did the Apache use these heights, and the sacredness is about as specific as references to the sky.... As an ordained priest and trained theologian as well as historian and anthropologist, I know that anthropological appeals to this court regarding the sacredness of Mt. Graham to the Apaches is little more than a preposterous misuse of academic status and the poorest manifestation of sound methodology that I have witnessed in recent times.[27]

In theory, the project was supposed to be about pure science. "Mt. Graham is the only way ground-based astronomy will advance in the state at the cutting edge level," says Peter Strittmatter, director of the University of Arizona Steward Observatory.[28] But Roger Lynds, a nationally respected astronomer with the National Optical Astronomy Observatory, thinks otherwise. The project is about "self-aggrandizement," he says. "It's got nothing to do with science, technology and truth or the best use of taxpayers' money."[29]

Guy Lopez from the Center for Biological Diversity echoes these sentiments. "In terms of the whole telescope building enterprise, it's not so much about cosmology any more, [but] more about cosmetics, sort of a beautifying their image in their own mind approach."[30] There are some 37 better observatory sites in the continental United States.[31]

In 2001 and 2002, the University of Minnesota also became embroiled in the controversy, as it debated a $5 million investment in the project. Although the university's regents ultimately approved the project, it was only after numerous student interventions and appeals. The controversy also highlighted that access to the telescope is not only about pure science or self-aggrandizement; it is also about lucrative military research contracts.

Lamenting that the University of Minnesota's ownership in two other research telescopes was "still not big enough to do a lot of the things we want to do," Minnesota astronomy professor Robert Gehrz argued that the Mt. Graham telescope would allow researchers to view objects with incredible detail. Noting that the University of Minnesota's astronomy department drew in just $1.6 million in sponsored research in 2001, a number dwarfed by the University of Arizona's $22 million, Gehrz and the astronomy department were anxious to land new NASA and Air Force contracts. Gehrz is presently working on an infrared map of the sky, which the Air Force could use to track a "star wars" type missile defense system. Considering that the Department of Defense's budget dwarfs education budgets, the possibility of new military contracts was a likely element in the University of Minnesota's decision to approve the project.[32]

Native Hawaiians have also raised telescope concerns, in particular about the desecration of Mauna Kea, the world's premier astronomy site, hosting the largest and most advanced astronomy facilities in the world. In a letter to the editor of the *Minnesota Daily*, Kealoha Pisciotta, of Hilo, Hawaii, wrote:

> I am a former employee of one of the world's largest submillimeter radio telescopes...atop Mauna Kea. We here in Hawaii have similar problems with our university and the astronomical development of our sacred temple, the mountain Mauna Kea.... The

upper region of Mauna Kea is considered the highest and most sacred temple of native Hawaiians, it is the burial ground of our highest born and most sacred ancestors.... Corporations pay only $1 per year in lease rent for the use of our land. They introduce hundreds of thousands of gallons of human waste into the principal aquifer of our island and use hazardous materials such as elemental mercury.... Universit[ies] push their developments...in the name of "education and research" [but] the technology developed on the telescopes is used to attract military and corporate contracts worth millions of dollars.[33]

In the end, money, the military, and university politics are all elements of a larger cultural dilemma. That dilemma, in part, is about very different views of the universe. Astronomer Gunther Hasinger told the Apaches, "We look differently at the stars. I know this is a different type of religion, but this is our religion. Scientists have to go out there, and do things that are inconsistent with the Bible. Every improvement we have has to do with science."[34] Echoing centuries of missionary violence, the director of the Vatican Observatory puts a more blunt, political edge to the conflict: "It is precisely the failure to make the distinctions [between insignificant nature and spiritual human beings] that has created a kind of environmentalism and a religiosity to which I cannot subscribe and which must be suppressed with all the force that we can muster."[35]

The Apache do not concur. Apache elder Franklin Stanley responds:

If you take Mt. Graham away from us, you will take our culture. You have killed many of us. You killed my grandfather. You have tried to change us, you forced me to go to your schools. But still I treat you with respect. I do not go to your church and hold my services. Why do you come and try and take my church away and treat the mountain as if it was about money instead of respect? Nowhere else in the world stands another mountain like the mountain you are trying to disturb. On this mountain is a great life-giving force. You have no knowledge of the place you are about to destroy.[36]

As Jack Hitt wrote in the *New York Times*,

In a sense the battle of Mount Graham signals a profound change in the way all of us look at nature—a paradigm shift, as scientists call it: If Galileo shocked the old order by stating that the earth is not the center of the solar system, the environmentalists and the Apaches are asserting that man is no longer at the center of nature.[37]

Salt, Water, Blood, and Coal

Mining in the Southwest

I am like the desert shrubs out there. The wind may blow, it may change, but I have deep roots and I know where the water is at.

—Laurie Weahkee, Diné and Zuni[1]

Zuni Salt Lake lies majestically surrounded by purple mesas, lush grasses, and tenacious trees, the center of a gentle sanctuary. This is the domain of the great Salt Mother. She is called *Ma'l Oyattsik'i* by the people of Zuni Pueblo, and stories are remembered of her movement across the land to her present resting place. It is told that in the earlier world she lived closer to the Zuni, but their actions and disrespect had offended her. So she traveled to the place where she now rests. Today, as in centuries past, great pilgrimages are taken by the men not only of Zuni but also of Acoma, Navajo, Apache, and other neighboring peoples to collect salt for their ceremonial life, indeed, their lifeblood. That is perhaps why this sanctuary, *A:shiwi A:wan Ma'k'yay'a dap an'ullapna Dek'ohannan Dehyakya Dehwanne,* has existed from time immemorial.

"Over there is the Zuni trail," Zuni writer and historian Jim Enote tells me, pointing with his mouth toward a spot invisible to my eye. "The Apaches come in over there, the Navajo here. They would all pretty much respect each other in here, each staying in their own camps, even if they were fighting."[2] Zuni Cultural Preservation Coordinator Andrew O'Thole explains that "the trails are umbilical cords tying the tribes to their salt deity and tying the sacred salt lake to the tribes' other holy places."[3] Softly trodden paths, traversed for a millennium, remain today as vibrant a part of traditional cultures as they were in the past.

This lake is sort of a miracle in itself, a spring-fed body of water in the most arid of regions, a hundred or so miles west of Albuquerque. Salty as tears, the lake is shallow from shore to shore, at no point more than four feet in depth; a cone of salt rises in the middle of the lake. That salt is known as the flesh of the Salt Mother. It is this salt that is used by the Navajo and the Zuni when an infant first cries and smiles. It is this salt that nourishes life.

"I am as much of the clouds as they are of me."

About 200 miles as the crow flies to the west of the Salt Mother, the heartland of the Colorado Plateau rises toward the sky, and eagles and kachinas dance to meet the rain clouds. Here the Navajo and the Hopi peoples—linked by their languages, their desert existence, their encounters with colonizers—tenaciously continue their lives in the longest continuously inhabited settlements on the continent.

Life at Hopi is austere, yet rich with 1,000 years of cultural practice and life in one place. It is rich in terms of a culture that cannot be purchased at a mall, austere in terms of the land's limits. There are few excesses allowed here, and only a carefully planned way of life could exist on these mesas—the fingerlike projections from the Colorado Plateau. Only those who heed the limits can survive and thrive here.

"There was a sacred covenant, between the Hopi and the Creator, in order for us to stay here," Vernon Masayesva, past Hopi tribal chairman and current executive director of the Black Mesa Trust, tells me.[4] Oral tradition explains that the Hopi followed the ant people up into the fourth world. There, they were greeted by Maasaa, who they asked if they could join. They were given a corn planting stick and a water gourd. "According to our creation story," Vernon remembers,

> only water existed at the dawn of time. From water came land; from land and water all forms of life were created, including man-

kind. Because all life comes from the same source, we are all interconnected, and I am as much a part of the clouds as they are of
me.... Hopi see the water underneath us as a living, breathing
world we call *Patuwaqatsi* or "water life." Plants breathe moisture
from the sky, and cloud people reciprocate by pulling the moisture
to the plants' roots. Hopi believe that when we die, we join the
cloud people and join in their journey home to *Patuwaqatsi,* and so
all Hopi ceremonies are tied to the water world, and all the springs
along the southern cliffs of Black Mesa serve as religious shrines or
passageways to water-life. The water model developed by western
scientists does not include any of these values because they cannot
be measured or quantified.[5]

While the Hopi see a single water world under the land's surface,
"western science" sees unconnected aquifers. So it is that in the new
millennium, two separate worldviews have come to live in the same
land, and, some would say, they do not reconcile well.

Asabakeshiinh, the Spider

When the Zuni look westward from the great Salt Mother, they
can see the destruction caused by the *asabakeshiinh,* the spider that has
been feeding off the water and land of the Hopi and Navajo for more
than 35 years. An intricate network of mines, power plants, pipelines,
train tracks, and roads, the spider has gouged and drained the liver of
Mother Earth, the Black Mesa. It is assuredly the mother of all ecologically destructive mining complexes. At Peabody Coal's Black
Mesa Mine and adjacent Kayenta Mine, huge draglines have made
deep holes that straddle the white man's borders between the Hopi
and Navajo reservations. More than 17,000 acres are scarred. The
spider was born of controversy even before the first lease was signed
in 1964: Backroom dealings, unscrupulous lawyers, and convoluted
legal loopholes allowed the development of what would become the
largest coal strip mine complex on the continent, bereft of almost any
environmental considerations.

The 1960s saw a remarkable binge of neocolonial expansion.
The rise of Third World nationalism, whether in Chile or the Middle
East, combined with a U.S. push for energy self-sufficiency. At the

same time, the passage of the Clean Air Act set the groundwork to carve out western low-sulfur coal, a good portion of which lies under Native lands in the Southwest and Montana. So it was that the big-time companies and their lawyers came to the Third World of North America: Indian Country. The flurry of mining agreements signed in the '60s dizzies the mind; their terms nauseate the stomach. While the federal government had a trust responsibility to protect the interest of the tribes, those interests were pretty much disregarded.

Today, the disparities are widely recognized as vast environmental injustices. Many a lease was signed with the terms "for as long as the ore is producing in payable quantities," shackling tribes into agreements with minimal recourse. The royalties themselves were often set for a pittance of the value of the resource, and attorneys representing the tribes were also, secretly, on the payrolls of the mining companies. The spree in development, not only of coal, but also of oil, uranium, and natural gas, meant a rapid transformation of a largely agricultural economy to one both dependent on, and heavily impacted by, energy development. While hundreds of Native Americans are employed by Peabody Coal and in related jobs, the benefits of the mine are decidedly lopsided. The coal energizes much of the Southwest's economy, yet many Native households lack access to basic electricity.

The Mormons, the Lawyers, and the Coal

There is, perhaps, no case more blatant in terms of collusion and deceit than that of John Boyden. Through a set of relationships between the Mormon Church, the Bureau of Indian Affairs, and Peabody Coal, Boyden came to be the attorney representing the Hopi. "Boyden was like a father to the Hopi," Vernon Masayesva remembers. "Everything he said the Hopi believed. The progressive people [many of whom were Mormon converts or had come to work closely with the Bureau of Indian Affairs and the Mormon interests] literally worshipped the guy and he deceived us." Vernon recalls from oral history how the Hopi Tribal Council met regarding the mine: "Boyden asks them how they would like to move the coal to market, they say 'train.' Boyden adjourns the meeting apparently dissatisfied.

They come back out with the proposal for slurrying the coal in the power plant, far away in Nevada." Slurrying means using water to wash crushed coal through pipelines instead of putting it in trucks or on trains for transport. Of course it was the tribe's precious groundwater that was to be used—practically for free. Only years later would Boyden's conflicts of interest become apparent to researchers like University of Colorado law professor Charles Wilkinson.

> John Boyden represented both Peabody Coal and the Hopis at the same time and Peabody got a highly favorable lease and the Hopi didn't. The reality was that the Hopi were in a highly strategic bargaining position...the whole development of the southwest hinged on this lease...and Boyden clearly and indisputably represented the interests of Peabody Coal.[6]

Once the initial lease agreements had been signed, the Bechtel Corporation got the call to design and build the massive 273-mile pipeline to Laughlin, Nevada, the site of the Mohave Generating Station.

Not only was Boyden the architect of the Black Mesa mining complex, he was also the underlying legal power in the drafting of the notorious mid-1970s' Hopi-Navajo Relocation Act, calling for a division of the so-called joint use area between the Hopi and Navajo and the subsequent relocation of 10,000 Navajo and approximately 1,000 Hopi who happened to be living on the wrong side of the fence. The Relocation Act and its subsequent heart-wrenching turmoil have pitted many members of the two tribes against each other. All the while, the water beneath the contested earth was being siphoned off.[7]

Sucking the Mother Dry

The devastation of strip mining is compounded by the region's aridness. Black Mesa is the heartland of the Colorado Plateau, and is the region's largest and most productive watershed. It is also a coal deposit, representing at its prime over 22 billion tons of coal. But the largest community in the area, Tuba City, Arizona, receives only a scant seven inches of rainfall annually. The Navajo–Aquifer, also known as the N–Aquifer, is the sole source of dependable drinking water for the region. Hence, the combination of massive mining development, with the use of water from the aquifer, has been a huge blow to the ecology of the region.

For the past 35 years, 1.3 billion gallons of pristine water has been sucked annually from the Navajo–Aquifer, just to move coal. Peabody, with its affiliate, the Black Mesa Pipeline Company, uses 3 million gallons of water a day to push coal in a pulverized powderlike consistency through the pipelines.[8] The irony of waste is not lost on the Hopi. Vernon Masayesva has lived in the shadow of the mine for a good portion of his life: "I've watched it for 35 years. All you could do is watch it, because no one had information on what it was doing." For years, both the traditional Hopi and Navajo have opposed both the mine and the slurry, but their arguments have been based on spiritual and cultural principles, quite a contrast to the lawyers, water rights adjudicators, and company-paid hydrologists.

The spiritual teachings form the foundation of the elder's opposition to the mine. "There was tremendous opposition by the Hopi elders," Vernon tells me, "because we'd violated a religious covenant: Treating water like a commodity—selling something sacred." That is a far cry from the water rights allocation formulas in widespread use in western law.

This is not to say that the Hopi and Navajo have not tried the white man's courts: scores of court cases over the past decade reflect problems with Peabody or various aspects of the Department of the Interior's trust responsibility. When Peabody Coal negotiated the initial lease agreement in 1966, then-Secretary of the Interior Stewart Udall included an escape clause to be triggered if there were any adverse impacts by the company on the aquifer and its users. Specifically, the clause allows Interior action if the N–Aquifer withdrawals are "endangering the supply of underground water in the vicinity or so lowering the water table that other users of such water are being damaged."[9] Although the Department of the Interior holds this powerful trump card, to date it has refused to play it.

For over a decade, Peabody has continued pumping water through an interim permit. According to Vernon Masayesva,

One billion gallons of our ancient, sacred water—water upon which we have survived for a millennia, upon which we depend today—mined to slurry coal, fouled beyond reclamation—evaporates each year in Nevada's desert skies. One billion gallons of living water, enough to provide Hopi for 100 years, dies on a dry wind, and Moenkopi Wash is dry.[10]

Water levels in some Black Mesa wells have dropped more than 100 feet, and many of the springs are dry. Hopis contend that by the year 2011, the dewatering will leave the Hopi village of Moenkopi without water. At present, Alvin Honyumptewa, a 70-year-old Moenkopi farmer, describes what many local residents have noted: "For the first time in my memory, I have not seen any water in Moenkopi Wash. We used to swim there all year long."[11] As well, shifts in the water pressure have allowed contaminated water from an adjacent aquifer to leak into the pristine aquifer. According to Leonard Selestewa, another Moenkopi farmer and board chair of the Black Mesa Trust, Peabody added insult to injury by claiming control of surface water flowing toward Hopi farms—water that recharges local springs. Thinking about Peabody's 200 surface water impoundments, Selestewa recalled, "Last year our reservation went dry. We needed one more water in our corn, and we didn't get it."[12]

In the fall of 2000, the Natural Resources Defense Council (NRDC), at the urging of the Black Mesa Trust, analyzed data collected by the Department of the Interior's Office of Surface Mining Reclamation and Enforcement, the U.S. Geological Survey, and the coal company itself. That data demonstrated that the water levels have decreased by more than 50% in most of the region. The NRDC recommended that "Peabody should cease groundwater pumping from the N–Aquifer no later than 2005,...[and] implement an N–Aquifer use-reduction plan,...[and that] [t]he Interior Department should complete the three-part study of coal transport alternatives it began in the early 1990s,...recalibrat[ing] its model and improv[ing] its monitoring." The NRDC argued that "federal trust responsibility required action" by the federal government to "restrain Peabody's uses of the N–Aquifer and, more generally, assure an adequate supply of water to the tribes."[13]

The Peabody Group, today the world's largest private coal producer, countered with a $2 million study, claiming that the water pumped for the coal operation had virtually no effect on the aquifer. The company contends that it will use less than 1% of the aquifer during the lifespan of the mine. Peabody issued a second study in the fall of 2003, arguing that the mine has no impact on the water supply of the region.

Peabody's vice-president for legal and external affairs, Fred Palmer, has repeated Peabody's claim that the mine can continue and even expand without hurting the local water table: "Ten years from now, I see two power plants using coal from Black Mesa. Mohave Generating Station has installed scrubbers for better air quality, which require more coal. But I envision water coming from the Lower Colorado River system and the N–Aquifer will be untouched."[14] The track record of the Bush administration gives Peabody executives like Palmer reason to hope that their interests will continue to be prioritized over that of the Navajos and Hopis.

Opposition to Peabody's continued use of the aquifer has united Hopis and Navajos, as evidenced by a summer 2003 rally held in front of the company's Flagstaff offices. Former Hopi tribal chairman Ferrell Secakuku told a Flagstaff crowd, "Every time you breathe, Peabody is pumping 50 gallons of water. Soon the aquifer will crumble and no longer be able to take recharge." Roberta Blackgoat, a Navajo elder and Big Mountain relocation resister, described coal as the Earth's liver and that because of the mining, "Mother Earth is really suffering. She is having a lot of pain."[15]

A new millennium has begun since the opening of the Black Mesa mine. Although the Bush-Cheney "Energy Policy" calls for more use of fossil fuels and nuclear power, there is only so much water. Our water today is the same water that dinosaurs swam in. Our water today is the water of the Ice Age. There is no more water. Indeed, as Hopi runners traversed some 265 miles of the Arizona desert under the sizzling sun of August, they brought a message to the city of Phoenix and the Bureau of Indian Affairs. "Water is sacred, a gift from the Creator, not a commodity to be bought and sold for a profit." The runners delivered a petition to end the Mesa Black coal mine's use of the N–Aquifer or, better yet, to end coal mining in the area altogether.[16]

There are no easy answers to this one. The Black Mesa Trust, the Hopi Tribe, the NDRC, and others have asked Peabody to end its use of the N–Aquifer by 2005 at the latest. The alternatives forwarded at present include bringing water in from Lake Powell and the Colorado River Basin to continue the slurry of the coal. This is highly controversial since the water level in Lake Powell has already dropped at least 30 feet in the last decade due to drought. Another proposal would move the water source to the C–Aquifer, once again taking Hopi and Navajo water. Other longer-term options include installing a rail line to eliminate the slurry or closing down the mine entirely. All have complicated facets: Tribal revenues are generated from the mines, as is employment, and electricity is generated using the coal.

Today 37% of Navajo households do not have electricity. Sixty percent of Hopi and 25% of Navajo tribal resources come from Peabody royalties.[17] The estimated value of the Black Mesa mines is $85 million a year in royalties, employment, and secondary spin-offs to the two tribes. The only plausible proposals for a transitional economy in the region will likely involve state-of-the-art, efficient coal plants and, eventually, solar and wind development on potentially a large scale. Since both the Hopi and the Navajo communities are well trained in energy and transmission systems, the potential for a renewable economy is particularly significant.

It is an intricate web the *asabakeshiinh,* the spider, has made. It is not easy to unravel, and there is an immense amount of money and interest involved in each strand. The studies of the white man scientists will argue on and on, but perhaps the Hopi elders had some premonitions about the future more than a decade ago when they said:

> Water under the ground has much to do with rain clouds. Everything depends upon the proper balance being maintained.... Drawing huge amounts of water from beneath Black Mesa in connection with the strip mining will destroy the harmony.... Should this happen, our lands will shake like the Hopi rattle: land will sink,

land will dry up…plants will not grow, our corn will not yield and
animals will die. When corn will not grow, we will die—not only
Hopis, but all will disintegrate to nothing.[18]

The National Academy of Sciences issued a report suggesting
that in arid areas like Black Mesa, "restoration of a landscape dis-
turbed by surface mining, in the sense of re-creating the former conditions, is not possible." The Academy suggested that if such lands
were mined, it was more feasible to deem the land "National Sacrifice
Areas" than to attempt reclamation at all.[19] Reclamation is but a distant dream for the Hopi and Navajo as Peabody continues to dig out
the coal and slurry it away with precious groundwater. The liver of
Mother Earth is sore from cutting; the lifeblood is draining away.

The Salt Mother Still Rests

The Zuni know only too well how the *asabakeshiinh* of Black
Mesa has taken the water out from under the farms of the Hopi and
the Navajo. They have felt the threat of their own spider, one called
the Salt River Project. From its headquarters in Phoenix, Arizona, a
giant sucking sound can be heard as the project draws in water and
coal from the region—a good portion of it coming from Native land.
The Salt River Project provides both electricity and water to hundreds of thousands of people and businesses in Phoenix and greater
central Arizona. It is the nation's third-largest public utility. The Salt
River Project *asabakeshiinh* is hungry, its appetite voracious. In the
1980s, the utility set its sights on 80 million tons of coal at Fence
Lake, New Mexico, a microdot of a town, just 11 miles from Zuni
Salt Lake.

The Fence Lake mine itself threatened not only to alter the terrain of the Salt Lake sanctuary, it also laid claim to 20.4 billion gallons
of water, the equivalent of 85 gallons of water a minute for 40 years.
That level of water use in a desert would more than likely affect
spring-fed Salt Lake, especially in this time of global climate change
when there is no assurance of rain. Edward Wemytewa, from the
Zuni Tribe's cultural preservation program, expressed his peoples'
concerns: "We can't resuscitate the springs when they are dead." In
Wemytewa's mind, there might be "a message as to why we should

protect the water resources.... When Zuni Salt Woman got angry and left, she taught us a lesson. We should learn from that.... We can't afford to lose any of the water. When it's gone, it's gone."[20]

Stanley Pinto, a Zuni conservation officer, connects the ecological and spiritual disruption the tribe would face if the lake's springs were a casualty of nearby mining: "If it does dry it up, I doubt that it would start up again. And the salt, you probably won't see it any more. A lot of Native Americans, I don't know what they would do. They wouldn't be able to do any of the things they need to do with the salt."[21]

The Zuni have fought long and hard to protect their Salt Mother. Zuni attorney Paul Bloom explains:

> Due to obscure legal determinations made in the late nineteenth century…Zuni Salt Lake had been treated as a salt harvesting resource of the territory of New Mexico, and had been put under the control of the Territorial Land Commissioner rather than of the Tribes that annually harvested salt for religious and practical purposes from the Lake. It was only in 1977, after decades of struggle, that the Congress instructed the Secretary of Interior to arrange whatever land exchanges were necessary to effect the return of this land.[22]

It took another nine years until, finally, 600 acres of land and the Salt Lake itself were transferred back to the Zuni Tribe, where the land was once again designated as a "neutral zone," allowing for the continued use by all the Native people in the region.[23]

Washington, D.C., politics are always a challenge for environmentalists and Indian tribes, no less, certainly, under the Bush administration that came to power in January 2001. In the face of dwindling options to stop the issuance of a Life of Mine Permit, the Zuni Tribe reached out and built the Zuni Salt Lake Coalition, linking the tribe's work with that of the Environmental Justice Program of the Sierra Club, the Water Information Network, the Tucson-based Center for Biological Diversity, the Seventh Generation Fund, and the Citizens Coal Council, in addition to interested individuals. Each time a proposal to approve the mine permit found its way to the desk of the Secretary of the Interior, it was countered with thousands of e-mails and letters opposing the permit. The Zuni Tribe tried for a number of months to negotiate some concessions from the utility, to no avail. When the negotiations with the Salt River Project broke down, Edward Wemytewa urged persistence: "We've been in this situation before, and the Zunis are going to just have to get tougher emotionally."[24]

Zunis are some tough Indians. They have lived for centuries in some of the most trying of terrain and have made it flourish. When something has been taken from them, they have worked to recover it. For years, the Zuni Tribe's conservation program has been internationally recognized for its restoration not only of traditional agriculture but also of traditional waterways and ecosystem-based management. That work is extending further, even off the formal reservation. "We're restoring our cultural lands...Zuni heaven," Wemytewa tells me, referring to a territory about an hour's drive west of Zuni near St. Joseph:

> That area was once lush and that is one of our sacred sites.... The river was diverted and the river died out. We finally got it back.... We are restoring the wetlands, and we know how hard it is to restore those lands. You have to start buying water rights.... We are starting to buy ranches around there, so we can harvest the runoff, the surface waters.... We are restoring it.[25]

Hopi spokespeople also echoed the concerns about the mine raised by the Zuni. The Hopi Tribe's Land Committee chairwoman, Lenora Lewis, noted the "devastating and long-lasting effect on the tribe" that the mine would risk. The Salt River Project itself has documented over 550 archeological sites in the proposed coal mining area and 50 sites along its proposed 44-mile rail transportation route that would send the coal to a nearby power plant. The rail line would transect the trails of pilgrimage used by the Zuni, Navajo, Hopi, Acoma, Laguna, and Apache peoples. The company offered, generously, to place strategic culverts so that the pilgrimages might continue without traversing the rail line. The federal government also recognized 185,000 acres, including the lake, as eligible for listing on the National Register of Historic Places.

The Zunis and their allies were diligent, holding 24-hour prayer vigils at the Salt River Project, marches, and rallies, along with legal and administrative wranglings and press campaigns. The coalition also proposed an alternative: generating electricity through renewable energy sources instead of burning more coal. Many local people became involved in the organizing. At one meeting in Grants, New Mexico, about 130 people came to voice their opposition to the New Mexico Department of Mines' renewal of the original five-year permit for the Fence Lake mine site; another meeting held nearby drew 75 people. Perhaps the most interesting question posed was not about the mine itself but about why the meeting was not held in the Pueblo communities most deeply affected by the permit.

After a sustained and concentrated campaign in opposition to the mine, the Zuni and their allies were able to claim victory. On August 4, 2003, the Salt River Project announced that it would relinquish the permits and the coal leases that it had acquired for the proposed mine. "It has been a long 20-year struggle with a lot of mental anguish and frustration for our people, but we have had our voices heard," Zuni head councilman, Carlton Albert, said.

> I feel relieved, and it sends shivers down my back to realize how long this struggle has been and now it has come to closure. So many people have supported us in this struggle and there is no word that can express our appreciation.... If there is a lesson to be learned, it is to never give up and to stay focused on what you want to accomplish.[26]

The Zuni victory demonstrates the power of individual and community activism where everyone is given a chance to be heard. The determination of this environmental justice coalition was noted by Andy Bessler, a Sierra Club regional organizer and founding member of the Zuni Salt Lake Coalition: "This victory is a testament to the spirit of the Zuni people, other Native American tribes, and non-Native supporters who would not relinquish Salt Woman in the name of cheap coal."[27]

Recognizing the importance of water to life as well as the significance of persistence in fighting for what you want, Salt Woman may rest easy in her home, and the Zuni, Hopi, Apache, and Navajo may continue their pilgrimages to Zuni Salt Lake to harvest their salt. New proposals loom on the horizon: coal methane leases and the endless possibilities for new combustion. That is the nature of the *asabakeshiinh*. For now, the Salt Mother still rests peacefully. Gentle footsteps come toward her to collect her flesh. She sighs and returns to her rest. The *asabakeshiinh* looks on.

Klamath Land and Life

We do prayers at the center of the world here, but they are not just for us. It is for the whole world. We are trying to save the world.

—Jeanerette Jacups-Johnny, Karuk Tribe, Klamath Basin[1]

From high in the mountains of southern Oregon, the lifeblood of the region springs forth. The Klamath River, nourished by its mountain tributaries, gathers strength and feeds into great wetlands in the territories of the Klamath and Modoc tribes and the Yahooskin band of Snake Paiute and, eventually downriver, those of the Karuk, Yurok, and Hupa tribes. Bordered by ponderosa pine and a sagebrush desert, the intricate river and marsh system forms a lush ecosystem called by some the "Everglades of the West." For centuries the Klamath, Modoc, and Yahooskin peoples have lived well on this land, honoring in their songs and ceremonies a multitude of relatives with wings, fins, roots, and legs. They were there, it's said, to see the eruption of Mt. Mazama and the creation of its successor, Crater Lake, one of the geological wonders of the world. The Klamath peoples have continued to live by this river despite the fact that the federal government has been consistent in denying them their land and their identity. The government even declared their tribe "terminated" in the 1950s. After a decades-old fight to regain recognition of their status as a tribe, now they are fighting for the survival of the fish relative that is so much a part of their way of life.

To some, the Klamath Basin suckers may not seem an important fish family, but to those who rely on fish for their nutrition, the sucker has been a mainstay for many a feast. The annual First Sucker ceremony of the Klamath people recognizes the significance of this fish and honors their annual return to their stream spawning grounds, despite dams, algae, drought, and diversions.

Writer Erika Zavaleta remembered as bittersweet the initial First Sucker ceremony held on the banks of the Klamath River since the restoration of the tribe's status in 1992:

> A quiet fell over the group when in the morning we went to the river to meet with the fish. Water diversions, logging and pollution are driving the sucker—the center of the Klamath's most important ceremony and subsistence practice—to extinction. On this morning, the men who carried out two of the fish for the elders to bless handled them gingerly, aware that in ten years the abundant sucker had become precious and scarce. One man commented that in years past, the sucker choked the river on the day of the ceremony, so that the people could pick them up from the surface of the water. That morning we did not see one go by. Said [Klamath tribal member] Gordon Bettles later in the day, he fears that in time they might only have a Last Sucker Ceremony to celebrate.[2]

The 1992 ceremony marked the return of a people to their territory and their fish, but although the Klamath Tribe had its tribal status reinstated under federal law, the Klamath land base has not yet been restored. And although the Klamath people (along with the Hupa, Karuk, and Yurok further downstream) have retained their water and fishing rights throughout the worst of U.S. policy toward Indian people, the question remains as to whether they will have enough water to support the suckers.

The Stronghold

From the lava beds at Tule Lake, one can get a panoramic view of the Klamath Basin. The wind whistles through vast unforgiving and jagged lands to the west and a huge marshland to the east. This is the land where the Changer and the animals sat together to discuss the Creation of man. This is the land where the people of the river have lived for 14,000 years or more.

The deep ravines, rushing rivers, and lava beds kept the white people at bay for many years. Then the California gold rush precipitated a ruthless slaughter of the Native people of California, forcing the Modocs and other mostly coastal tribes further into the up-river region of the Lost River and the Klamath. The U.S. Calvary and settlers came right after them.

Modoc headman Captain Jack wanted to be able to stay on his peoples' traditional lands near Tule Lake, but the small Indigenous nation did not have the same power as the gold and lumber interests that had moved into the area and were ravaging it. Representatives of the Klamath, Modoc, and Northern Paiute bands of southern Oregon and northern California agreed to negotiate a treaty in return for a territory that would be free from settlers and their violence. The negotiations cost them all but about 5% of their 20-million-acre territory. The remaining 1.1 million acres were designated the Klamath Reservation under the 1864 Treaty.[3]

The Modocs, and the Yahooskin band of Snake Paiutes, ended up on the Klamath Reservation, where there was conflict from the start. The reservation had been created from the Klamath's traditional territory, and now they had to share it. When appropriations of food, clothing, and tools came to the reservation, there were meager allocations for the Klamath and even less for the others.[4]

Promises of livestock, farm equipment, and rations were not kept, and Captain Jack was unwilling to let his people starve. He led his followers off the reservation and, back to the Lost River Valley, where his people had lived for centuries before. Here they felt they knew the land and could support themselves. The return of the Modocs did not sit well with the white settlers and gold seekers who had now moved into the territory. In November 1872, the Cavalry under Major Jackson was dispatched from Fort Klamath to bring the Modocs back to the reservation. Thus began a nightmare year for the Modoc people.

Where the fog from the Tule Lake meets the impenetrable fortress of the lava beds, the Modocs held camp. Captain Jack's Stronghold, as it is known, is a complex cave system in the form of a horseshoe that overlooks the lava beds. The jagged edges of the lava made it impossible to traverse by any set of wheels, and only sure-footed horses and Native people could find their way through the beds. There, for three weeks the Modocs held off a huge force of the Army, frustrating the soldiers immensely. "We fought the Indians through the lava beds to their stronghold...the center of miles of rocky fissures caves, crevices, gorges and ravines," the Army commander reported. "One thousand men would be required to dislodge them from their almost impregnable position, and it must be done deliberately, with a free use of mortar batteries.... Please send me three hundred foot-troops at the earliest date."[5]

On the edge of these same lava beds six months later, negotiations for a homeland for the Modocs took place. Those negotiations had little resonance. Captain Jack asked for nothing more than the most barren part of the Modoc homeland: "Give me this lava bed for a home. I can live here; take away your soldiers, and we can settle everything. Nobody will ever want these rocks; give me a home here."[6]

The federal government, now represented by General Edward R.S. Canby (fresh from the Indian Wars in the Southwest), was unwilling to grant even this small request. The negotiations worsened, and Captain Jack ended up killing General Canby on Good Friday, 1873. The fighting escalated, and the Modocs retreated back into the Stronghold. When the soldiers finally stormed the hideout, it was empty. Captain Jack's followers continued to move, but they had few resources left. The chase became like a sport of men and hounds chasing a fox. The remaining Modocs were vastly outnumbered, without food, and on foot. When Captain Jack finally surrendered, there was a trial of sorts. The Modocs were not allowed to have a lawyer and had little ability to launch a defense in a foreign language. Captain Jack and two others, Schonchin John Boston Charley and Black Jim, were convicted of murder and hanged on October 3, 1874. The surviving 153 Modocs were exiled to Indian Territory in Oklahoma. A generation later, only a third of the Modocs remained alive. These 51 Modocs—except for two who were sent to Alcatraz Prison—were allowed to return to the Klamath Reservation in Oregon in 1909.[7]

This is the bitter history that opened the Klamath Basin to the settlers; this is the living memory of the Klamath peoples today.

Unhealed Wounds of Federal Policy

Another, slightly subtler form of land appropriation quickly supplemented the military assault on the Klamath Basin peoples. While the Klamath viewed their territory as stretching from one peak to the next, government surveyors grabbed over "600,000 acres of treaty lands by adopting straight lines between points well inside of the peak-to-peak boundaries."[8] While the Klamath leaders protested, settlers poured into their territory. A subsequent government survey returned some land sections to the Klamath, but most were never returned, and the tribe received only a paltry payment in return. Congress took additional reservation lands for the construction of roads. This land grab included not only the roadbed but also alternating sections of land for a right-of-way. The checkerboard was eventually deemed inefficient for development so it was returned to the tribe and 87,000 acres of prime forestland in the northeast corner of the reservation was taken instead.[9]

Not content with merely whittling down Indian land, federal land-taking policy expanded radically under the Dawes Act of 1887. The law forced a European land tenure institution—privately held property—on tribal peoples whose land had been held collectively through traditional institutions of use rights and lineage systems. Under the Dawes Act, 118 reservations were divided into 80-acre plots "allotted" to individual families. Not only could these families now sell to non-Indians, large portions of reservations were deemed "surplus." It may be that the act's primary intent was to open up Indian lands to homesteaders. Since Indian people were deemed to be a dying race, access to those lands was seen as an inevitable part of Manifest Destiny. Klamath lands by the turn of the century came under immense pressure from prospective homesteaders, and in 1924, Bureau of Indian Affairs superintendent Fred A. Baker reported that the

whites were acquiring title to Klamath lands at a rate that he estimated would "render the Indians homeless in 25 years."[10] By 1957,
almost two-thirds of the reservation had been taken through the allotment process. The Klamath were left with 75,000 acres.

Termination: The Trees and the Land

There is no word like "termination" to strike at the heart of Indian Country. Termination—the federal government's essentially
unilateral withdrawal from all government-to-government relations
established through treaties and laws—was the icing on the cake of
military domination, shady surveys, and divide-and-conquer allot-
ments. The termination policy articulated under House Concurrent
Resolution 108 and adopted in August 1953, declared Native people
to be "subject to the same laws and entitled to the same privileges and
responsibilities...as other citizens of the United States" by "freeing
them from all federal supervision and control."[11] Although cast as a
way to free Indians from the limitations of trustee status, at its essence termination became an open invitation to private enterprises to
exploit Native land and resources. More than 100 bands and tribes
were terminated, affecting more than 1.5 million acres of land.

Between 1954 and 1960, the federal government terminated
most small Native communities with little political power. Oregon
Indians were especially hard hit by the termination policy, largely due
to the fact that Douglas McCay, a former governor of Oregon, was
then-President Dwight Eisenhower's Secretary of the Interior. In his
position of trustee of Indian Country, McCay determined that "Oregon would be the prototype of the new Indian policy."[12] The
Klamath and the Menominee were the largest tribes terminated.[13]

Despite the fact that the majority of Klamath people opposed
the termination of their relationship with the federal government,
Public Law 587, the Klamath Termination Act, was enacted in 1954.
In trying to fathom the government's reasons for terminating his
tribe, Leonard Norris, a Klamath active in the subsequent Klamath
restoration struggle, points to the fact that the tribe controlled "the
largest ponderosa pine stand in the U.S. It's not hard to figure out
why they did this."[14]

Enrolled Klamath adults were given a choice of receiving a large cash settlement up front or becoming beneficiaries of a privately controlled tribal fund. Knowing that many Klamath tribal members were cash rich from the termination settlement, the area was flooded with snake oil peddlers: unscrupulous purveyors of anything that could be bought at a ballooned price. Gordon Bettles remembers the time well:

> I would liken it to a dream time. Salesmen used to show up and take everything out on the lawn. Vacuum salesmen, furniture salesmen, people selling everything you can put in a house. The Indian way is to feel sorry for people like that. My aunt, she bought just a token from all of them, a plate here, a spoon there. She ended up with a house full of junk she couldn't use.[15]

As some get rich, others get poor. The Klamath Bar Association emerged in the settler town, which had been established largely to benefit from the Native community's assets. The bar association set a fee for administering the Klamath trusts that was triple the rate charged to others. Other attorneys defrauded the Klamath of tens of thousands of dollars.[16]

Even those Klamath who remained as beneficiaries of the tribal fund were not even given control over the proceeds of the sale of their land. The U.S. National Bank of Oregon, appointed by the federal government as trustee for the remaining 474 tribal members, made it difficult for many tribal members to get access to their trust funds. Elnathan Davis, Klamath tribal member, remembers the change from the federal government as trustee to the bank: "We got off one bus, we got on another bus.... We were never given the chance to drive the bus."[17] In 1969, an exasperated tribal membership voted to dispose of the U.S. Bank of Oregon as its trustee. The bank responded by selling all of the remaining lands and distributing the proceeds to the tribal members individually, as the earlier termination settlement checks had been distributed. The Chiloquin Fund, a fund started in the mid-1970s by Edison Chiloquin and his wife,

Leatha, to fight for the right to maintain their land, would later write, "The bank did what even the federal government had not dared to do. They terminated a tribe without even consulting its members."[18]

Along with selling off the land, termination also ended the decades of sustainable forest management under tribal authority. During the termination process, conservation interests lobbied successfully to have 500,000 acres of tribal landholdings allocated to the Winema National Forest. Since the Forest Service itself had little interest in preserving the ecosystem of the region, timber companies were given free rein and the vast ponderosa pine stands quickly fell. The Winema National Forest became virtually a joke in national forest management.

In contrast to the sustainable pace at which the Klamath had harvested the forests for decades, timber company harvesting reached up to five times more than the Klamath had harvested annually in the previous years. Indeed, Oregon was, in many ways, a logging state—*until* most of the big trees were cut down by Weyerhauser and the like. In the land where the 1990 spotted owl decision originated as a result of ruthless logging in pristine national forests, tribal land areas, and forested mountains, the lumber did little to support the local economy, beyond the relatively few years when the mills were active. Chuck Kimbol, former tribal forester, noted that some 70% of the trees harvested from the Winema in a 15-year period, ending in 1988, left the county as unmilled logs, while in the same period, 80% of the county's lumber mills closed down.[19]

The Winema National Forest is named after Winema, a Modoc woman also known as Toby Riddle, who worked to keep the peace between settlers and the Modoc. The naming honor is ironic, given how little of the local forest remains in the hands of her descendants. Watching their trees move to the lumber mill, the Klamath people also saw their own social and economic stature decline. Before termination, the Klamath had managed their fisheries, livestock, and timber industries well enough to give a modest annual stipend to each tribal member, along with maintaining a hospital and medical team, and even making payments to the federal government for Bureau of Indian Affairs administrative costs. This relative wealth made the

Klamath a prime target for termination, but the policy did not take into consideration that it was the tribal organization that created the economic security for its individual members. Termination cut to shreds the tribal safety net.

Without the tribal clinic or funds for private care and insurance, the health of the Klamath worsened dramatically. Discrimination against Indians hardened in the public school and at the local welfare department. In 1965, there was only one Klamath receiving welfare, even though a full 40% of them had no settlement money left. Tensions and divisions in the community intensified, leading to violence, family breakdown, and a threefold increase in juvenile delinquency. When a Senate committee came to Klamath in 1969, it reported that the "termination of the Klamath reservation in Oregon has led to extreme social disorganization of that tribal group. Many of them can be found in state penal and mental institutions."[20]

Edison Chiloquin and Tribal Restoration

In the heartbreak of the Klamath people, there is also hope. Edison Chiloquin was an ember for that hope. Born during the August moon of 1923, in a small home on the confluence of the Sprague and Williamson rivers, Edison would become the first Native person in the United States to have land returned to him. His grandfather had been the headman of the Plaikni people, one of several bands that would become known collectively as the Klamath, and had signed one of the treaties in 1864. Edison grew up in the town of Chiloquin, named for his grandfather.

After returning from World War II and the Pacific, Edison Chiloquin was discharged with both a Silver Star and a Purple Heart. When he returned to his land, he was homeless, yet Edison vowed to work for his people and for the return of his land. After the liquidation of the last tribal trust, Edison refused to accept almost a quarter of a million dollars' worth of settlement checks, becoming the only Klamath who refused to cash the government checks for termination. "The Earth is my mother; I cannot sell my own mother."[21]

Edison did not give up his quest for the return of the land and in the end he prevailed. On December 5, 1980, President Carter signed into law the Chiloquin Act, granting Edison Chiloquin the trust deed to the Plaikni village. The government set up 580 acres in the Wimena National Forest as "Special Trust Land." This land is to remain part of the national forest, with the Chiloquin family having stewardship as long as they keep the land for traditional cultural purposes and do not commercialize it. The act is unique in that it is the only return of land to an individual Native person. Like Edison, the Klamath people also kept struggling until they won restoration of their tribal recognition in 1986. Unlike Edison, however, they have not yet seen the restoration of their land.

Since the restoration of the Klamath people under the Restoration Act of 1986, the return of the land has remained a focal point. One might wryly suggest that there are still too many trees in the traditional Klamath territory and far too many drained wetlands to return anything of value to the Klamath people. Under the Restoration Act, the Klamath people were "required to come up with a plan for economic self-sufficiency," explains Bud Ullman, attorney for the Klamath Tribe. "The return of reservation lands is a natural centerpiece of that goal."[22]

That proposition would be challenging, particularly when your expected allies oppose you. At the end of 2003, the Klamath Tribe came up with a forest management plan intended for the return of what they would call the Klamath Reservation Forest, including parcels from both the Winema and the adjacent Fremont national forests. Klamath proposals include a diverse management plan for 690,000 acres, reflecting a "state-of-the-art forest management plan that could become a model for the nation."[23]

The potential for the Klamath proposal can be seen in the experience of the Menominee Tribal Forest. Recognized as the first "green certified" forest in North America, the Menominee set a benchmark for sustainable timber harvesting practices. The Menominee have cut their forest the equivalent of three times over, but the same amount of trees remain in the forest today, as well as an ecologically diverse canopy, as when the Menominee signed their treaty with the government in the 1800s. The Menominee forest is the model for all tribal forests nationally.

Klamath proposals for actual economic self-sufficiency and the return of land have historically been opposed by the Oregon Natural Resources Council (ONRC), an alleged environmental organization. The ONRC has advocated for "cobbling the reservation together out of tracts currently under private ownership."[24] Recently the ONRC has softened its stance but remains concerned about public lands being turned over to tribal hands. Jay Ward, conservation director for the ONRC, acknowledges that Indians "have suffered greatly at the hands of the federal government." But, he says, Americans "[should not] be asked to give up public lands, natural resources, and the...national forest legacy."[25]

In response to ONRC suggestions, Klamath tribal chairman Allen Foreman remains steadfast: "The Klamath Tribes do not and will not support ONRC's proposed alternative. The conservation group's opposition will not deter us from working to restore what was our homeland for 14,000 years before being designated National Forest only 42 years ago."[26] That far sighted approach will likely serve the Klamath well in the years of negotiations ahead. The Klamath, however, also have thrown some major legal challenges into the federal courts that may help to push the hand of federal policy toward restoration of the land that ultimately belongs to the people, the deer, the fish, and the trees.

A River Runs through It

> There is a story which goes something like this. "Grandmother," said the young Indian girl, "What are those big things in the river?" The grandmother raised her eyes towards the broken blocks of massive concrete through which the river poured. "Daughter," the old woman replied, "Those are the dams the white people left."
>
> —Jean Johnson, journalist, *Indian Country Today*[27]

Draining almost 10,000 square miles of southeastern Oregon and northern California, the Klamath River at one time supported the third-largest salmon population in the country. The natural salmon runs are today impeded by seven dams, 45 pumping stations, 185 miles of canals, and 516 miles of irrigation ditches that stretch like a web over the land. Less than 25% of the original wetlands remain, and within those wetlands, some 25,000 acres have been leased out to farmers, adding to the 200,000 acres of farmland remade in the area. It is, of course, a familiar story in the arid West—water is moved from where it was to places it likely should not be, then a century later, the ecological karma of the situation returns. The Klamath River Basin has become the waste drain for over 470,000 acres of agricultural runoff from well-fertilized farmland.

A "blue-green algae" is sold in health food stores across the continent as a panacea for health concerns and is a direct beneficiary of the nitrogen-laden runoff into the Klamath. That algal bloom sucks dissolved oxygen from the water and suffocates fish. Frequent fish kills plague the Klamath River system, including one of up to 300,000 fish in 2000, and scientists surmise that the lack of dissolved oxygen in the water is the likely source.[28] The agricultural runoff has altered the chemistry of the lakes and wetlands, and waterfowl have declined by two-thirds. Given the state of the environment, however, this is still one of the best places to rest if you are a migratory bird. It's estimated that 80% of the migratory birds in the Pacific flyway, or around 2 million winged creatures, pass through the Klamath refuge every fall. Close on their tails are an estimated 1,000 eagles who follow their prey to this refuge, waiting for a meal. Those eagles remain there most of the winter in rookeries around the basin, where they continue to pick off waterfowl at any opportunity. This is said to be the largest concentration of bald eagles of any area in the lower 48 states.[29]

"What we have," explains Bud Ullman,

> is an overcommitment of the water resource and general ecosystem degradation. There have been promises of water initially to Indians in the treaty…. Then there were promises to the farmers in a big irrigation project, from 1905 until the 1960s, then promises for water to other farms. This all adds up to more water than nature gives us to work with. This year, we have the mother of all droughts here. It's not a simple matter of the dunderheaded fed-

eral government taking water away from farmers. The situation is too often and incorrectly portrayed as fish against farmers. That is both incorrect and a deep disservice to the community.[30]

Indeed. Think about it this way: The 15,600-square-mile Klamath Basin starts high in the Cascade and Siskiyou mountains. Water at the top is siphoned off for the other side of the mountain—the Rogue Valley's lush pear crop and the newly sprawling housing developments get a big slurp before the water even gets to the Klamath Lake. Then it's leftovers. The farmers and the wildlife refuges need, according to National Wildlife Refuge manager Phil Norton, half a million acre-feet of water a year. Double that, if you want to actually protect fish in the ecosystem. That is more than there is, upstream and downstream. Bad math means bad water policy. Add global climate change to that math, a couple of drought years, and dams without fish ladders, and you have the recipe for an ecological nightmare.

"The management of that water project," explains Yurok Tribe executive director Troy Fletcher, "controls the flow to the main stem of the Klamath River, which is a major concern, so fish can migrate out to sea. An acre-foot of water left in the rivers that feed Upper Klamath Lake would do just as good, for the fish, as an acre-foot kept from flowing out of the lake for agriculture. You can debate how much water fish really need," Fletcher adds, "but it's hard to say they don't need any." Arnie Nova, a fisheries technician for the Yurok Tribe, echoes Fletcher's comments: "They can grow potatoes somewhere else, but the fish in this river can't go somewhere else."[31]

Let's talk about fish. The word for sucker in Klamath is *c'wam*. Asked for the Klamath word for salmon, Bud Ullman responds wryly, "gone." The dams obliterated the salmon in the upper Klamath River system. Downstream the coho are listed as "threatened," but the Yurok (whose reservation spans 44 miles on either side of the lower Klamath River) still rely on the salmon for their way of life. "The river is critical for our cultural survival," Troy Fletcher says, whose family has fished the lower Klamath for generations.

"We depend on the fishery resources in the basin for ceremonial, subsistence, and commercial purposes. We have since the beginning of time."[32]

The Klamath Tribe, under its 1864 treaty, and in each subsequent federal law involving the Klamath, including a termination act, a restoration act, and a federal court ruling in *United States v. Adair*, had reaffirmed the tribe's inherent right to the water. Despite having their reservation whittled down from 2.2 million to 880,000 acres, the Klamath survived. They also survived the Termination Act of 1954, and the seizure of their land, largely for Winema National Forest. Through it all, their water remained, perhaps the only constant in the raging tides of federal Indian policy.

"In short," says Bud Ullman "the fish are endangered now, the tribe's fishery is closed, and the tribes are suffering terribly because of the inability to fish." In terms of just money, revenues from the farming operations in the Klamath project area represent around $100 million, largely from potatoes, peppermint, onions, and horseradish. According to U.S. Geological Survey estimates, fishing in the Klamath watershed (despite its ecologically compromised situation) represents an $800 million industry.

The Bush administration, which hasn't been particularly supportive of small farmers (as opposed to large corporate farms), has weighed in on the side of the Klamath Basin farmers with unusually avid support. In turn, anti-Indian and "Wise Use" groups are fanning conflict between the Native community, environmentalists, and the farmers, with convoys of farmers reportedly on their way to take a stand with their water-strapped allies. In a future with global warming and increasing scarcity over water resources, there are no easy answers. Conservation groups, however, are forwarding proposals to buy out willing farmers and retire some land from production, or at least diminish the water demand. At present, conservation groups have options on about 30,000 acres of farmland, at a hefty $3,000–4,000 an acre. There are other proposals to farm crops needing less water. Given that the Klamath peoples have seen some of the most ludicrous examples of past Indian policy, a federal buy-out of non-Indian lands is another reasonable suggestion. As Oren Lyons,

Faithkeeper of the Onondaga Nation, and other great Native leaders have said countless times, "The only compensation for land is land."[33]

The Bush administration has not signaled much indication of fulfilling its trust responsibility to the Klamath peoples. In the highly politicized 2001 water war along the Klamath, when some 1,400 farmers pried open irrigation gates out of the Klamath system to water their fields, the White House intervened. The Bush administration, through Secretary of the Interior Gail Norton, opened the headgates of a dam on Klamath Lake, allowing the water to flow to the farmers and cutting off the water for the fish in the Klamath River system. By fall 2002, over 30,000 salmon had died in the river system, not to mention a multitude of suckers.[34] As bloated, dead fish floated down the Klamath River, the Klamath people, and theYurok, Karuk, and Hupa communities downstream, joined with fishermen and environmentalists in opposing the Bush administration's environmental management policies.

The three- to five-year reproduction cycle of the fish means that the impact of the 2002 fish kill will be felt for years ahead.[35] In September 2003, the salmon population experienced yet another catastrophe. An accident at a PacifiCorp dam on the Klamath River killed off most of the fish in a salmon hatchery. As the story goes, after routine maintenance, a PacifiCorp employee at the Irongate Dam accidentally forgot to restore the water flows. As a result, 40,000 Chinook salmon offspring that had survived the previous year's massacre, as well as 30,000 steelhead, perished at the nearby hatchery.[36]

Valuable Stuff

The United States is the largest hydraulic society on the planet.[37] Our huge cities and industrialized agriculture have only been possible through the enormous efforts of the U.S. Army Corps of Engineers. The Klamath River Basin is one of some 17 major river systems in the western United States that are focal points for litigation, policy debate, and huge conflict over Native water rights in the face of di-

minishing water quality and increasing demands.[39] All told, explains
Dan Israel, an attorney hired by the Klamath Tribe of Oregon to sue
for protection of the Klamath River system,

> these rivers in the West are becoming more like national parks be-
> cause of the high degree of federal legislation influencing public
> streams. A century and a half ago, many tribes were put on reserva-
> tions right in the middle of these water basins. Today, the tribes
> probably control about half of the unused water in the West, and
> that stuff's getting real valuable.[40]

The destruction of the salmon of the Klamath River has taken its
toll on tribal communities spiritually as well as economically. In summer 2004, the Klamath Tribe (following related lawsuits by the
Yurok Tribe against the Bureau of Reclamation) filed suit against
PacifiCorp and its parent company, Scottish Power. The suit challenged the legitimacy of the five dams that span the Klamath River,
destroying virtually all of the salmon runs reaching the Klamath people. While most Native communities would be hard-pressed to put a
price tag on their river system, lawyers are good at numbers. That
price tag is a billion dollars. The tribes and environmentalists are also
opposing the relicensing of PacifiCorp's dams; its federal license ex-
pires in 2006.[41]

Dan Israel has been successful in water rights litigation for a
number of other western tribes, securing two of the largest river water judgements ever, including a $450 million settlement for the Col-
orado Ute and a $250 million award for the Northern Ute. The legal
precedents may be of some concern to Scottish Power, whose stake
in the Klamath is relatively small in terms of its electric-generating capacity: the 160-megawatt project on the river generates enough
power for 77,000 homes. The Klamath dams represent less than 2%
of PacifiCorp's power.

If the lawsuit is not enough to impress the Scots, seeing the
Klamath people may help. In 2004, representatives of the Klamath
people traveled to Edinburgh, Scotland, to Scottish Power's annual
general meeting.

"I have traveled all this way because the dams mean that I have never been able to see a salmon in my part of my river. They have denied me my birthright," Gail Hatcher from the Klamath Tribe told a reporter. Leaf Hillman, Karuk Vice-Chairman, added, "We have lived there since time began and so have the fish. Our dependence is reciprocal. The fish and the river have provided for us for all those years. Now it is our turn to pay them back."[42]

The trip resulted in a meeting with Scottish Power and PacifiCorp executives and a commitment to at least consider removing the dams. PacifiCorp director Judith Johansen told the delegation that "there is no fixed vision on the final outcome of the [Final License] application and we are open to the idea of dams coming out."[43]

Downstream on the Klamath, the Karuk, Yurok, and other peoples continue to pray for their salmon. They have also raised a new twist in the PacifiCorp dam licensing. The Karuks have urged the Federal Energy Regulatory Commission to recognize the high levels of diabetes, heart disease, and other ailments among the Klamath River tribes as a result of the dams. "Government bureaucrats look at you a little bit sideways when you raise the issue of human rights," explains Leaf Hillman. "It's only credible when you raise the issue in Sudan or South America. But whenever you deny or taint a food source for a people, it really is about human rights."[44]

The lawsuits, politicians, power companies, and biologists will continue to argue. In the meantime, the Klamath will persevere. They are a people who have lived along the Klamath River for 14,000 years, and they intend to stay. They will continue to struggle and pray in their First Sucker ceremonies, and one day there will be suckers and salmon in the river again. And one day, the people will have their land—the land with a river that runs through it.

Part 2

Ancestors, Images, and Our Lives

Sonja Holy Eagle, Lakota
(Photo by Keri Pickett)

Imperial Anthropology

The Ethics of Collecting

They called him Ishi in our language, Pit River. "Is" means man, and our people are called the Iss-ahwii people. That means the Ab-alone or Shell people.... If they called him Ishi it's because he was saying that I am a man, I am a human being.

—Mickey Gemmill, tribal chairman, Redding Rancheria[1]

It is said that we are 99.9% the same, at least in terms of our DNA. What accounts for the amazing difference between peoples, colors, cultures, and worldviews is one aspect of the wonder of being human. The way one comes to understand this diversity is neither through measuring a person's head nor through crushing that skull with a rock; understanding only can come through the nuance of relationships. Through relationships can we perceive how language determines thought and reality, illuminating the gift of the Creator to humans—a gift that one might think of as our minds.

That's not, however, the history of the continent, not least in California, where the Spanish invasion, followed by the discovery of gold, meant the death of whole cultures and languages. It is the story of imperialism and it calls into question the ethics of "collecting" things that belong to other cultures, including their bodies. It is a story told, in this instance, by a people about a man and his brain: Ishi of the Yahi people of the northern reaches of the Sierra Nevada Mountains. It is the story of imperialism and anthropology.

With the crush of industrialization and greed comes the loss of life. Species after species is obliterated from the face of the Earth, from frog diversity to human diversity. California was and continues to be one of the most diverse regions on the continent, containing some of the most amazing differences in Native America. Of the six great linguistic "super-families" of Indigenous North America, five are spoken in California, and those five language families were expressed through 113 dialects.[2] Within these there is still more complexity. In some communities, like the Yana, there are both male and female dialects. Anthropologist Theodora Kroeber notes, "Take the word for 'grizzly bear,' a two-syllable word in the male form, *t'en'na*, the syllables separated by a glottal stop; it becomes *t'et*, a single syllable in the female form."[3] That nuance is definitely not uncovered at the point of a gun or in dissecting the brain of a person.

The Spaniards remade most of coastal California, enslaving Indigenous communities to the work of the Lord in 32 missions created for the perpetuation of this work. Father Junipero Serra accomplished a great deal with a whip and a sword, and when he was proposed in the late 1990s for canonization, the Indigenous community raised a great outcry that *slaveholders should not be saints*. By 1848, through the ministering of Serra and his compatriots in the Church, the so-called Mission Indians had been decimated by the diseases and cruelty of the Spaniards. At the northernmost reaches of rivers like the Trinity and the Sacramento, and in the shadows of Mt. Lassen, however, the Native people—the Wiyots, Yurok, Karuk, Yana, Yahi, and many others—escaped the Spanish onslaught. Unfortunately, the "Forty-niners" would follow these very rivers in their ever-widening search for gold.

"California was so rich in gold and everything that [the settlers] wanted, all the Indians in California moved to Oklahoma or whatever," Mickey Gemmill tells me. "Closed-door hearings were held in Washington…and Congress appropriated approximately $2 million in [the] 1850s—money to basically exterminate the Indians of California. You could go out and kill any Indian man, woman, or child in California and get a bounty." Gemmill, a bear of a man, is a Pit River Indian, and has ancestors from the Yahi, Yana, and other peoples of the region. For three decades he has been recognized as a national leader in Indian Country. "I grew up listening to the horror stories of the slaughter of people in this area. The Indian children, the babies had their heads smashed against oak trees or against rocks. All of those people they killed."

Hiram Good was one of many bounty hunters who participated in the creation of California and the legend of the Forty-niners. According to Kroeber, "The Captain was always entitled to the scalps. At one time Good had forty hanging in the poplar tree by his house. Good was one of the best Indian trailers in northern California and was a dead shot."[4]

Settler historians showed little interest in recording the deaths of the Native people they encountered or much of the slavery and ongoing rape of Native women. Records account for "several," "many," or "few" Native people killed in any given instance, while exact numbers of settler deaths are recorded. The most meager data from the battles and skirmishes of the Mt. Lassen region suggests that one white person would have been killed for every 30 to 50 Indians. Such is the accounting for the destruction of a people. The Native oral history breaks the silence on the genocide, and recent writings by Jack Norton, David Stannard, and others have documented the widespread massacres that occurred in northern California. As Stannard states:

> From almost the instant of first human contact between Europe and the Americas, firestorms of microbial pestilence and purposeful genocide began laying waste the American natives.... [D]isease and genocide were independent forces acting dynamically—whipsawing their victims between plague and violence, each one feeding upon the other, and together driving countless numbers of entire ancient societies to the brink—and often over the brink—of total extermination...from fifteenth-century Hispaniola to nineteenth-century California.[5]

Then there was the forced assimilation of thousands of those who survived. Kroeber notes that the soberly estimated numbers of kidnappings of Indian children by whites in California to be sold as slaves or kept as cheap help was, between the years 1852 and 1867, from three to four thousand, and every Indian woman, girl and girl child was potentially and in thousands of cases actually subject to repeated rape, to kidnapping and to prostitution. Prostitution was unknown to aboriginal California, as were venereal diseases, which accounted for forty to as high as eighty percent of Indian deaths following the gold rush.[6]

In a time of immense violence, it only takes a short time for life to be totally transformed. In the ten or so years before Ishi's birth, the Yana lived a nomadic life in over 2,400 square miles of land recognized by other tribes as Yana territory, in the upper reaches of the river systems near what is presently Sacramento. Life was still somewhat as it always had been. By 1872, 22 years later, there were no Southern Yana left, and only some 20 or 30 scattered "individuals of the Northern and Central Yana remained alive. As for…the Yahi, they were believed to have been entirely exterminated, and so they were except for a handful, Ishi among them."[7] A few from each community had been absorbed into their neighboring communities.

"I am a man"

So it was, that on September 4, 1911, a man considered to be the last Yahi, the man who came to be named Ishi, walked out of the killing grounds of northern California and into the town of Oroville with an oral history of it all. Rescued from the Oroville jail by famed anthropologists T. T. Waterman and Alfred Kroeber, Ishi was taken to live in a San Francisco anthropology museum, where his closest friends were Kroeber and other scientists, who referred to him not only as the "last wild Indian in the United States" but as a friend as well. Kroeber worked with Ishi to record language, rituals, toolmaking, and history. The pressed-wax recordings of Ishi singing Yahi songs are still valued today, among many from other peoples, as Indigenous communities work to recover their languages.

Until he succumbed to tuberculosis, Ishi lived for five years as a "living specimen" in a complex life that challenged the boundaries of anthropology, ethics, and society. Knowing that he would pass on to the spirit world, he had informed Kroeber and other anthropologists of his wishes to be returned to the earth in his own world. Kroeber agreed, and in a letter dated March 24, 1916, argued to his colleague who was attending to Ishi on his deathbed:

> there is no objection to a cast death mask. I do not, however, see that an autopsy would lead to anything of consequence, but would resolve itself into a general dissection. Please shut down on it. As to disposal of the body...if there is any talk about the interests of science, say for me that science can go to hell. We propose to stand by our friends. Besides, I cannot believe that any scientific value is materially involved. We have hundreds of Indian skeletons that nobody ever comes near to study. The prime interest in this case would be of a morbid romantic nature.[8]

Ishi died on March 25. Kroeber's letter was not received until after the autopsy had been performed, and so began the mystery of Ishi's brain and the changing of Kroeber's thinking.

Enter the head measurer. The Anishinaabeg people of White Earth called him the "Doctor Who Knows Who Indians Are," or the "Head-Measuring Doctor." Remembered for his odd requests to measure the breadth of a head, the span across cheekbones, the size of the forehead, and then scratch the skin, Dr. Ales Hrdlicka was the preeminent physical anthropologist of the Smithsonian Institute.[9] In 1916, Hrdlicka was fascinated with such measurements as the femoral-cranial index, the greatest facial breadth in the plane of the aygomatic arches, and suppositions as to the relationship between brain size and cultural groups.[10] Hrdlicka's work was instrumental in the creation of "blood rolls" on the timber-rich and fertile White Earth Reservation in Minnesota. His data was used to categorize "mixed bloods," whose land could then be alienated under federal Indian policy.

When Hrdlicka received a letter from Alfred Kroeber offering him the possibility of securing Ishi's brain, he must almost have peed his pants. "Dear Dr. Hrdlicka," Kroeber wrote, "I find that at Ishi's death last spring, his brain was removed and preserved. There is none here who can put it to scientific use. If you wish it, I shall be glad to deposit it in the National Museum collection." Hrdlicka replied exuberantly, "My Dear Dr. Kroeber: I hardly need to say that we shall be very glad to receive and take care of Ishi's brain and, if a suitable opportunity occurs, to have it worked up." And so the brain was sent from California to the Smithsonian.[11]

For 83 years, Ishi's brain sat preserved in a chemical soup, eventually coming to rest in a storage facility in Maryland. In the meantime, the state of California grew, and the Yahi, Yana, Round Valley, Pit River, and other peoples of northern California tried simply to survive. Ishi, it turned out, was not the last of his people. They had intermarried throughout the river systems of northern California, and their memories and blood remained.

Ishi's Descendants

There is a direct relationship between the price of real estate, the diminishment of Native title, and subsequent complications in legal redress. California is a case study of theft, politics, and betrayal.

During the early years after California became a state in 1850, Native peoples had come close to securing over 7.5 million acres in the state, but before the 18 pertinent treaties could be ratified, political pressure by the gold prospectors and other politically powerful interests killed the treaties in the U.S. Senate. With limited policy options open and the continued decline in Native community health and social conditions, some wealthy Californians began to take an interest in the Indigenous peoples. Several groups of influential women ("'the robber barons' wives, the rich ladies," as Mickey Gemmill calls them) lobbied on behalf of California Indians and helped create the California Rancherias, state-designated reservations where much of the Native community resides today. It wasn't until almost 75 years after statehood that the 18 "lost treaties" were given renewed legal impetus through the federal California Indian Reorganization Act of 1928, also known as the Lea Act. On the basis of the Lea Act, people of the Pit River and other California tribes pursued a set of claims to California lands through the federal Indian Claims Commission created in 1923.

"I became involved in the land claims in the 1960s," Gemmill continues.

The Consolidated Indian Claims Act paid for 94 million acres out of the 150 million acres of land [in California]. The Pit River Nation began organizing a movement for return of 3,386,000 acres taken illegally from us without consent and without compensation. We had a separate land claim than the Consolidated Indian Claims Act, and...we won. That was the largest compensatory claim at that time, and we refused the money because we wanted our land. We began organizing to support each other (with Native people from across the continent and the Americas), and we began occupying national forests, large corporations' land, and national parks, like Lassen National Park. Lassen National Park was closed for a year [in 1970] during the Native occupation. People came from everywhere to support us in reclaiming our lands, and we were arrested again and again.

Federal relocation programs had made the Bay Area and Los Angeles two of the largest urban Indian communities in the country, and, as a result of the gains of the Civil Rights movement, the Native community began entering the university system in significant numbers during the 1960s. Mickey Gemmill was a student at San Francisco State in the '60s, and took part in the student strike in 1968, which "basically shut down the university." The creation of Third World Studies departments at these schools further galvanized not only Native students but also other students of color to discuss issues of ethics, universities, and history. Campus organizing also provided fertile ground for renewed activism off campus, including the 1969 takeover of Alcatraz Island led by California Indian peoples. The activism of the Native community resulted in the passage of a number of federal laws, including the Indian Self-Determination Act, the American Indian Religious Freedom Act, and the Indian Child Welfare Act, to name a few. The ancestors, however, remained cached away.

In the California university system, Native students came face-to-face with their ancestors' body parts and ceremonial items in one of the largest collections of human remains known. Some of them had earlier, similar experiences. Gemmill remembers, "The first time I went to the Smithsonian in D.C., I was met with a glass case that was 10 feet high, 20 feet wide, filled with human skulls of Indigenous people. I am a Native American person. I could never understand that." He recalls another incident, a bus trip through Salt Lake City. "In their museum [in the basement of the Mormon Church], they had basically a so-called natural setting with nine Indians all in their skin, their hair, everything that the Mormon Church had supposedly found them naturally mummified. They were on public display."

At the universities, the Native students were horrified to learn the scope of collecting that had occurred. With the creation of Native American Studies programs at many of these universities, Native people, who had previously been objectified by academics, became vital proponents of change in institutions. The Native students at Berkeley, Stanford, and other universities pushed for accountability, and found allies as well as opponents within the university systems. As Gemmill describes it, "There was all these rumors that they had dissected [Ishi] and removed his brain. During the 1990s, there was a movement by the Indians of northern California, particularly Oroville, to confront the government and find out 'what you guys really did with Ishi.' And if they had his brain, we wanted it returned."

Nationally, pressure was mounting for the passage of a federal law that would come to be known as NAGPRA, or the Native American Graves Protection and Repatriation Act. California Indian people continued to push for return of their ancestors, and Ishi quickly became the most well-known case. Gemmill tells the story. "The Oroville Indians had been back to Washington and they didn't get very far. But they had some friends like Nancy Rockafeller and Orin Starn, who found the paper trail and the brain. [The Smithsonian had] just discovered it a month before, and they had to admit they had Ishi's brain, and they had to return it."

The problem now would be reuniting Ishi's brain with his ashes, which were in a private cemetery in the Bay Area. The cemetery was reluctant to repatriate the ashes, and the Smithsonian was reluctant to return the brain unless it joined the ashes. Under those circumstances, Gemmill testified to the California legislature. The times were changing for California Indians, largely for monetary reasons.

By the 1990s, tribal casinos had increased the political power of Native Nations. That money helped spur the California legislature into action, and this time, even the state attorney general for California joined in with the Native people to seek the return of the ashes from the cemetery so that Ishi would be reunited.

When the time finally came to reunite Ishi, Gemmill remembers:

> There were two people, Floyd Buckskin and myself, who went to D.C. We had many ceremonies. Then we sewed up those brains in a silver fox skin. That fox is like the Seventh Creator. We had to go through all the airport screening. There was all this public attention, so we had to have a group divert them.... We never let him out of our hands. We flew back with him like that.
>
> When we first got the urn with the ashes, we had them in a private room. You could just feel this powerful spirit. We became aware that no Indians, and no women, had been involved, and so we had women and grandmothers in the final ceremony. We left [Redding Rancheria] in the middle of the night because we wanted to elude the press. We even put his brain into a locked safe while we prepared to take him out. We collected plants for his final journey, and put him in a bearskin, a sacred textile from Guatemala, and a beautiful basket. There's a mountain ridge between Mill Creek and Deer Creek, and in a real beautiful spot in an unmarked grave, that's where he is. We wanted him to be in the heart of his land.
>
> There is nothing easy about the recovery of ancestors, for the living or the ancestors. It's a real emotional thing. Women needed to cry for Ishi; men needed to cry. You feel at peace and you know he's at peace. It's a part of healing.

That healing process remains in sharp contrast to America's colonizers' traditions. The conflict remains.

The Ethics of Collecting

The practice of collecting buried bodies and cultural properties finds its origins in the paradigms of imperialism, science, racism, and the bounty of war. While some of the Europeans who settled North America came for religious refuge, others came in search of adventure, bent on discovering the exotic. In the process of leaving behind their histories in the old lands, the colonists became a people in search of a history—a desire that led many to collecting the history of other peoples. The desecration of Native American remains and sacred objects began with the arrival of Europeans in the Americas: Pilgrims looted graves after arriving in Wampanoag territory on Cape Cod, Thomas Jefferson looked into burial mounds and documented his findings, and priests and ministers often took great pleasure in collecting and then destroying sacred items.[12]

Perhaps it is in an effort to feed the immense spiritual void inherited from its colonial past that the mainstream culture has maintained a persistent tendency toward wanting to discover, classify, and collect everything the mainstream considers exotic. Descendants of settlers are, in a sense, haunted by nostalgia for the lost cultures and fabled pride their forebears worked so hard to annihilate. The sociopathology of the United States rests on its colonialist history and, in particular, on the awesome weight of genocide. In attempting to dispel this burden, science has been instrumental.

Lewis Henry Morgan, the "father" of American anthropology, published the first ethnography of a Native American nation in 1851.[13] Historian Robert Bieder notes that although Morgan was "critical of the insensitivity expressed toward Indians by government policies to promote civilization among tribal peoples," he was responsible for placing the process of acculturation within biology, thus strengthening both the political and the academic arguments that would justify the collecting of human remains.[14] Morgan's biological determinism allowed American policy and the collective American psyche to divorce itself from the responsibility later associated with colonialism—that is, the colonizers' responsibility to care for the colonized. As Bieder explains:

> The shift from an emphasis on external characteristics linked to the environment to internal characteristics linked to heredity allowed Americans not only to retain confidence in the American environment as a positive force for change but also to place the fault of Indian deficiency on their biology and heredity. This freed Americans from having to assume responsibility for the condition of tribal peoples and their future.[15]

In short, if the poverty and social chaos apparent in Native American communities in the 1700s and 1800s could be shown to be based in biology rather than colonialism, then the United States would be absolved.

The colonizers' expectations that Native people would disappear altogether, coupled with the furor of westward expansionism and privatization, fueled a competitive increase in the mining of Native cemeteries in the late 1800s. Take, for instance, the story of the Pawnee. During the 1870s, the Pawnee were forcibly removed from their Nebraska homeland to Oklahoma, 400 miles to the south, leaving behind their vast villages and the graves of their ancestors.[16] When the Pawnees were removed, local citizens and collectors began a mass looting of Pawnee graves. It was not unusual for private collectors to charge admission for the privilege of seeing shellacked bones, like a freak show exhibit at a carnival. Eventually most of the "booty" from the Pawnee graves became housed at the Nebraska State Historical Society and the Smithsonian, including the contents of the graves of two very important Pawnee chiefs: Pitarisaru and Pitaresaru, whose graves yielded treaty medals as well as remains. Also collected were the skulls of six Pawnee men who had been "discharged" from the Army and subsequently massacred by soldiers and Kansas settlers.[17]

The booty of war included the skulls and body parts of many Native people. For instance, many of the Cheyenne who died at the Sand Creek Massacre in 1884 were decapitated by order of the surgeon general of the Army, for the Indian Crania Study. According to the assistant surgeon general in 1868, "The chief purpose had in view in forming this collection is to aid in the progress of anthropological science by obtaining measurements of a large number of skulls of aboriginal races of North America."[18] In 1900, Ales Hrdlicka led an expedition to Larson Bay, Alaska, and, in front of the anguished villagers, dug up and departed with the remains of 800 Koniag people.[19]

An estimated one million Native American remains were held in public and private institutions by the late 1900s. That is, however, a conservative estimate, considering the vastness of private collections and the remains that have been shipped to Europe, Japan, and else-

where.[20] One of the most ambitious of many twentieth-century collectors of Native American objects was Asa T. Hill, a used-car
salesman and amateur archeologist in the 1920s who bought a farm
containing the ruins of a Pawnee town and began his hunt for graves.
He boasted of his interest: "I don't play golf.... My only recreation is
this Indian investigation. I come out Sundays and dig up Indians....
This hill is my golf course."[21]

During the 1960s and '70s Native communities and organizations, including American Indians against Desecration, the American
Indian Movement, the International Indian Treaty Council, and
more mainstream organizations like the Native American Rights
Fund and the National Congress of American Indians, advocated at
local, national, and international levels to find some redress for the
problem of imperial archeology and its appropriation of Native history and peoples.

Most of the stories of successfully repatriated remains and relics
are of individuals who use their voices to build a community of opposition. Such is the story of Maria Pearson, a Lakota elder who lived
near Des Moines, Iowa, and was an outspoken member of the Native
community. It was in 1971 that Pearson learned that archeologists in
Iowa had just dug up human remains from a "pioneer cemetery."
The remains were immediately reburied, with the exception of those
of a young Indian woman. Iowa's state archeologist decided to study
her remains rather than rebury them. It was Maria Pearson who challenged this decision as "totally arrogant." Her work and the growing
public pressure eventually resulted in the first state law requiring the
reburial of Native remains found in unmarked graves.[22]

Millions of dollars of university and donor funding have gone to
collection programs. Harvard's Museum of Comparative Zoology,
the Chicago Field Museum, and the American Museum of Natural
History were some of the first in the field. Other large collections
were amassed near the residences of the leading anthropologists of
the time—the Phoebe Apperson Hearst Museum at Berkeley, near
Alfred and Theodora Kroeber, to name one example.

As Devon Mihesuah writes, "The fact that Indians exist allows
these people—[anthropologists and archaeologists] as well as histori-

ans—to secure job tenure, promotion, merit increases, fellowships, notoriety, and scholarly identity—all without giving anything back to Indian communities."[23] While peer, academic, and donor review is common for academic researchers, Mihesuah argues that more stringent guidelines are needed, such as: "how will your research benefit the people you study?"[24]

Native agitation provoked discussion by organizations like the American Anthropological Association, which in 1971 adopted new standards of ethical conduct. These standards state that "in research, an anthropologist's responsibility is to those he studies. When there is a conflict of interest, these individuals must come first."[25]

It was the work of the Pawnee and many other communities that resulted in the 1989 passage of the National Museum of the American Indian Act, creating a Native museum within the Smithsonian and specifically requiring the Smithsonian to inventory, identify, and return human remains to the appropriate Native nations.[26] The act provides Native people the hope that "one day their ancestors will finally be given the resting place that they so deserve," according to Arizona Senator John McCain, of the Senate Select Committee on Indian Affairs. McCain reiterated the importance of this initial step in beginning to challenge the collecting process and ownership associated with the museums and their relationship to Native peoples. McCain noted that the bill "sends a clear signal to those in the museum community who have dismissed repatriation as a transitory issue that they would be wise to carefully consider."[27]

The museum bill was followed closely by the enactment of the NAGPRA on November 16, 1990. NAGPRA sets out the procedures and standards for the repatriation of human remains, funerary objects, sacred items, and objects of cultural patrimony, and provides for the protection and ownership of materials unearthed on federal and tribal lands by institutions that receive federal funding.

Thirty-four states had passed unmarked burial protection laws by 2000, and two laws had been passed to protect funerary objects and cultural patrimony. Under Nebraska's law, the Pawnee tribe finally repatriated over 400 dead Pawnee in 1990, despite continued resistance from the Nebraska State Historical Society.[28]

There is still much to do. A decade after the passage of NAGPRA, only 10% of an estimated 200,000 remains in public collections has been even inventoried, according to federal records. Leading collections include the Smithsonian, followed by Harvard University and then the University of California at Berkeley, with 8,000 remains.

Showing moral leadership on the issue, the University of Michigan returned 16-18 human remains in the spring of 2005 to the Whitefish River band of Ojibwe after holding them for 60 years. The remains had been dug up in 1938 by Emerson Greenman, a university professor, and preserved by the Museum of Anthropology. After 20 years of requests by the Ojibwe, the university finally agreed in March 2005 to return the remains.[29]

Many institutions evidence a lack of compassion in their attempts to abstract and objectify Native remains into the realms of academic freedom and academic properties. Powerful academic institutions have contributed to the delays, and federal "white tape" has augmented the process. The most recent example is that of the "Kennewick man," a 9,600-year-old ancestor whose bones were discovered in the Columbia River in 1996. In this case, forensic and other anthropologists have waged a fierce struggle to keep him from being repatriated by the Columbia River tribes, arguing that he is a "national treasure" and the "common heritage of all Americans that should be studied for the benefit to all."[30] Scientists opposed to his reburial seem to argue that if the ancestor is old enough, the law does not protect him. Citing academic freedom and the need for scientific knowledge, many academics and curators forestall repatriation, and the recent legal decisions regarding the Kennewick man have given academics a bit more leeway. (See the "Vampires" chapter for more on Kennewick man.)

At the center of the discussion, however, there still remains a difference in worldviews. "It really comes down to a distinction between thinking that you own remains or sacred objects versus understanding that you are custodians or stewards for them," explained historian Martin Sullivan, who spent eight years on the national NAGPRA advisory committee.[31]

Mickey Gemmill says that the University of California has been

fighting NAGPRA tooth and nail. They've returned a few bones. They called me [in 2004] because they had to figure out how to return some 60 human remains.... After we got there, they were on a table going 40–50 feet long one way, then another 60 feet going the other way. They started out with skulls, some with bullet holes, down to baby skulls. They kind of like it categorized in that way. All along with them are all kinds of stacks of bones, rib bones, finger bones. You see little baby rib bones that are really tiny, and it's a very emotional thing.

Many tribes are unsure of whose ancestors are held where; many have limited repatriation capacity. Some Indigenous communities have discussed opening their lands for repatriation of ancestors from other tribes, just to ensure that the ancestors are allowed to go back to Mother Earth, the land.[32]

Our Relatives are Poisoned

Everything we make, whether it's basketry or regalia, comes from our heart, from our feeling of goodness, from our creator making our dances carry on forever. When the regalia don't dance, they cry. We believe that very strongly.

—David Hostler, director, Hoopa Valley Tribal Museum[33]

As the Trinity River cascades down from the deepest woods of northern California, it finds the Hoopas, down river from the Yahi. At the center of Hoopa ceremonial life are the Earth Renewal ceremony, the Jump Dance, and the Brush Dance, all performed with some continuity over the past millennium. That in itself is an amazing feat, considering the level of destruction wrought by the California gold rush on the Indigenous people of the region.

The Hoopa Valley Reservation bridges the Trinity River for a good span of trees, river, and people. Here is the home of the Hoopa Valley Tribal Museum, a modest place where some of that which is treasured by the Hoopa may come to rest. The Hoopa, like most other Native peoples, had their cultural patrimony, their most sacred regalia and the objects essential for their ceremonial practices, hauled off to museums elsewhere. The closets of the collectors are full of skeletons, full of ancestors, and full of sacred items. When the Hoopa found that much of their history was at Harvard's Peabody Museum, David Hostler, director of the Hoopa museum, went to Cambridge to look through the closets.

Hostler describes the moment when he got the first inkling of the problem with retrieving their lost patrimony. "As we started going through the collections, I was forewarned to wear gloves and a breathing apparatus. They said, 'We don't know what's on this stuff, but to be safe, you should wear gloves.' I didn't get no clear understanding of the problem until I got back, but that's when I first learned about the poison." He is referring to the broad array of chemicals that collectors had been using for around 100 years to ward off bugs, rodents, and any other pests that could be imagined. Those toxic pesticides included mercury, arsenic, thymol, DDT, and naphthalene, used individually or in unique combinations.[34] "I've always told people that if it's organic, if it's fur or fiber, and it's over 50 years old, it's been dosed pretty heavily," explains Richard Hitchcock, the repatriation coordinator at Berkeley's Hearst Museum.[35]

Herein lies a core complication with the provenance of collecting and undoing the collecting. First, Native people are subjected to genocide. Then, when their extermination seems very likely to be complete, anthropologists raise alarms about the culture being "lost." Bones are dug up and the other sacred items are taken to far-off museums. The survivors are separated from all the things that make life meaningful, and the academics get tenure. Communities suffer under an immeasurable loss: the loss of the people, the ancestors, the songs, the ceremonies, and the sacred items that are part of the ceremonies. If communities survive through it all and finally begin to find redress, they feel glimmers of hope. The collections are identified and the tribes retrieve their items, their people, their relatives. But after retrieval comes a new difficulty, described by journalist Matt Palmquist.

> Their regalia, after being stolen by whites, contaminated in museums and returned at great expense to the tribes, are too poisoned to use and too precious to pack away. If they bury the items, they

risk contaminating the soil and poisoning their groundwater; if they burn them, they risk scarring their lungs by inhaling the pollutants.[36]

That is where what Palmquist refers to as the "dirty little secret" of the museums becomes a public health problem. Indeed, the problem is so significant that when the Hopis finally recovered their Kachina masks, one of them was so contaminated that Arizona scientists classified it legally as toxic waste. The Hopis, and other tribes, are now noticeably more cautious and concerned with the repatriation process.[37]

Tribes lack the infrastructure and hundreds of thousands of dollars worth of equipment needed to test the items, and there is no simple recipe for decontamination. Universities, by and large, may have the equipment, but lack the grant money needed to undertake the effort to identify the contaminants and assist tribes with decontamination. San Francisco State University helped the Hoopas with their items, testing some 17 of the items the Hoopa brought back from Harvard, but this is the best-case scenario of academic responsibility.[38] While universities often directed and applauded a good portion of the historical collecting, university chemical departments and laboratories today do not have the interest to do the analytic chemistry that San Francisco State professor Pete Palmer refers to as a community service.[39]

Tribes, in many cases, believe that the institutions that contaminated their sacred items should clean them up, but most institutions point out that the poisoning was unintentional, that their own workers have a high risk of contamination, and that the funds for cleaning are just not there. Paulette Hennum, NAGPRA coordinator for California's Department of Parks and Recreation, helped get some funding for testing at San Francisco State University, but still feels challenged for solutions. She gives some easy advice, like using mylar strips on a contaminated headband to avoid contact with the skin, and tells tribes to "assume the worst." "We go out and open this huge can of worms," she says, "and we give them a little Band-Aid: 'Now you know, now you're scared, here's a smock and good luck.' "[40]

There is no easy answer to this quandary. Sacred items often remain encased in plastic on the shelves of tribal historians, mummified and only able to watch the descendants of their makers from their high perch. Hostler tells the story of going to view some sacred objects held in a collection: "I was looking at the most beautiful regalia. And I looked at it and I literally cried, like a little baby out loud, and I felt embarrassed when I got through. But what that was telling me was that the regalia was crying, so it made me cry. I was told that, but I never knew it until I literally cried out loud."[41] So Hostler took some of the sacred regalia to the Brush Dance, and draped a few items across a bench. From there the items could participate in the dance only as a spectator, but at least the songs were not muffled and 3,000 miles away.

Spoils of War

History is filled with fascinating ironies and contrasts. The horrors of the Nazi Holocaust remain indelibly etched in the memories of survivors and descendants, and hopefully on the psyches of all alive today. Yet the ethics applied to one holocaust experience are not necessarily applied to another.

A forum titled "The Spoils of War: World War II and Its Aftermath: The Loss, Reappearance, and Recovery of Cultural Property" was held at New York's Bard College in 1995, with panelists presenting the story of works of art stolen by German Nazis during World War II. Right after the war, some 200 of these works of art were transferred by the U.S. Army from high-security warehouses in Wiesbaden, Germany, to the National Gallery in Washington, D.C. A major outcry from those responsible for the care of the collection resulted in the Wiesbaden Manifesto, which declared:

> We are unanimously agreed that the transportation of those works of art [to Washington, D.C.] undertaken by the United States Army, upon direction from the highest national authority, establishes a precedent which is neither morally tenable nor trustworthy.... No historical grievance will rankle so long, or be the cause of so much justified bitterness, as the removal, for any reason, of a part of the heritage of any nation, even if that heritage be inter-

preted as a prize of war.... There are yet further obligations to common justice, decency and the establishment of the power of right, not might, among civilized nations.[42]

The Wiesbaden Manifesto was so compelling that it resulted in President Harry Truman ordering the return of many masterpieces to Germany. The exemplary language and process of the Manifesto sets a moral foundation that should be more broadly applied to the Native American art market, argues Elizabeth Sackler, former director of the American Indian Repatriation Foundation, affiliated with the Association on American Indian Affairs. Most collectors of Native American arts and crafts are unable to provide provenance for the artifacts due to the questionable origins of the material and the inappropriate methods of sale. Examples might include a pair of moccasins collected at Wounded Knee or a Cheyenne parfleche from Little Big Horn. Those two items were sold together at an auction for $11,385.[43]

The Wiesbaden Manifesto has not been applied to the collecting of Indigenous regalia—a moral and legal loophole that has been incredibly lucrative and convenient for both institutional and individual collectors, and a source of major anguish for the Native community. There is no doubt that the repatriation process is fundamental to the healing of the community. The Native community requires that the collectors clean out their closets, and, indeed, at some level, that America looks at its psychology of collecting from other cultures. And, one might easily propose that more doctoral degrees should be given for applied work, like maybe decontaminating "collections" for their homecoming.

White Earth Anishinaabe writer Gerald Vizenor has an interesting proposal for the legal standing of ancestral remains: bone courts. "Bones have a right to be represented and heard in court. These rights, not the assumed rights of science or the interests of politicians, must be the principal concern in court..... Tribal bones [must] cease to be the neocolonial research chattel of the...sciences."[44] One might add that brains also have a right to standing in court, a right that might have helped Ishi and his descendants.

Pawnee scholar James Riding In has a sort of pragmatic set of be-liefs. "I simply advocate that American Indians receive what virtually every other group of Americans enjoys: that is, the right to religious freedom and a lasting burial."[45] I remember my own conversation with one of our Midewiwin leaders on this subject in Anishinaabeg country. I asked what the word was for the ceremony where the an-cestors were reburied. "The Sending Them off Again Ceremony," was Eddie Benton Benais's response, from the Three Fires Midewiwin Lodge. "There was no word for that ceremony in our lan-guage; we had to make it up. Who would think we would have to bury our ancestors twice?"[46]

Quilled Cradleboard Covers, Cultural Patrimony, and Wounded Knee

The [Wounded Knee] massacre and the theft of 7.3 million acres of Black Hills land have always been interconnected in important ways in Lakota thought and history; ways that non-Indian historians have rarely understood. The Ghost Dance religion and resulting Wounded Knee massacre in 1890 were caused by (among other things) the theft of the Black Hills in 1877, and of nine million additional acres of land in 1889, not other reasons given by apologists in history. Lakota people were looking for salvation in a messiah that would rid them of the non-Indian intruders and the terrible conditions they were living under in the late 1880s, the famine, sickness and death. They wanted their stolen lands and way of life restored.

—Mario Gonzales, Oglala Lakota attorney[1]

Alex and Debra White Plume's house sits perched in a canyon overlooking Wounded Knee Creek. Each summer, their herd of 50 or so horses is set into motion, ridden in the local horse races that commemorate the 1875 Little Big Horn victory of the Lakota over George Custer—or other informal tournaments in which Lakotas dare anyone who is crazy enough to race them on Pine Ridge Reservation.

The willows still stand by Wounded Knee Creek, the cottonwoods and the clay, just as they have for a thousand years or more. It is as if the relatives with roots in Lakota teachings are watching the horse races, most likely the same kinds of races that were run and

87

won 150 years ago on the same banks. While the world around the Lakota has changed dramatically, there is something constant about Lakota culture and perhaps their spiritual blood itself. The Lakota may adapt to new times, but in their essence they remain, like their ancestors, the Lakota Oyate, the Lakota Nation.

Not far from the White Plume's home is an environmental disaster of toxic tailings, ponds, cyanide, and a hole in the earth a mile wide and 1,000 feet deep. This is what's left of the Homestake Gold Mine in *He Sapa* or *Cante Ognaka,* the Heart of Everything That Is, what the Lakota call the Black Hills. The mine had taken billions of dollars of gold out of the Black Hills—a fortune for families like that of William Randolph Hearst.[2] In the winter of 2001 South Dakota's leading senator, Tom Daschle, negotiated a Christmas present for Toronto-based Barrick Gold Mining Company, which had operated the mine with George Bush, Sr., on its board of advisers.[3] Daschle organized a deal to let the company off the hook for cleanup, with the federal government assuming costs estimated to be around $50 million. Attorney Edward Lazarus quipped, "It reaffirms an unsurprising truth: This country deals far more generously with foreign corporations that buy [U.S.] land than with the native peoples from whom we took it."[4]

As disparate as the negotiations of mining corporations with the U.S. Congress and the White Plume horse races may seem, they are related by time, money, blood, and bullets. The complexity of unraveling a historic event, tracing its causes and implications 100 years later, amazes me. Such is the story of the Wounded Knee Massacre, that fateful winter day in 1890 when more than 300 men, women, and children were killed by the troops of the Seventh Cavalry under the command of Colonel John Forsyth.

Cankpe Opi, Wounded Knee

The wind blows over the grave site today, touching the faces of both ancestors and descendants, stones and bones, all related somehow through the passage of time, by a touch, a song, or a bullet. I feel the wind as I climb the hill to the mass grave, joined now by the graves of the more recent residents of Wounded Knee village, and I wait my turn to enter the church on the site. A family has come to bury one of their own, a longtime resident of Wounded Knee village who has passed on. An elderly man smiles at me as I enter.

Time is different at *Cankpe Opi,* the village of Wounded Knee. In this one place two very important moments stand side by side. Here is where the sacred hoop of a people and a way of life was broken in 1890, where people's lives and dreams were shattered. And this is also where, 83 years after the Massacre, other dreams were remembered and a flame rekindled with the armed takeover of the Wounded Knee church and trading post by Lakota people and allies from the American Indian Movement. The second Wounded Knee, in many ways, began to rebuild the sacred hoop. The 1973 takeover, on the heels of the occupation of Alcatraz Island, the Trail of Broken Treaties caravan to Washington, D.C., and numerous other demonstrations and takeovers, marked a renaissance and rebirth in Native America. It also marked a time when the United States itself, amid the emotional and political fallout from its own struggles over the Vietnam War, watched as Native American people stood vigilant against an immense show of force by the U.S. military and survived. There is a sense of amazing power at this place. I look out on the village from the hillside from whence the ancestors must look also. This place, if any, is where a people must be allowed to heal.

Wounded Knee village is used as a cliché by the U.S. media; almost every major magazine and network has visited it in the past decade, all to talk about the economic poverty on the Pine Ridge Reservation. It is a dubious honor—Shannon County on the Pine Ridge Reservation is one of the poorest in the United States, and has retained that position for the greater part of this past century. In his tour calling attention to U.S. poverty, President Clinton made a visit to the Pine Ridge Reservation in 1998, becoming only the second president in U.S. history to set foot on an Indian reservation.

Here is a good question to ask the president, or any representative of the federal government—a question directed from Wounded Knee but echoed in the heart of Native America: *How can people recover or heal themselves without reconciliation, without apology, and without addressing the crime?* Since the 1993 transition in South Africa from a state of legalized slavery to a nation led by those who had been oppressed, South Africa's Truth and Reconciliation Commission has set an international standard for a country trying to deal with its past of genocide and oppression. The process of allowing those whose pain is not healed to begin a dialogue is critical to building a healthy nation. It is a process still foreign to the United States, but there is always hope for truth, hope for peace.

There was one formal attempt in South Dakota to heal from the devastation of Wounded Knee. In 1990, South Dakota Governor George Mickelson declared a Year of Reconciliation, an acknowledgement of the Wounded Knee Massacre. It was an opportunity to begin healing between the settler and the Native. The year was intended to begin a discussion on the conflicts exemplified by the Massacre, which continue today in jurisdiction issues, law enforcement, racism, and economic and political battles between the state of South Dakota and the Lakota Nation. Although the renaming of Columbus Day to Native American Day is a result of Mickelson's initiative, it produced little else. There were, at the outset, some significant subjects omitted in the framing of the reconciliation dialogue, including return of the Black Hills to the Lakota Nation, congressional apology for the Wounded Knee Massacre, revocation of Army medals awarded for the Massacre, and the return of items and clothing stripped from the bodies at the Massacre site.

Instead of following the model created by South Africa's Truth and Reconciliation Commission, South Dakota–style reconciliation is more like a victim of sexual abuse having to sit down in a counseling session with the perpetrator present, only there is no discussion of the crime. The primary beneficiary of the crime of Wounded Knee is the federal government, the second is the state of South Dakota, both of which today hold vast sections of Lakota land. The victims of the crime, the Lakota, continue to struggle with laws not of their own making, economics derived from the theft of land and life, and the scars that remain with the victims of horrendous crimes. It is a hundred years later, and these issues remain, glaring and connecting each generation to the past in a way that makes it difficult to heal. Through it all, the people and the land remain.

Cante Ognaka: The Heart of Everything That Is

The center of the Lakota universe lies in the *He Sapa*, the Black Hills. The Lakota Oyate originated, it is said, from the Black Hills, as did the *Pte Oyate,* the buffalo nation. The Lakota say that in the beginning things were different, that, for instance, the buffalo ate the humans. Then at one point, there was to be a race to determine who would eat whom in the future. The great race, it is told, was held on a path that surrounds the Black Hills. The four-legged were on one side, and the winged creatures and the two-legged were on the other. Each side put forth its best runners, and the arduous race began. The magpie, in the end, won the race for the two-legged and the winged creatures, and the race track remains, it's said, surrounding the *Cante Ognaka*, the Black Hills. Still visible, it is seen in the Geographic Information System and satellite pictures of the region. The *He Sapa* is the place where visions are sought and found to this day. Here, Lakota people and many others continue their vision quest ceremonies and reaffirm their relationship to the land.

The Lakota Oyate, in each treaty with the U.S. government, reserved this sacred land as the heart of their homeland. The 1851 treaty with the Lakota and 1868 Fort Laramie Treaty both recognized Lakota control of these lands, allowing U.S. citizens only passage through this territory. It took less than ten years after the Fort Laramie Treaty for the United States to abrogate its commitments.

In 1874, Lt. Colonel George A. Custer left Fort Lincoln (near Bismarck, North Dakota) and entered the Black Hills from the north. His expedition dispatched reports of huge gold deposits in the *He Sapa*.[5] There is nothing like gold fever to ensure the theft of land. The "Thieves Road," as Custer's route was called by the Lakota, was the entryway for hundreds of miners and settlers, and created pressure for the illegal seizure of the Black Hills. In 1876, the federal government created a commission headed by a federal treaty negotiator, who had just "negotiated" the transfer of most of the copper and iron ore country of Minnesota, Wisconsin, and Michigan, which belonged to the Ojibwe. The approach was relatively simple and well proven: Cut the rations and then negotiate.

Although starved by cuts to their rations, the Lakota would not relinquish their Black Hills. The treaty negotiator was unable to secure the agreement of three-quarters of all adult males, the percentage required to alter the Treaty of Fort Laramie. Unimpressed by this display, the government took the land anyway. The Black Hills Act was a unilateral "eminent domain taking," through which the United States confiscated the Black Hills in 1877.

By the 1880s, the Lakota were trying the white man's legal system, talking about filing a claim against the United States for the seizure of their lands. After four decades of legal maneuvering, Congress waived its sovereign immunity and granted jurisdiction of Indian claims to the Court of Claims, a federal court that was to be the process, essentially, for legalizing the theft of Turtle Island.

In 1946, the Indian Claims Commission Act was created by a U.S. Congress interested in legitimizing the federal government's relationship to Native America.[6] The Indian Claims Commission Act defined the bases on which Native nations, as sovereigns, might litigate in the courts. These included:

> Claims in law or equity arising under the constitution, laws and treaties of the United States; Claims which would result of the treaties, contracts and agreements between the claimant and the United States were revised on the grounds of fraud duress, unconscionable consideration, mutual or unilateral mistake, whether of law or fact or any other grounds recognizable by the court of inquiry.[7]

A Lakota suit, filed in 1923, began a process that would take 57 years. In 1980, the Court of Claims in an eight-to-one vote awarded the Lakota $105 million for the Black Hills and $40 million for the land east of the Missouri River taken by the government. The claim was, at that time, the single-largest legal award against the government in U.S. history.[8]

The Lakota position for the past 100 years has been the same: They want the return of their land. "The problem is two worldviews and a lot of gold," explains Oliver Red Cloud, chairman of the Black Hills Treaty Council and great grandson of Chief Red Cloud, a treaty signer. "We don't want to settle. We want our land back."[9] The bands of the Lakota Nation knew that the monetary settlement was immense, and that a starve-or-sell strategy was the federal government's way of doing business. The federal government fully expected the Lakota to cave-in to the settlement. For the past three decades, the Lakota have resisted the settlement being forced upon them. Even federal management of the financial accounting on the settlement money remains dubious, illustrating in some ways that which the Lakota know: Land is forever, money is just for today. [10]

Despite the fact that the government's starve-or-sell practices remain very much intact, a hundred years after the taking of the Black Hills, despite the fact that every social and economic indicator remains stark here, the Lakota position remains firm: "The Black Hills are not for sale."

There is much that could be done to return land and begin a reconciliation process. The Black Hills itself includes over 1.3 million acres held by the Forest Service—lands that could easily be returned to the Lakota Nation. Other lands include the Badlands National Park, more than 240,000 acres, including the Stronghold, a significant cultural and spiritual site to the Lakota Nation, and the last Ghost Dance site for Big Foot's band before the Wounded Knee Massacre.

The Lakota have made many efforts to seek the return of some of their lands and begin the process of redress. Frankly, there has been little support from U.S. politicians. Two stand out for illustrating some courage in their approach to correcting a huge injustice: James Abourezk of South Dakota, and Bill Bradley of New Jersey, both of whom pushed for legislation to return to the Lakota people the Black Hills public lands.

The Bradley Bill, as it was eventually called, embodied the beginning of a reconciliation process, but was not supported by Abourezk's South Dakota congressional colleagues, particularly former senator Tom Daschle. "Daschle not only voted against it, he organized against it," remembers Abourezk. "He organized white citizens against it."[11] The organization Daschle helped start was called the Open Hills Association, a group of miners, people with timber interests, and ranchers who rallied against the return of the public lands within the Black Hills to the Lakota Nation.[12] "You can kind of understand if some of his constituents opposed the bill, but to organize his constituents against the bill, that's something else," said Abourezk.[13]

Although South Dakota representatives to Congress are increasingly reliant on the Native American vote to swing their way, in general, Daschle was quite supportive of turning Lakota assets over to private interests. Actor Kevin Costner was able to secure 639 acres of Forest Service land in exchange for his privately held land in nearby Spearfish Canyon. At the time, Costner and his brother Dan proposed to build the Dunbar Resort in Deadwood, South Dakota, with $13 million in government subsidies.[14]

In 1999, Daschle arranged the transfer of jurisdiction of 90,000 acres of Missouri River lands from the U.S. Army Corps of Engineers to the state of South Dakota. Those lands had been taken from the Lakota Nation and contain many burial sites along the riverbanks. A coalition of Lakota traditionals and the Lakota Student Alliance occupied LaFramboise Island, a sandbar in the Missouri River, near Pierre, for over a year as a protest.[15]

While Daschle supported federal appropriations to tribal colleges, wind energy, and the tribes themselves, his leadership was not the best on redressing the conflicts in South Dakota or caring for its natural wealth. Besides securing the clean-up exemption for the Barrick Mining Company, Daschle attached a rider to a military appropriations bill in 2002, opening up the last roadless area in the Black Hills to loggers. The bill was supported by a compromised Sierra Club and Wilderness Society, but not by the Lakota or other local environmental groups like the Biodiversity Conservation Alliance.[16] In this instance, Daschle mimicked the Bush administration's preemptive logging approach to fire prevention on public lands.[17]

The Lakota were also concerned with a federal Housing and Urban Development appropriation for a recreation center in the city of Sturgis, South Dakota. The facility would have included a shooting range, with a projected 10,000 rounds of ammunition to be shot off daily. The proposed shooting range was within four miles of Bear Butte, the preeminent vision-questing place for the Lakota and a violation, in Lakota perception, of the sacredness of that place. Both Native and non-Native South Dakotans united to oppose the shooting range, and were successful in 2004 in stopping the project.[18]

What appears clear is that South Dakota politicians are, in general, quick to give away lands that are not theirs to those who do not need them, and remain entirely opposed to actual reconciliation with the Lakota Nation. It is also clear that each year there is a need to reconcile on more crimes and more theft from Lakota people. That conflict has its origins in the making of wealth and the letting of blood that founded South Dakota.

The Road to Wounded Knee

What I do as a lawyer is base my legal paradigms on the Indian perspective of treaties: that the Treaties are the Supreme Law of the Land. Unfortunately, others see these treaties as less than sacred. What I mean to say about the 1868 Treaty of Fort Laramie is that it was a Treaty of Peace, not a treaty for cession of Lakota territory. What I say about the Wounded Knee Massacre of 1890 is that it was a crime against humanity for which the United States must be indicted.

—Mario Gonzales, Lakota attorney[19]

There is perhaps no event that so embodies the history of American westward expansion as the Wounded Knee Massacre, a senseless tragedy resulting from a media campaign of lies joined with a misinformed and malicious government policy. Indeed, the military plan itself was so bungled that most of the U.S. Cavalry fatalities at Wounded Knee resulted from friendly fire.

It had been a scant 14 years earlier that the Lakota and their allies, the Cheyenne and Arapaho, had celebrated a resounding victory against Custer and the Seventh Calvary of the U.S. Army in the Battle of the Little Big Horn in June 1876. It was a victory that galvanized the Lakota Nation, placed the military strategies and leadership of Sitting Bull forever in the annals of military history, and carved into the U.S. military a deep resentment toward the Lakota and all Native people.

The Lakota chiefs were not only military strategists; they were pragmatic leaders of their people. Since the Army had brought roads and miners to the Black Hills, the great buffalo herds and smaller game had been killed or frightened away. Surviving off their land and the lush ecosystem of the Black Hills was no longer an option. Sitting Bull quickly took his band to Canada to find sanctuary from the American military. Over the next year, Crazy Horse and Red Cloud brought their bands into the Great Lakota Reservation. Sitting Bull finally surrendered in 1881 at Standing Rock Agency.

Although peace and rations had been promised in every treaty after the discovery of gold in the Black Hills and the Black Hills Act, the Great Sioux Nation increasingly became prey to settlers and their depredations. The U.S. government, not content with the Black Hills eminent domain taking, continually pushed for more of the Great Sioux Reservation to be sold or ceded. And it continually cut rations in order to force concessions. Sitting Bull was frank with the negotiators in 1883:

> The Great Father owes us money now for the land he has taken from us in the past. You white men advise us to follow your ways, and therefore I talk as I do. When you have a piece of land, and anyone trespasses on it, you catch them, and keep them until you get damages, and I am doing the same thing now.... I see my people starving, and I want the Great Father to make an increase in the amount of food that is allowed us now, so that they may be able to live. We want cattle to butcher—I want to kill 300 head of cattle at a time. That is the way you live and we want to live the same way.... When the Great Father told me to live like his people, I told him to send me six teams of mules because that is the way white people make a living, and I wanted my children to have these things to help them make a living.... I never ask for anything that is not needed. I also asked for a cow and a bull for each family, so that they can raise their own. I asked for four yokes of oxen and wagons with them.... It is your own doing that I am here; you sent me here and advised me to live as you do, and it was not right for me to live in poverty.... I want to tell you that our rations have been reduced to almost nothing, and that many of our people have starved to death.[20]

The Black Hills Act of 1877 promised a ration of food necessary to sustain the Lakota until their farming and implements allowed them to support themselves, but the implements were many fewer than needed and the rations were reduced much faster than the slow progress of learning farming. By 1886, the annual authorized issue was 8,125,000 pounds of rations, and in 1889, it was 4,000,000 pounds of rations, a reduction of more than 50% in three years, with no corresponding reduction in the Lakota population nor an increase in their ability to support themselves. In 13 years, more than one-third of the Lakota perished from disease and starvation.[21] What followed, however, was worse. A great drought in the Dakotas shriveled the meager Lakota crops, and epidemics of measles, grippe, and whooping cough ravaged a community already weak from hunger.

In this time of discontent the vision of Wovoka, the Paiute Messiah, and the teachings of the Ghost Dance found resonance with the Lakota. Wovoka's vision, it is told, occurred during a solar eclipse on January 1, 1888, and revealed a new, peaceful world where the buffalo and the Native people would live again, and the white man, with the shaking of the earth, would be gone. It was the dancing, prayers, and fasting of the Native people that would save them from being lost as the new world came. Word spread through the communities of the new Messiah, and for thousands of miles delegations were sent to see Wovoka. The Lakota as well sent delegations to see Wovoka.

Word of the new religion did not sit well with the Indian agents or the missionaries who had come to prey on the communities. The spread of the religion and the Ghost Dance that was its expression became fodder for the popular media. The eastern press dispatched reporters to the Dakotas. Although the teachings were of peace, "describing the Ghost Dance as a war dance made good copy. Some of the dispatches were inaccurate due to the ignorance and ineptitude of the correspondents, but a few were intentionally exaggerated or blatantly untrue," writes William Coleman, author of the most extensive compilation of interviews and documents on the Massacre.[22]

As the media whipped eastern policymakers into a frenzy, new Indian agents were sent to the Dakotas, many selected out of political patronage rather than experience. The lack of knowledge of Indian Country and federal budget cuts to the Lakota and other nations combined to further exacerbate an already bad situation. A sense was rising of an explosion about to occur, fed by sensational newspaper articles, such as this: "Joseph Buckley...came in today and says every Indian on the reservation will shortly go on the warpath and that they have got possession of Custer's rifle, which the United States Army never found.... Local hardware men have in the past few days sold their entire stocks of ammunition to the Indians."[23]

With a misrepresentation that the "weapons of mass destruction" were at hand, it was not surprising that almost every military regiment in the region was dispatched to the Dakotas. The *Omaha World Herald* reported the deployment to be the largest to date, and the Indian agents at Rosebud and Pine Ridge noted that the Lakota were increasingly concerned by the massing troops in their region. President Benjamin Harrison's order to use military strength to quell Lakota unrest underwrote the large movement of troops. By November 17, 1890, General Nelson Miles had dispatched the Ninth Cavalry to the Pine Ridge and Rosebud reservations. On December 15, the Eighth Cavalry at Standing Rock Reservation arranged for the assassination of Sitting Bull by Indian police, allegedly in an attempt to arrest him for refusing to stop his people from participating in the now-outlawed Ghost Dance.[24]

In the last three decades of Sitting Bull's life, the Lakota and neighboring nations experienced a radical degradation: from a nomadic, self-sufficient way of life companioned with the buffalo nation, to confinement on shrinking reservations with the destitution of meager rations supplemented by gardens and chokecherry harvests. The destruction of the great buffalo herds by the military and game hunters was another form of the scorched earth policy the U.S. government had always used against Indigenous Americans. By 1890, the Lakota had little material or nutritional wealth left, but they had their spiritual practice and determination to survive. Mining interests were greedily salivating over their land. The Army was looking for a way to earn medals in the quietude that followed the Civil War, and the Seventh Calvary in particular still wanted vengeance for its ignoble defeat at Little Big Horn.

The Killing Fields

Stripped of their most powerful leaders and nourished by a mystical vision of peaceful delivery from the white man's hell, the Lakota of Chief Big Foot's band were hoping for shelter and supplies to survive the winter when they agreed to be herded into a U.S.

military encampment at Wounded Knee that December. They knew
of the growing military concentration on their land, and they saw the
guns and soldiers who surrounded their camp. When the soldiers
demanded that all Lakota guns be surrendered before any rations
were distributed, a struggle ensued between a soldier and a Lakota
who wouldn't give up his rifle. Alice Ghost Horse was 13 years old
that day. She described the weapons search and the slaughter that
followed:

> Cavalry men...started to search the wagons for axes, knife, guns,
> bow and arrows, and awls. They were really rude about it. They
> scattered the belongings all over the ground.
>
> The soldiers picked up everything they could find and tied
> them up in a blanket and took them. They also searched the
> Lakotas in the center. They emptied the contents on the ground
> at the center in front of the officers and continued to argue with
> the Lakotas but the Lakotas did not give in....
>
> At this time, there were cavalrymen all on bay horses all lined
> up on top of the hill on the north side. One officer rode down to-
> wards the center at a full gallop. He made a fast halt and shouted
> something to his commanding officers and retreated back up the
> hill and they all drew their rifles and long knife [swords] and you
> can hear them load it with bullets.
>
> In the meantime, some more cavalrymen lined up on the
> south side. A big gun was also aimed down towards the center
> and towards where we were.... I heard the first shot coming from
> the center followed by rifles going off all over, occasionally a big
> boom came from the big guns on wheels. The Lakotas were all
> disarmed so all they could do was scatter in all directions. The two
> cavalry groups came charging down, shooting at everyone who is
> running and is a Lakota.
>
> My father made it back to our wagon and my horse was trying
> to bolt so he told me to jump off, so I got off and the horse ran
> for all its worth toward the creek. We fled to the ravine, where
> there was lots of plum bushes and dove into the thicket. The gun-
> fire was pretty heavy and people were hollering for their children.
> With children crying everywhere, my dad said he was going to go
> out and help the others. My mother objected but he left anyway.

Pretty soon, my father came crawling back in and he was wounded below his left knee and he was bleeding.... My father said we should crawl further but my mother said it's better we die here together and she told me to stand up so I did, but my father pulled me down.[25]

The Aftermath and the Medals of Honor

Only about 50 of the Lakota in Big Foot's band survived the onslaught from the Calvary's powerful, rapid-shooting Hotchkiss guns. As Massacre survivors like Alice Ghost Horse ran for their lives, more than 300 Lakota lay dead or dying that December 29, 1890. Dead soldiers were buried almost immediately, but it was five days before the frozen Lakota dead were buried. Soldiers and civilians in the burial detail had photographs made of themselves amid the carnage. The Lakota dead were stripped of valuables, then packed into a mass grave. Even a survivor, eyewitnesses suggest, was buried alive.

One of the many photos from the killing fields shows Peter MacFarlan, who worked for the Army as a civilian teamster, with a Sharps rifle said to have been turned over by the Lakota that fateful morning. Suspended from the gun are some feathers, rattles, and a moccasin, which he claims he took from Big Foot's body. He is pictured in a buffalo coat he allegedly "allowed Big Foot, who was very ill from pneumonia, to sleep on the night before he was killed."[26]

News of the Massacre spread quickly, but newspapers tended to confirm the white community's belief in the inherent threat of the Indians and the innocence of the Army. On the day after the Massacre, this headline graced the *Iowa State Register:* "Treacherous Red Devils." The article proclaimed:

Members of Big Foot's Band shoot down soldiers after having surrendered. The troops undertake to disarm the Indians, when a fight occurs. One captain and five soldiers killed and a lieutenant and fifteen others wounded. None of the Indians seem to have been hurt, and no report the fire was returned. Some of them got away and further trouble is feared with other straggling bands—no good Indians but dead ones.[27]

Colonel Forsyth commended his soldiers for their "gallant conduct...in an engagement with a band of Indians in desperate condition and crazed by religion," and the Army awarded 23 medals of honor to soldiers who participated in the Massacre. [28] The most famous enlisted man to receive a medal for the Wounded Knee Massacre was Corporal Paul H. Weinert, the gunner from Company E, First U.S. Artillery. Weinert was cited for "firing his howitzer at several Indians in the ravine."[29] The ravine, according to researcher Jerry Green, was adjacent to the Lakota camp and many noncombatants sought shelter there. Since his gun was less than 300 yards away, Weinert's firing was capable of inflicting terrible damage and destruction on women and children. At the close of the century, Weinert, sporting his Medal of Honor, toured with the Buffalo Bill Cody's Wild West Show as a member of its color guard. Not all of Forsyth's superiors were uncritical, however, especially General Miles, who urged Congress to acknowledge the wrong and compensate the survivors.

> Wholesale massacre occurred and I have never heard of a more brutal, cold-blooded massacre than that at Wounded Knee. About two hundred women and children were killed and wounded; women with little children on their backs, and small children powder burned by the men who killed them being so near as to burn the flesh and clothing with the powder of their guns, and nursing babes with five bullet holes through them.... Col. Forsyth is responsible for allowing the command to remain where it was stationed after he assumed command, and in allowing his troops to be in such a position that the line of fire of every troop was in direct line of their own comrades or their camp.[30]

The notoriety of the Wounded Knee Massacre is unrivaled in Native American history, although there were many infamies of that scope. Other massacres (Pequot, Shasta, Wiyot, and Sand Creek) are missing from the pages of most history books, and were not much noted by the popular press of the time. That is perhaps why the collecting of Wounded Knee memorabilia became such a frenzied affair. There is no question that it was a ghoulish period. Collections that advertised scalp locks, clothes, or fingers from those who died at the Wounded Knee Massacre offer a grisly reminder of this. Journalist Avis Little Eagle describes the scene in the days and weeks that followed the Massacre:

> Calvary vultures circling around the people they had just murdered, stealing their finest possessions, going as far as cutting off the foot of a murdered infant for its beautiful handmade moccasin. Such ghoulish items as skeletal remains, scalps and clothing stripped from bodies that lay on the icy killing fields of Wounded Knee are on display for curious gawkers at museums and historical societies across the country.[31]

The desire to make a buck off the Massacre was captured well by an observer in 1891 who commented on the prolific displays of Wounded Knee relics in Omaha, Nebraska: "Every old duffer that owns a camp knife or bridle snap with brass tacks in it or a buckskin pouch, or a painted stick has them 'on view' in some window tagged 'Big Foot's'.... It is amusing to see the eagerness with which Eastern people swallow the dose."[32]

The Collection

There is a sentimental attachment between curator and collection. One of the largest collections of goods and clothing associated with persons who were killed at the Wounded Knee Massacre is housed at the Woods Memorial Library Museum in Barre, Massachusetts. Audrey Stevens serves, in her spare time, as the museum's primary curator. Audrey has a weathered face, tiny frame, and tenacious spirit. A farmer, like her father before her, she is also in charge of the Barre ambulance service.

It is a pilgrimage of sorts to Barre, a town that began in 1774, more than 100 years before the Massacre. Spared submersion by the

Quabbin Reservoir, Barre lies in the hinterlands of Massachusetts, linked to the world by winding two-lane roads, dotted with farms and piled stone walls that have survived a century of development and suburban sprawl that has crushed most of the region. There are around 4,000 town residents, many of them from old Yankee families who have lived there for generations.

Increasing numbers of Lakota and other Native people have made a pilgrimage to Barre as they seek to recover remnants and memories torn from communities and placed far away, behind glass in tagged cages or in boxes, rarely to be seen. There are moccasins detailed in beadwork and quillwork, a Ghost Dance shirt, and a beautiful dress for a child. The most difficult items to view are the cradleboard covers and dolls, for it is not likely that their owners survived that day. Yet the red lines of quillwork remain brilliant atop the brain-tanned hide.

The Barre collection is remarkably well preserved, largely a result of Audrey Stevens's Yankee common sense. "I never did anything with it. Frank Root [the collector who loaned the materials to Barre in 1893] built these display boxes, and I've never let anyone touch them. We've got a few mothballs in there, that's it. We don't take them out, and we don't touch them." One shirt Audrey associates with Sitting Bull is a geometric and line-patterned garment in colors of the period. "That one is as if you could just put it on now, a hundred years later," she tells me.[33]

The big question is: how did Frank Root come to possess this remarkable collection of Lakota things? This is the story as Audrey first learned it:

> There were two men; they were civilians. They were hired by the Army to move the bodies and put them in a mass grave. They had these wagons and mules, which the bodies were on. One of the mules stepped in a hole. They looked in and found all of these clothes. Big Foot's band had buried them there on their way to Wounded Knee. They found their cache; it was all there in the ground.[34]

Audrey tells me that Root purchased the cache from its finders.[35] That is the story the museum tells of how the clothes, pipes, dolls, and moccasins came to Barre.

Bill Billeck, director of the Smithsonian's Office of Repatriation, questions the likelihood of a starving people burying clothing and other items while traveling in a state of great apprehension: "I don't know if anybody at Wounded Knee expected [the Massacre] to occur. Why would they go there if they thought they would be killed, and certainly, why would they take off their clothes in the dead of winter?"[36]

So, there are questions about the collection, most of all about how the items were taken in the first place. But in the end, all that concerns the Lakota is that they are items of cultural patrimony: locks, amulets, pipes, and clothes that have grieved them by their absence.

The Spirits Still Linger

In December 1992, attorney Mario Gonzales wrote a letter on behalf of the Wounded Knee Survivors Associations from both the Cheyenne River and Pine Ridge reservations to the Woods Memorial Library. The Lakotas had heard of the exhibit, and wanted an inventory and some answers. Gonzales wrote:

> It is our belief that the artifacts and objects belong to the families and descendants of massacre victims. These items are uniquely important to the cultural and religious heritage of the Sioux Nation. The theft of these items from the dead and wounded is still a source of great anguish and suffering to the victims' descendants and the entire Sioux nations. The public display of these items in a non-Indian museum far removed from the Sioux communities involved is also a matter of urgent concern to the Survivors Association, whose membership consists entirely of massacre victims' descendants."[37]

It was January 27, 1993, exactly 100 years after the day Root had brought the collection to Barre, that Nellie Two Bulls, Alex White

Plume, and Edgar Fire Thunder came from Pine Ridge to see the items that had belonged to those killed at the Wounded Knee Massacre. Alex White Plume described his visit as "one of my saddest expeditions I had ever had. We didn't know at all what to expect, but it was really sad. The reason was all the children's clothing and the *cekpognaka*, the amulets for the umbilical cords. Everything had bullet holes in it, blood and Big Foot's hair."[38]

Nellie Two Bulls's grandfather was a Wounded Knee survivor. "It brings a sad memory of my people," Two Bulls said. "These things should be given back to us so we can have a sacred ceremony and bury them. Many of these items should have been buried with their owners in order for their spirits to rest." Two Bulls doubts that the pipes or other items had been sold to the soldiers. Some of the bags were used to carry umbilical cords. "It would be carried with a child all his life, it has to be buried," Two Bulls explained. "The spirits still linger in the museum; I hear their voices and cries."[39]

NAGPRA: The Homecoming Law

A century after the Wounded Knee Massacre, Congress passed a law that is starting to bring home some of that which was lost. Unfortunately, there are loopholes in NAGPRA so large, and the lack of enforcement is so dire, that you can drive an entire collection through it. Private institutions without federal funding, for example, are not covered. The Barre museum argues that it is exempt from NAGPRA, even though it has received at least one small federal grant in the past. "There is a lot which doesn't fall under the categories of the law," Billeck tells me. "For instance, they must be objects buried with the dead, sacred objects or objects of cultural patrimony or be taken off of people's bodies." The key question of course is: was an item stolen or legitimately sold or bartered? Dan Monroe, director of the Peabody Essex Museum, another private museum in Massachusetts, believes that "an institution has right of possession only if an individual or group with the authority to alienate an object freely transferred title. Clearly the Sioux and other groups did not freely transfer title to the objects in [the Barre collection]."[40]

Audrey is reluctant to let the items go all at once, and hopes that something can be worked out to replace them one at a time. "I always thought of them as artworks," Audrey told a *New York Times* reporter. "I'm sorry I didn't realize the significance of these things."[41] Audrey might be able to keep the "artwork" under a plan called a "win-win" solution by Mario Gonzales: Lakota artists would be commissioned to create exact replicas of each item. The museum would get to keep the replicas and the Lakota would get the originals. The museum has been slow to raise the money needed to inventory the collection and replace it, but the Lakota hope that continuing public pressure will bring the items home one day.

In the meantime, the Barre exhibit is slowly changing. A lock of Big Foot's hair has been repatriated to one of his descendants. A caption for an item that once read, "After the battle of Wounded Knee, a Trooper of the Seventh Regiment, under command of Colonel Forsyth took these moccasins from the feet of Flying Horse, a Chief of the Bloody Brules who is on his way to the Happy Hunting Grounds," has now been removed.[42] Also missing are two scalps, one from an Indian man and one from a white woman, that were contained earlier within the exhibit.[43]

Since NAGPRA was passed, other collections of Indian items have shrunk, sometimes inexplicably. Their first inventory of the Coffin Collection at the Nebraska Historical Society included around 30 items identified as somehow affiliated with Wounded Knee. Of deep concern to the Oglala and Minnecoju Lakota is a baby's foot, still wearing a moccasin, that was held at the Nebraska Historical Society. Kathleen Danker, a student working on the collection, discovered the foot, which was in a mummified condition.[44] Asked about it in 1992, then-curator Gail Potter initially said she wasn't aware of the child's foot, but later said it had been located, and that tests were being done on it. That foot was no longer in the collection when I visited.

By the time I visited the Nebraska Historical Society, eight months after this inventory was made public, the number of items considered affiliated had dwindled to around four, including, as in the Woods Historical Society, a cradleboard cover with red-lined quilling on it, unique to the period and community. From the Omaha Charlie's "Bristol Collection," object 173 is labeled "porcupine decorated papoose hood found on Wounded Knee battlefield." Looking at it, a sick feeling rose in my stomach, a feeling that did not subside quickly. I knew that the baby had not survived the Massacre.

Marvin Many Horses (Burnette), a Sicangu Lakota from the Rosebud Reservation, lives in New Hampshire. He was influential in finding a necklace that belonged to Sitting Bull and securing its return to the Yankton Sioux Tribe. The shell necklace, according to reporter Avis Little Eagle, was taken from the body of Sitting Bull after he was killed on December 15, 1890, by one of the officers involved in his arrest. The necklace was given to Alfred Beard Kittredge, a native of Nelson, New Hampshire, who traveled out West and later became a senator for South Dakota. When Kittredge died, some of his items were returned to Nelson, where they were stored in the basement of the Olivia Rodham Memorial Library. There, for 100 years, Sitting Bull's necklace lay, dwindling to little more than a shell.[45]

There are a number of collections rumored to contain items from the Wounded Knee Massacre, both nationally and internationally. When the Barre museum story appeared in the *New York Times,* a number of separate institutions placed calls to Alex White Plume from the Survivors Association and expressed interest in returning items. Those names have thus far been kept confidential.

Healing and Reconciliation

The return of clothing and cradleboards is an integral part of a larger set of changes needed for healing the scars of the Lakota com-

munity and building, eventually, a foundation for reconciliation between Natives and settlers.

The Lakota have demanded return of the Black Hills since that
land was seized by eminent domain. They have also consistently demanded restitution to the survivors of the Massacre. William Horn
Cloud remembers that his father, just before his death in 1920, sold
all his "good things" to take a trip to Washington, D.C., on behalf of
Wounded Knee Survivors Association. Horn Cloud requested that
Congress support a museum, an eternal flame at the mass grave, a
national day of mourning, and monetary compensation in such
forms as scholarships to the survivors and descendants of the victims of Wounded Knee.[46]

There are no easy answers, as evidenced by the complexity of
the stories, the ancestral memories, the clothing, and the economics
of Pine Ridge today. Perhaps one must look outside the continent,
outside the laws and institutions of the United States, to find a path
toward healing. South Africa's Truth and Reconciliation Commission built on lessons learned from the Nuremberg Trials following
World War II. The South African model has since been replicated
and adapted for use worldwide. Since 2001, the International Center
for Transitional Justice has worked in war-torn societies as well as
societies in which the repercussions of great atrocities in the distant
past still remained unresolved in the present. The center works with
communities in a process that involves a mix of judicial and
nonjudicial mechanisms, different levels of international involve-
ment (or none at all), individual prosecutions, truth seeking, institutional reform, vetting and dismissals, and reparations.

Today, some 30 transitional justice projects exist internationally. There is even one underway in the United States. The Greensboro (North Carolina) Truth and Reconciliation Commission stems
from decades of racial violence, including the 1979 murders of five
activists by members of the Ku Klux Klan, American Nazi Party,
and Greensboro Police Department. Survivors of the Greensboro
Massacre hope that the process of public listening involved in this

people's tribunal will augment the limited legal resolution they have experienced so far. In the case of the Lakota and other Native American peoples, it is likely that some elements of the resolution must come from well outside the realm of the laws of the United States, which has been one of the primary perpetrators of the crimes against Native Americans.

When the state of South Dakota initiated its own reconciliation commission, former senator James Abourezk offered this advice to the commissioners: "What you need is to have Indian leaders sit down with white leaders and have a confrontation session, to have them understand a little better." Abourezk's advice was ignored, and he is not optimistic about the reconciliation efforts of the future. "I think racism is so damn deeply ingrained, I am just afraid that nothing will happen."[47]

A hundred years after the Massacre, new voices emerged from Lakota country asking for some redress and some dignity. Rosebud tribal member Tillie Black Bear, settler descendent Sally Wagner, and attorney Mario Gonzales began a campaign to urge the federal government to rescind the Wounded Knee medals of honor. Governor Mickelson refused to get involved in the campaign. His press secretary, Gretchen Lord Anderson, was quoted as saying, "He, the governor, wants to concentrate his efforts on things that will happen, and that plan won't happen."[48]

In turn, a group associated with the Seventh Cavalry also decided in 1993 that it would try and make some sort of reconciliation. "It was a Seventh Cavalry Hobbyist Club, or something like that," says Alex White Plume, describing for me the day one of the club's members came to Pine Ridge.

> He met Frances White Bird. He gave him one of the gridirons and a Cavalry hat. And he was supposed to set up several meetings with the tribe, and he was supposed to come and apologize for what they did at Wounded Knee. They had tons of manure that they used for gardens and lawns, and they were going to donate 100,000 pounds of manure, as a part of it.

The word got around the community about the Seventh Cavalry, their apology proposals, and their manure. Alex recalls:

> Uncle Mark Big Road had a ceremony, and we asked him if we could accept an apology from them. He said, "They can't just apologize. There's too much things they did bad, and it's humungous. So an apology won't do it. We had to wipe the tears of our nation, what that means is the return of land with the sacred sites especially." So we told them they couldn't just come in and apologize and take off, like it was a cheap incident. It was a really strong incident for us. Those were our relatives that they killed. So in not so many nice words, I told him to leave the rez.

The revocation of the medals of honor would be a critical, though not sufficient, component to healing the unresolved historical grief identified by White Plume and other Lakota. White Plume has observed that "our relatives who lost people at the Massacre were the most poverty-stricken people on the reservation, the most *unkshila*. There was no [explicable] reason for that. It was the pain."

Marie Yellow Horse Brave Heart–Jordan and others have researched the ongoing desolation at Pine Ridge. Brave Heart–Jordan points to the massacres, starvation, boarding schools, and displacement from the land as having continuing repercussion for the Lakota and other Indian communities. Brave Heart–Jordan quotes the words of psychologist Utng Erickson: "Step for step, the Sioux have been denied the basis for a collective identity formation and with it that reservoir of collective integrity from which the individual must derive his stature as a social being."[49]

The Pine Ridge community is working to rebuild its collective soul. Starting in 1990, the community initiated the Big Foot Memorial Ride, an annual event in which descendants and community members retrace the midwinter horse ride taken by Big Foot's band to the Massacre site. White Plume explains, "We started this ride to empower the survivors." In 1990, hundreds of people rode to the Wounded Knee grave site for ceremonies and to heal the sacred circle.

The Lakota people are ready to heal; it is now time for the United States to begin making amends to those who grieve, to those whose land and blood forms the foundation for this country—its prosperity and its awful history. In many ways, Wounded Knee and the Black Hills, intertwined, remain central and symbolic of all that is wrong with an unreconciled past.

It is the summer of 2004. At Alex and Debbie White Plume's house, the horse races commemorating the Little Big Horn battle draw a crowd. Hot dogs and chips are served while the onlookers take bets on who is the fastest.

The federal policies ebb and flow. Politicians come and go, and a collection of people's lives and pride awaits its homecoming. On the banks of Wounded Knee Creek, the Lakota horse races carry on. There is a healing process under way in Lakota territory, despite the federal government's inaction. Truth waits. But on the banks of Wounded Knee Creek, it is clear that the Lakota and their way of life will continue, and they will continue to heal. In spite of it all, the Heart of Everything That Is will always be there.

Vampires in the New World

Blood, Academia, and Human Genetics

First, I would like all of the blood returned to us. There are people, loved ones who gave their blood and who have passed away. But their blood is still out there somewhere, I think. Blood is very important to us. We need a ceremony with [Arizona State University] officials present to bury that blood.

—Dianna Uqualla, Vice-Chair of the Havasupai people[1]

Say that you are a member of a remote Indigenous community situated at the bottom of the Grand Canyon. Approached by what you believe are some trusted researchers who propose to do a study of the incidence and possible solutions to diabetes, hundreds of community members donate blood. Some are given general consent forms to sign, while others receive only an oral explanation of the project. Those blood samples disappear into the laboratories of Arizona State University, along with copies of other medical records, taken surreptitiously without anyone's approval.

A decade later, Carletta Tilousi, Tribal Chairwoman of the 650-member Havasupai Tribe, is shocked listening to a doctoral presentation reporting on the use of Havasupai blood samples to uphold the Bering Strait Theory, directly challenging Havasupai oral history. The tribe's blood—which they thought they gave to end the diabetes epidemic in the community—had found its way into a wide range of genetic research in numerous labs, including those at Stanford University and in the private sector pharmaceutical industry.[2]

That's the story of the Havasupai people of Arizona and Therese Markow, the geneticist who seems to be the key person responsible for the misuse of the blood samples. Markow has profited professionally from this pirated genetic material. Honored by President Bush in December 2001 as one of ten scientists nationally to win the Presidential Award for Excellence in Science, Mathematics, and Engineer Mentoring, Markow's recognition was followed closely by a million dollars in grants from the National Institutes of Health.[3] Blood moves—not only within bodies but also between them and, increasingly, into laboratories. Today it is the subject of international profit. That loss of control over part of a human being, the potential for unethical practices, and indeed patenting of life-forms has shocked many Native communities.

In an era in which humans can create custom-tailored medicines and designer babies, there are millions of children who do not have access to basic drugs and inoculations, clean drinking water, and adequate food. While simple, preventable diseases like dysentery kill huge numbers of children every year, today's investors in medical research choose to support people like Markow.

Captain Hook and the Biopirates

> Indigenous peoples are entitled to the recognition of the full ownership, control and protection of their cultural and intellectual property. They have the right to special measures to control, develop and protect their sciences, technologies and cultural manifestations including human and other genetic resources, seeds, medicines, knowledge of the properties of fauna and flora, oral traditions, literatures, designs and visual and performing arts.
>
> —UN Working Group on Indigenous Populations[4]

Debra Harry, a Paiute woman, lives in Nevada not too far north of the Havasupai Reservation. A political activist who in her youth enjoyed barrel racing at Indian rodeos in Nevada and throughout the West, Harry now leads a group—Indigenous Peoples Council on Biocolonialism—focused on roping in genetic pirates.

Victoria Tauli-Corpuz is an Igorok woman from the Philippines, a leader for 25 years in groups like the Cordillera Women's Organization and the Tettebba Foundation. Like Debra Harry, Tauli-Corpuz works against biocolonialism—a new frontier of colonialism where even the genetic matter of the world comes into the realms of patenting and individual ownership. When I ask Tauli-Corpuz why she does political work like this, she says, "We fought the World Bank and we fought Ferdinand Marcos. We will continue to fight for justice."[5]

Indigenous activists like Tauli-Corpuz and Harry are working to stop the crime of biopiracy: the misappropriation of life, whether microorganisms, plants, or animals (including humans), as well as the cultural knowledge that accompanies it. Biopiracy violates international conventions but manages to continue under protection of various international trade agreements and patents laws. "It is quickly gaining momentum because of the amount of money going into biotechnology," explains Harry.[6] And most of the piracy is from Indigenous and Third World communities to First World corporations.

In the marketplace of biopiracy, there are few bigger players than Monsanto, distributor of genetically modified seeds (such as its Roundup Ready product line). From before the advent of written history, seeds have been the common property of farming communities, with a percentage of every harvest carefully saved for the next planting. Monsanto has worked hard to privatize that common heritage, creating sterile seeds or requiring farmers to sign contracts stating that they will not save seeds from Monsanto's crops. Monsanto has sued hundreds of farmers that it accuses of replanting its patented seeds.

In Monsanto's notorious case of Percy Schmeiser of Bruno, Saskatchewan, a lifetime's work in seeds garnered from careful plant breeding was almost ruined by pollen blown in from neighboring fields of Roundup Ready canola. For its predatory practices of allowing its seed stock to drift in the wind and then sue farmers for "theft" of Monsanto's patented seeds, Monsanto has been awarded the Captain Hook Award by the Coalition against Biopiracy.[7] It is against this background that the discussion of the Human Genome Diversity Project (HGDP) is held. Through all its permeations, the project has reached deep into the hearts of Indigenous communities.

The HGDP is an offshoot of the Human Genome Organization (HUGO), a nonprofit, nongovernmental group of scientists that plays a role in coordinating studies of human genetics around the world. For 13 years, the leading edge of genetic research was the scientific quest that succeeded in 2003 in creating the first complete map of human DNA. Funded largely by the U.S. National Institutes of Health and the U.S. Department of Energy for around $20 billion, this project focused on the similarities that all humans share. Now that they have a template of a seemingly generic human, some scientists view the HGDP as the next step in their research. As Debra Harry explains: "The HGD Project seeks to map the variance, that is, the genetic differences of groups that differ from the monotype genome...identified by the HUGO effort."[8]

Indigenous communities house a mother lode of genetic diversity. Where the mobility of industrial cultures has led to something of a genetic melting pot, rare genetic traits have been preserved within territories of Indigenous peoples. HGDP scientists refer to Indigenous peoples as "isolates of historic interest." "The populations that can tell us most about our evolutionary past are those that have been isolated for some time, are likely to be linguistically and culturally distinct and are often surrounded by geographic barriers.... Isolated human populations contain much more informative genetic records than more recent urban ones," according to prominent geneticists.[9]

Intact Indigenous communities also have a comprehensive knowledge of their own genetic histories. Harry remarks, "There are few places where you can find this: who had which disease, and who had what."[10] HGDP researchers have identified 722 human communities for DNA sampling, and plan to collect as many as 15,000 samples before they are done, all at a cost of somewhere around $35 million. Leading geneticists have called for an aggressive pace for the sampling. Tauli-Corpuz notes the irony of trying to save a genetic record instead of the people who could themselves perpetuate those genes: "The scientists are aware that their target populations are fast vanishing, so for them, time is of the essence. [One of the scientists] calls the HGDP an 'urgent last-ditch effort' to collect DNA" before disease and dispersion make Indigenous communities either biologically or culturally extinct.[11]

Ethical Question Number One: Why would so many resources be involved in collecting the genetic materials from "vanishing populations," rather than working to preserve those peoples and their cultures?

Native communities in many regions of the world face major threats to their survival. Millions face relocation due to dam and mining projects. Other Native communities, like the Western Shoshone and the Paiutes of Nevada, are deeply impacted by radiation exposure. Environmental degradation creates dire health circumstances in many Indigenous communities.

Indigenous communities are often found in the most geographically isolated regions and lack the political power to get basic services. Many of these communities are also the focal point for natural resource extraction: The Uwas in Colombia, the Mbuti of the Congo, and Indigenous peoples in Papua New Guinea, Indonesia, and elsewhere are faced with powerful entities seeking to exploit natural resources. As mining and oil companies increasingly crowd into Indigenous peoples' territories, it is no surprise that the health of those environments and peoples deteriorates.

Expenditures for military conflicts over resources mean that expenditures for basic health care and infrastructure are further compromised. Infectious diseases like tuberculosis, malaria, and cholera, anticipated to be on the decline by 2000, instead have spread, often in more drug-resistant forms. Hepatitis C and AIDS are also wreaking havoc, along with an additional 30 diseases previously unknown to these communities.

Lack of access to clean water is a key factor to diarrhea and other common life-threatening diseases that constitute roughly a fourth of preventable illness worldwide, according to the Worldwatch Institute. In 2002, Worldwatch estimated that 505 million people live in countries that are water stressed or water scarce, with that number projected to more than quadruple in the next 25 years.[12] Climate change exacerbates these problems in many ways, diminishing water quality and increasing the habitat available for mosquitoes and microbial organisms, such as those that cause cholera.

Economic stress means that patients in many countries under-use medicine either because it is under-prescribed or because they cannot afford the full treatment. A 1997 study in Vietnam, for instance, found that more than 70% of the patients monitored were given too few antibiotics. The widespread use of some but not enough antibiotics encourages the evolution of drug-resistant strains, making common infections life threatening. Ultimately, far more expensive medications are needed to effect a cure.[13]

Victoria Tauli-Corpuz notes that money is rarely spent on curing poor people's diseases:

> You know, in the South, a majority of people die of communicable diseases, of malaria, of tuberculosis. But do [health sector investors] ever put funds there? Of course not. They will put funds into diseases that are diseases of the wealthy because that is where they will get money. This is the whole rationale behind genetic therapy.[14]

A 1999 study reported that only 13 out of 1,223 medicines commercialized by multinational drug companies in the 1975-97 period were designed to fight tropical diseases. Meanwhile, the market for treatments for obesity, toenail fungus, baldness, impotence, and wrinkles runs into the billions of dollars.[15]

In the end, this question must be reiterated with all its ethical implications: Instead of a costly last-ditch effort to collect DNA samples from these communities, why are these resources not used to ensure the survival of these communities?

Ethical Question Number Two: How have those samples been collected and how are they used?

Tauli-Corpuz tells some stories of DNA collection in the Pacific, noting that many of the methods of collection are unethical.

> One example is the attempt of [the] Hoffman-LaRoche [company] to collect the genes of the Aeta people of the Philippines. Since the

Aetas became the victims of the eruption of the volcano Mt. Pinatubo in 1991, there are medical missions that would visit them once in a while. In 1993, Hoffman-LaRoche approached the Hawaii-based Aloha Medical Mission, which often visits the Aetas. They tried to link up with this group to collect the genetic materials they need. For people facing calamity, any group that offers charity will be warmly welcomed.[16]

A classic example of controversial medical/anthropological research was a project led by University of Michigan researchers Napolean Chagnon and James Neel with support from the U.S. Atomic Energy Commission in the late 1960s. Neel's research focused on the "formation of antibodies to newly introduced diseases in isolated populations."[17] The researchers took samples of blood from Yanomami individuals in Brazil and determined that the Yanomami lacked measles antibodies. A schedule of vaccinations was begun, but an epidemic of measles broke out in 1968 and spread from Brazil into Venezuela. The researchers are alleged to have responded inadequately to the epidemic by not speeding up the vaccinations.[18] The project cost the lives of many Yanomami and became an international scandal. At the center of the controversy is the question of whether the researchers infected the Yanomami as an intentional or unintentional aspect of their research.

Almost 30 years after the 1968 epidemic, Patrick Tierney published a book, *Darkness in El Dorado,* using the Yanomami example to frame a discussion of the ethics of scientific researchers and their academic institutions. The University of Michigan and various associations that supported the Yanomami project spent far more time trying to discredit Tierney's writing than they did addressing the concerns of the Yanomami. Indeed, the blood samples themselves continue to be a source of great concern to the Yanomami, since neither the initial taking of the samples, represented as a charitable effort to assist the Yanomami, nor the final disposition of the samples involved truly informed consent.[19]

In North America, the Havasupai case has emerged as one of the most controversial. While the blood samples were collected from tribal members on the pretext of doing diabetes research, Markow was actually writing research grant proposals focused on studying schizophrenia in the community. In 1990, the tribe learned that Markow had assigned a researcher to look for mental health diagnoses in confidential medical records, obtained without any consent. Finding little to no information to back up her hypothesis, Markow was frustrated, but continued to search for support, ultimately having a hand in 23 academic papers using the Havasupai blood, 15 of which were on schizophrenia.

In a lawsuit against Arizona State University, Markow, and her associates, tribal members point to the large volume of research grants and money awarded based on illegally procured information and dubious science.[20]

Debra Harry's research indicates that the Havasupai case represents larger dynamics in Native communities.

> I think we are really vulnerable because we're generous, giving people. If someone came to our community and said, "would you please participate because we want to find a cure for cancer, or asthma, or whatever," we're likely to participate, thinking that our contributions are going to be good. But we don't know the full intent of the people on the other side. You know, whether they are going for their own commercial interests, or they're trying to boost their own academic careers, or whether they have colleges who want access to those DNA samples.[21]

Concern over the taking of genetic samples has prompted many tribal governments to oppose the project. The World Council of Indigenous Peoples has consistently opposed genetic sampling, which it refers to as the "Vampire Project." The National Congress of American Indians (NCAI), the oldest national Native organization in the United States, also opposed the project with a 1993 resolution declaring, "NCAI does hereby condemn the HGDP and call upon all parties and agencies involved in it and related activities to cease immediately."[22] Representatives of many national and international Indigenous organizations and communities gathered in Panama in November 1997 to oppose the HGDP. As summarized by the Indigenous Peoples Council on Biocolonialism, the Ukupseni Declaration:

condemns the Human Genome Diversity Project, calls for a moratorium on the collection of genetic samples from indigenous peoples, demands the repatriation of genetic samples and data already obtained by unethical means, opposes the application of intellectual property law, and patents, to human genes, and calls upon scientists to denounce any research conducted in a manner that violates the protocols which protect the human rights of human subjects.[23]

The Yanomami are not the only people who are left wondering whether the genetic material taken from their bodies will some day be used in ways that are diametrically opposed to their spiritual beliefs. In the burst of genetic research activity in the 1990s, several other Indigenous nations learned that tissue samples from their community members had been used to propagate cell lines that the U.S. government was anxious to patent, as if a scientist could have authority over someone else's body tissue.

From the small bit of blood and skin scrapings taken from a study participant can come enough DNA for virtually unlimited numbers of research projects. The DNA from the original sample is in effect immortalized through the propagation of cell lines. HGDP researchers intend to make these cell lines "available to the world research community at no profit, or perhaps even a subsidized cost."[24] So it is that basic human needs in many Indigenous communities are not met, while scientists seeking to exploit the DNA gathered from those communities will have their research costs subsidized.

The controversy about the skeletal remains of a person alternatively know as "Ancient One" and "Kennewick man" brings up both the question of physical control of genetic material and the intellectual goals of genetic research. A primary interest of the HGDP, according to writer Sandra Awang, is to "clarify the history of specific indigenous populations around the globe, from a genetic perspective. Populations will learn what science believes to be their origin and history."[25] That would bring up another ethical question.

Ethical Question Number Three: What would be the impact of geneticists' assessment of peoples' origins on Indigenous land rights and sovereignty struggles?

The bones of the Ancient One were found in shallow water near the bank of the Columbia River near Kennewick, Washington, in 1996. James Chatters, the first archeologist to assess the skeleton, surmised, based on the skull alone, that the remains were "Caucasoid" and thus less than 300 years old. Examining the full skeleton days later, Chatters found a stone spear point embedded in the pelvis and realized the skeleton was indeed ancient. Carbon dating tests estimated the Ancient One to be more than 9,000 years old. A scent of new research potential wafted from the Columbia River, and a host of scientists appeared, drawn to the potential of DNA research and archeological discoveries. They started doing DNA research on bone tissue, but were stopped by the Columbia River Tribes (the Yakama, Nez Perce, Umatilla, and others) as well as the Army Corps of Engineers, which holds jurisdiction over the riverbank where the bones were found. The Columbia River Tribes asked for the Ancient One's reburial under the NAGPRA, the federal law addressing repatriation and graves.

Eight scientists filed suit seeking to do DNA testing and other research on the Ancient One, prior to, or in exception to, any re-interment by the Columbia River peoples. The scientists argued that they had a right under the U.S. Constitution to review the remains. Audie Huber is the Inter-Governmental Affairs Manager of the Confederated Tribes of the Umatilla Reservation and has represented the tribes of the Columbia River continuously in the discussions surrounding the Ancient One. Their argument, according to Huber, was based on "challenging that the government was hiding information, and that the First Amendment would protect their right to speak and receive information with regards to the Ancient One." This, continues Huber, meant they were comparing an individual ancestor "to a book that the scientists could read."

In 2004, the Ninth Circuit case was decided in favor of the scientists, with the court deeming that the ancestor was too ancient to be considered culturally affiliated with any tribe. This has raised major concerns in Native communities. Audie considers it to be a very significant case, "essentially challenging the basic tenets of NAGPRA," and allowing scientists to keep tribes from repatriating their ancestors until the scientists are done. "This is not about the Kennewick man; this is about any other Indian found in the future. The question is asked, do scientists have a constitutional or statutory right to study dead Indians. Knowledge is good, but every piece of knowledge acquired has a price."[26] Proposed legislation in 2005 would redefine "Native American" (in the context of ancient remains) as a member of a tribe or culture that is *or was* indigenous to the United States. That legislation, if passed, would protect future ancient ones from scientific study unless approved by Native nations.[27]

Native American human remains became property when European settlers started marketing them as prizes of conquest. NAGPRA was intended to reverse this desecration and say that the rightful trustees of the remains are the tribes—a claim that is now challenged. The Department of the Interior has determined that "cultural affiliation," the prior category under which Native people could protect the remains of ancestors found in their region, can now be determined by biological means. To many tribes this is a huge threat. Audie Huber is incredibly concerned about the future of graves protection because of the potential for misuse of DNA research.

The difference between biological affiliation and cultural affiliation can be quite large in Native American communities. That's why "Congress chose the line of cultural affiliation, not genetic affiliation under NAGPRA," explains Huber.

> Race does not exist as a biological concept; it is a social construct, not a biological construct.... In the future, the Department of Interior may determine that there can be scientific testing without tribal consent, and then, maybe, there will be a re-interment. That is the concern of many tribal members of the potential for misuse of DNA work and the research interests surrounding this work.

The controversy gives some indication of the conflicting impacts of genetic studies on prehistoric relationships between populations. Chatters contention that the Ancient One had "Caucasoid features" opened up a huge can of worms. The problems of science, genetics, and origin are augmented and politicized in the era of land struggles and sovereignty. "People saw that Chatters identified the remains as being Caucasoid," Audie explains, "which means an anthropological shorthand for long narrow face, and thought that meant Caucasian, which generally means white. But Caucasoid cranial features are shared by the Ainu of Japan, the Aboriginals of Australia, and most of India."

Europeans also have Caucasoid cranial features and that piqued the interest of a number of Nordic groups. The Asatru Folk Assembly of California, a group that practices pre-Christian Norse religious traditions, formally intervened in the dispute in 1996, filing their own arguments for further study of the skeleton. Audie suspects that the Nordic groups were "asking for DNA samples to prove that he was an ancestor of theirs. Proving that Europeans were here first, and the Indians wiped them out."

One can easily see how scientific speculation as to who came from where would eventually be used to politically disenfranchise Indigenous peoples. The Bering Strait theory posits that modern Native Americans are descended from Asian peoples who crossed the Bering Strait and eventually migrated across North and South America. The concept of Native Americans as simply "early settlers" not only negates these peoples' traditional understandings of their origins, it also leaves them undistinguished from later settler societies politically and legally. Indeed, as the Indigenous Peoples Council on Biocolonialism suspects, that "validation of the Bering Strait theory...can be used to challenge aboriginal rights to territory, resources and self-determination."[28]

Validating the Bering Strait theory is, in fact, what happened in the Havasupai case. As Carletta Tilousi explains, "They challenged our identity and our origins with our own blood and without telling us what they were doing."[29] Argosy University psychology professor Louise Baca echoes Tilousi's sentiments: "Think of how devastating it would be to learn that you unknowingly gave your blood for studies that went against your entire belief system of origin. What's really sad is that many people built their careers off the blood of these Indigenous people."[30]

Many governments have already sanctioned the use of genomic archetypes to help resolve conflicts and ancestral ownership claims—for example among Tibetans and Chinese, Azeris and Armenians, and Serbs and Croats, as well as German citizenship claims by ethnic Germans in Poland, Russia, and the Ukraine. The secular law in many nations, including the United States, has long recognized genetic archetypal matching as a legitimate technique for establishing individual identity.[31]

Genetic research applied to individuals can be extremely imprecise. While geneticists have identified some variations that occur in higher frequency among Native Americans than in the non-Indigenous population, tests for these markers can analyze only a small percentage of an individual's full genetic inheritance, and thus result in many false negatives and false positives.[32] For example, a person with one-sixteenth Indigenous ancestry might have the Native American marker while another with fifteen-sixteenth Indigenous ancestry might not.[33] Needless to say, the test completely fails to register individuals who are adopted into tribal cultures, or to distinguish between one tribe and another. Native American tribal affiliation is at least as much cultural as it is genetic. What is to prevent this Eurocentric scientific theory from being abused by greedy politicians and racists? In the end, this enters the slippery slope of eugenics.

Ethical Question Number Four: What if there were military uses of this genetic information, say, to make genetically specific biological weapons?

Military use of genetic information is hardly a new practice. Speaking about the enormous investments by the top agrochemical, seed, food, and drug corporations (Aventis, Monsanto, Bayer, Dow, and others) in genetic research, Debra Harry says, "You can trace the lineage of these companies, and some of them go back to the companies that made the gas for the gas chambers used in World War II."

Harry thinks it is no coincidence that the corporations that sought to profit from genocide have now turned to genetic research. "They are about capturing and controlling nature," she says.[34]

Just as the Abu Ghraib scandal revealed that the U.S. government had secretly shifted its policy on conducting torture, one wonders if the "War on Terror" will reveal a change in the U.S. government's policy on biological and chemical weapons. Under the terms of the 1972 Biological Weapons Conventions, the U.S. government officially halted the development of biological weapons. Yet research proceeds into vaccines and other measures to counter biological warfare agents—research that necessarily involves creating and studying active agents of biological warfare. Furthermore, the Armed Forces Medical Intelligence Center has been specifically directed to investigate the vulnerability of "foreign" populations to disease and infection.[35] Research units of the U.S. Navy have collected blood samples in Peru, Indonesian-occupied West Papau (Irian Jaya), and the Philippines. The National Institutes of Health, which is believed to control some of the world's largest collections of Indigenous peoples' blood and tissue samples, carries out much of its research on these materials at Fort Detrick, in Maryland, which also happens to be home to Department of Defense projects related to biological and chemical warfare.

Ethical Question Number Five: Who owns these genetic samples and who decides what will happen with them? Who decides the research and health priorities in our communities?

Corporations engaged in expensive genetic research, often in collaboration with universities and government entities, are interested in the privatization, through patents, of their research and the life-forms they are working with.[36] U.S. corporations get a great deal of assistance from the federal government in their efforts to make a profit from genetic research. In 1993, the U.S. Department of Commerce applied for a patent on a cell line propagated from a sample taken from a 26-year-old Guaymi woman from Panama.[37] Neither she nor her tribe had even been informed of the patent application.

The Guaymi Congress of Panama, the World Council of Churches, and other organizations protested in outrage. The European Greens introduced an emergency resolution to the European Parliament opposing the patent claim. They called for a halting of the HGDP. Faced with mounting pressure, the United States withdrew its patent claim in November 1993.

The U.S. government subsequently applied for two other patents on human genetic materials, these based on tissue samples taken from Solomon Islanders and from the Hagahai people of New Guinea. These applications were also eventually withdrawn due to protests.[38] The cell lines were, at latest word, on deposit at the American Type Cultural Collection in Washington, D.C.

Debra Harry believes that western property law has reached a legal/policy/moral bind when it comes to patenting organisms. She argues that genome research is "a science that paces ahead of social policy. The science basically has free rein to go where it goes because the public doesn't understand genetics. The public hasn't set limits on what is and isn't [acceptable] in this area."[39] Harry cautions that extending intellectual property rights into this realm is an attempt "to gain control over life and microorganisms, viruses, plants, human genetics, and even mining the minds of Indigenous peoples.... Western property law is its own ideology, and as Indian people we need to recognize its limits." Under the law, she points out, "something can be a commodity, it's alienable, can be bought and sold, reduced to a single entity." But Native Americans see things differently. "We're talking about something that has existed collectively. It doesn't belong to the present generation."[40]

The reality is that genome research involves groups' rights, further complicating the legal arena. According to Harry, the federal government is

> comfortable with coming to an individual and asking for our consent, but not to go to tribes and get approval of any findings, or consent from tribes. But that is exactly what we are advocating. We are saying that as tribal people, we have something that is very powerful to put into action; we have sovereignty, police power, and we have legal rights to protect our legal interests, and if [the

federal government] has any interest that impacts our people, the tribe has a right to deal with it. We have a right to decide whether or not anything [of ours] is commercialized, who owns the data, and what happens with the biological samples. Researchers are going to have to get used to dealing with that concept. There's a lot of questions and resistance. For too long [scientists] have been very happy in not including us in this discussion. We've got to get on board and up to speed to take action.[41]

A number of Indigenous nations have moved ahead to protect their genetic resources, enacting tribal codes and ordinances, informing the community so that people are prepared to respond to research requests, and training community members to review scientific proposals. Additionally, a number of national tribal organizations have not only opposed the HGDP but also demanded that federal spending priorities be shifted toward basic human needs.[42]

Indigenous peoples worldwide are extremely concerned by the April 13, 2005, announcement of a five-year, $40 million collaboration between National Geographic Society, IBM, and the Waitt Family Foundation, known as the Genographic Project. The project plans to collect 100,000 samples of Indigenous DNA from around the world. The Indigenous Peoples Council on Biocolonialism has called for a boycott of all programs, products, and services of the National Geographic Society, IBM, and Gateway Computers (the source of the Waitt family's fortune) until the Genographic Project ceases to exist.[43]

There are, without dispute, huge ethical questions and questions of basic survival involved with expenditures like those that support the HGDP. Harry observes that,

every day, grants are being made in our name, on our behalf, for research that looks at our health conditions or the genetic basis for conditions that we suffer from, and it's completely a misappropriation of funding because if you consider our health conditions today, we live in contaminated environments, we are eating unhealthy food, we don't have access to the natural lifestyles and the foods that we've always eaten, that have sustained our lives, and so we have horrible health conditions. We are suffering and dying from type II diabetes because our pancreases can't manage the amounts of insulin, yeah, the junk food, the carbs that we consume, and we see a lot of suffering every day. So what I'm saying is, our health conditions are a result of the environment and the economic, political, legal situations that we're in. They're not caused by our genetic, biological makeup. We are not dying from our physical inheritance. We are dying from the environments that we live in, and the conditions that we have to survive in.

There is a reductionist view of the world through scientific eyes. You would see far more benefit in cleaning up the water, in cleaning up contaminated environments, and making sure people have access to just standard health care, vaccinations, education programs around nutrition, organic gardening, all of those things that sustain healthy lives. That's where we are going to see benefit.[44]

Masks in the New Millennium

> In the twenty-first century, the battle to protect Indian land and culture has become even more complicated as it is now possible to steal Indian property, names, traditions and symbols without ever setting foot in Indian country or coming in contact with the tribes or individual Indians from whom these pieces of cultural property are being stolen.
>
> —Crazy Horse Defense Project[1]

The doorway through which one observes the controversy over Native American mascots and commercial imagery is full of fog and fire. It is the fog of myth that shrouds the history of this country and its icons of westward expansion, colonialism, and domination. It is also the fire of passion, as those whose flesh and bones have been turned into mere imagery challenge the foundations of the myths. While some people justify exploiting old stereotypes by saying that they are honoring Native Americans, Indigenous activists ask, "In whose honor" and by what rights are our names used?[2] It is, ultimately, a struggle for the minds of America—on ballfields, in bars, in boardrooms, and even on battlefields where Apache helicopters and the like serve as masks invested with the white man's violent dreams.

This controversy may appear to be solely about symbolism, but it is also about power relations between peoples. Journalism professor Robert Jensen points out that "Indians don't get to tell white people what to do. Why not? Polite white people won't say it in public, but this is what I think many white folks think: 'Whites won and Indians lost. It's our country now. Maybe the way we took it was wrong, but we took it. We are stronger than you. That's why we won. That's why you lost. So get used to it. You don't get to tell us what to do.' "[3]

There is power in naming, in renaming. That power is widely abused in the United States. Many communities struggle with the names given to them by others, and the deconstructing of the categories and borders placed on identity. African American scholars refer to the slanderous insult, "Are you calling me out of my name?" And Carol Spindel, in her book about Indian mascots, points to, "the Star of David worn on a chain by a Jewish person, the Star of David sewn by Nazi order to a prisoner's clothing. In one case, the symbol is chosen freely as a positive indictor. In the other it is coerced, the person is branded with it, and the values attached are all negative."[4] There is little difference in the Native community. While you would never find a Martin Luther King Malt Liquor or a Mahatma Gandhi Strip Club, both a Crazy Horse Malt Liquor and a Crazy Horse Strip Club do exist. The insult to the Lakota descendants of Crazy Horse is the same as it would be to King's or Gandhi's followers.

Often when I speak to non-Native groups, I ask audience members to raise their hands if they can name at least ten distinct Native nations in North America. Whether they are doctors of law, architects, or college students, it is rare that I find more than a handful worthy of the task. That is the amazing reality of a U.S. education. While most of our children can name a set of superheroes into obscurity, or a list of sports teams, presidents, designers, and fashion models, very few can name the Native nations that have lived on this land for millennia. *Even those in their own local territory!* When I have asked businesspeople in the town that adjoins my reservation if they could name ten different groups of Native people, a few were unable to name even the Indigenous nation in whose presence they lived, referring to them as "the Indians."

That is the sad truth. U.S. educational institutions have done a poor job in teaching North American history, particularly from the perspective of Native people. Few know either about the history of genocide in this country or about the Native origins of various democratic, medicinal, or agricultural foundations of modern U.S. culture. Even fewer know about the history of the treaty-making period. Outside of those areas near reservations, the American people are almost completely ignorant of the present-day struggles of Native people. By and large, most discussions regarding Native people continue to be framed in the past.

The most commonly known names of Native nations are those popularized through Hollywood "westerns": the Comanche, the Navajo, the Sioux, the Cheyenne, the Crow, and so forth. Ask non-Native crowds to name famous Native women in history and two will appear: Pocahontas and Sacajawea, those profiled most recently in Hollywood movies. (Increasingly, when a discussion of Native people arises in a non-Native setting, the most common association is with a casino, again illustrating the rather limited knowledge about the majority of Native Americans today.) Indeed, studies investigating children's perception of race and class in the media have found that "most children in America view Native Americans as far removed from their own way of life."[5]

We are faced with a strange irony. The vast majority of Native images that have drifted into the U.S. psyche are those from the mass media: television, movies, cartoons, commercial brands, and sports team mascots. In essence, Indigenous peoples as peoples in the present have all but disappeared from the U.S. consciousness, and our vital role in North American history is grossly misunderstood. The false representation of the Native in media augments America's persistent problem of historical memory and the related dilemma of historical revisionism. *In the end there is no victim, so there was no crime.*[6]

The Native in the Game

They are the Fighting Whites, an intramural basketball team at the University of Northern Colorado. The Reds, a nearby Eaton High School team, uses a Native American caricature for its logo and has, despite many requests, refused to change its name. Eaton School District superintendent John Nuspi has responded defensively to criticism, saying, "Their interpretations are an insult to our patrons and blatantly inaccurate."[7]

Organized by both Native and non-Native students, the college group "came up with the 'Fighting Whites' logo and slogan to have a little satirical fun and to deliver a simple, sincere message about ethnic stereotyping."[8] Their logo features a clean-cut white male in a business suit, and the slogan, "Every thang's going to be all white." "It's not meant to be vicious; it is meant to be humorous," explains Ryan White, a Mohawk team member. "It puts people in our shoes, and then we can say 'now you know how it is, and now you can make a judgment.' "[9] With an outpouring of interest in their T-shirts, computer mouse pads, and other items, the Fighting Whites are putting the profits of their T-shirt sales toward scholarships for Native students. By 2003, the group had raised $100,000 for scholarships, an excellent response to the issue of Native mascots.

A quarter of a century after Stanford University and Dartmouth College retired their Native American mascots, over 600 other educational institutions have joined them. In each case the institutions have transferred their loyalties to a new mascot without, one can presume, huge psychological trauma.[10] Nevertheless, at least 80 colleges and universities, hundreds of high schools, and a number of professional sports teams retain Native American mascots.[11] While it would be unthinkable for sports fans to wave Torah scrolls or crucifixes, they frequently wave staffs decorated with feathers, "peace pipes," or full feather headdresses, all of which are of great spiritual significance to Native peoples. "It says, 'Your religion is not as important as mine,' " explains Gary Brouse, from the Interfaith Council on Corporate Responsibility.[12]

From the grotesque smile of the Cleveland Indians logo to the video game "Custer's Revenge," which featured a cartoon of General George Custer raping Native women, the imagery is clear and it is demeaning. The prevailing commercial use of Native stereotypes is as insulting and dangerous as were the minstrel shows that depicted Blacks as lazy, smiling idiots. According to University of Kansas professor Cornel Pewewardy,

> In popular culture, using a person for your clown has always been
> one of the major ways to assert your dominance over a person or a
> group of people. Mockery becomes one of the more sophisticated

forms of humiliation in sporting events. Therefore, clowning and buffoonery during ball games became one of the primary ways in which Indian mascots are used as clowns while sports fans manipulate and keep in place negative images during school related events.[13]

Kate Stetson, an attorney who works on Native concerns, likens the mascot issue to a broader one. "What mascots do is trivialize and demean individuals and erase a culture. The less you think people are like you, the more you feel that you can be violent [toward] them with impunity. That's the argument with pornography and violence against women."[14] That violence continues.

Even in the absence of violence or insulting local teams, Native peoples have an increasingly difficult time maintaining an authentic Native identity in the era of MTV and the culture-consuming elements of globalization.[15] As mass media imagery from Disney and the like has percolated into the hearts of Indigenous cultures—even isolated ones—and non-Indigenous cultures alike, the struggle over Native American mascots and imagery has become increasingly urgent.

Charlene Teeters, a Spokane woman who has been a lightning rod for the present-day mascot struggle, equates the use of Native mascots with imprisonment:

> These caricatures and stereotypes are really intended as prisons of image. Inside each desperately grinning Cleveland Indian and each stoic Redskin Brave or Chief Illiniwek mascot, there is someone we know. If you look hard enough and don't panic, you begin to see the eyes and the hearts of these despised relatives of ours, who have been forced to lock their spirits away from themselves and from us. I see our brothers and sisters, mothers and fathers captured and forced into images they did not devise, doing hard time for all of us. We can liberate them by understanding this, and ourselves.[16]

In her role as a spokesperson for the National Coalition on Racism in Sports and the Media, Charlene fights the effects of this dangerous, subliminal racism on U.S. politics and justice. Chad Smith, Principal Chief of the Cherokee Nation, explains the problem with this question:

> How can the American public understand sovereignty when the foundation for their understanding of Indians is the 1940 release of *Peter Pan*—the Lost Boys versus the Indians? There's a poison that's been in the system since the creation of the first "Western," Indian myth, the Budweiser commercial, the European novelettes and the public domain cartoons of the 1930s and 1940s. In Oklahoma, the state where there's the most tribes, you see the greatest number of derogatory "Indian" mascots for sports teams, and the greatest tolerance towards them among Indians. So we come back to the point about marketing and public imagery and being smart enough to control that. I think we have to grasp a global perspective about what's in our own interests as tribes and set out a long-term plan to change the public imagery of Indians. A lot of folks say they're trite or petty, but mascot and public imagery issues have not only poisoned our people, but are the main reason why when I go to court, I have to tell the judge that our treaty has the same weight as the U.S. constitution. We all recognize that the time for Little Black Sambo passed long ago, and Little Red Sambo is overdue to join him.[17]

The Fighting Sioux

There are fewer examples of the image appropriation battle more ironic than that of the University of North Dakota (UND) "Fighting Sioux." It is a strange and twisted tale in which a neo-nazi makes a large gift to a university, ostensibly to support a sports team named *in honor of* the greatest opponents of his European forebears' settler society. Any pretense of morals and ethics are forgotten, and Native people find themselves, once again, at odds with a public institution pimping off their culture.

To understand the decades-long conflict, one must recognize the moral disparity between UND and the people whose name it has tried to coopt. You see, in 1978, the Indian Claims Commission issued a $100 million settlement check to the Sioux in lieu of ordering the return of their native land. The Lakota, as the people who were known historically as the Sioux now call themselves, refused this check, considering it to be blood money, and did so despite the dire economic needs of their communities, the lack of infrastructure, and the desperate lack of ways to generate income. The Lakota have some high moral standards. UND has none.

The opening of the UND Ralph Englestad Hockey Arena certainly has put the issue of racism in sports in the limelight. Englestad's donation of $100 million to UND was one of the ten-largest gifts ever given to a public university, but it has put a focus on the true price of corporate and private contributions to our university system. It also summons a puzzling question: How can anything built by a man who dresses up in a Nazi outfit be an honor to Native people?

Understand at the outset a bit about UND's hometown of Grand Forks. It is a city nestled on a floodplain, sort of spitting in the face of the natural world, daring the Red River to take its soul. Like most American cities, it was carved from the heart of Indian Territory. Little Crow's War, or the 1862 Dakota War, included the "largest mass execution in American history" when 38 Sioux were hanged on December 26, 1862.[18] Just north of Grand Forks is the city of Pembina, from which millions of buffalo hides were shipped to fur companies—a cornerstone of the near-extermination of both the buffalo and the Dakota, the eastern relatives of the Lakota. (The Lakota, the Nakota, and the Dakota make up the Sioux Nation.) The Dakota were able to keep a sliver of their original territory along the Minnesota River valley, and on small reservations in South Dakota and Nebraska. Subsequent treaties, like the 1868 Fort Laramie Treaty, secured the Lakota's land, only to be violated by gold prospectors and the Army (see the Wounded Knee chapter).

The state of North Dakota has engulfed four reservations: Turtle Mountain, Spirit Lake (also known as the Fort Totten Reservation), Standing Rock (Fort Yates), and Fort Berthold, home of the Mandan, Hidatsa, and Arikara peoples. The fact that three of the reservations are named for the forts pushed into the hearts of Indian Territory should be an indication of the degree of animosity between settler and Native. Twenty years after the assassination of Little Crow, the Army was given control of the Indian reservations in North Dakota and elsewhere, and from these it launched the operations that killed great chiefs like Sitting Bull.[19]

In the new millennium, the state of North Dakota continues to battle for its existence. Demographically, the state is affected by a net annual loss in non-Native population. Sixty-two percent of the state has returned to frontier status, as farms and populations dwindle. Native communities, on the other hand, seem to be increasing dramatically in population. The climate and landscape is more suitable for buffalo than for farming, hence an inherently challenged state economy. Then there is the military. With the Cold War came the creation of a string of military bases that could both defend the United States against the "Soviet threat" and attack as needed. It is said that the Lakota Nation itself (as circumscribed by the 1868 treaty that spans North and South Dakota as well as portions of Nebraska and Wyoming) constitutes the third-greatest nuclear weapons power on the face of the Earth. At present, the state of North Dakota controls the lion's share of that power.[20] The Grand Forks military base, with around 7,500 residents, remains one of the few economic boons for the region.

Indigenous students comprise less than 4% of UND's total student body of 11,000. Many feel like they are being spit on every day. They are still sporadically called "prairie niggers," accused of living off the government dole, and termed "crybabies," as if their protests against racism show them to be unappreciative of the presumed largess of UND. In addition to the routine pressures of university or graduate school, these students must face the difficulty of going to school in a town bedazzling itself with the money of racists.

Racism in the north looks different now than it did in Selma, Alabama in 1965. It is the racism of silent stares and closed-door meetings in which white men in power consistently vote down Native interests without Native dialogue. It is the racism that allows a story of a Native woman who is homeless, pregnant, and addicted to drugs to occupy the front page of a newspaper for a month, while never discussing the circumstances that make people homeless or the fact that the homeless shelters in the same town are entirely full of Native people.[21] It is in the oft-repeated comments that Indians are all drunks and that somehow we had it coming. Racism in the North Country is subtle. Scott Nelson, a former sports editor for the *UND Student,* told a reporter, "There are no hate crimes. It's not like the deep South in the '60s." Nelson, however, also mentions the irony of thousands of students who "will wear a jacket, with a mascot of an Indian, but won't talk to one."[22]

In the midst of this irony, UND's claim that the Fighting Sioux logo honors Native students is strange. Roland Barthes, the French semiologist, has noted the hollowness of the ubiquitous and particularly American adoption and re-creation of the crests of ancient knights and other mythic images. He argues that they are "half amputated, they are deprived of memory, not of existence. They are at once stubborn, silently rooted there and garrulous, and speech wholly at the service of concept." [23]

North Dakota is not a story of knights of honor. It is possible to make an argument that one can respect an "honored enemy." It would seem, however, that this respect would include the return of the enemy's lands and a respect for the dignity of that individual. UND's hockey house is emblazoned with the Sioux logo and a huge statue of Sitting Bull presides, but these "honors" were bestowed despite the written opposition of the Standing Rock Sioux Tribe and every other tribal government in North Dakota.

Ralph the Nazi

UND is a hockey powerhouse, viewing the world from a frozen corner of the prairie where ice hockey can be played outside for at least four months a year (absent the impacts of global warming). The university prides itself on having sent at least 50 players to the National Hockey League, and routinely makes at least the semi-finals of the college hockey playoffs. Hockey is the staff of life, it would appear, to some UND alumni.

It was in 1930 that UND decided to change its sports icon, the Flickertails, to the Fighting Sioux. The change came about, it seems, because the flickertail was not considered a formidable foe against the "Mighty Bison" of North Dakota State University. Native journalist Holly Annis found an internal UND memo, discussing the merits of the name change:

1. Sioux are a good exterminating agent for the Bison.
2. [Sioux] are warlike, of fine physique and bearing.
3. The word Sioux is easily rhymed for yells and songs.[24]

There was little debate, and the team re-emerged with its new face. With little popular attention to racism nationally and extremely few Native students, almost four decades passed without protest of the name appropriation. But when the first Native American students group was formed at UND in 1969, it called for the creation of a cultural center for Native students, an Indian Studies program, and the end of the Fighting Sioux name and the Sammy the Sioux mascot.[25]

A couple of years later, the cultural center was created, the Indian Studies program was started with two classes, and Sammy the Sioux was shipped off. The Fighting Sioux name, however, remained. With it came all the unfortunate embellishments, including those invented by opposing teams such as portrayals of Indian women having oral sex with buffalo (a reference to the North Dakota State University buffalo mascot) and team chants like "Scalp the Sioux."

Ralph Engelstad had come to UND on a hockey scholarship in the '50s. After college, Ralph became a building contractor, moved to Las Vegas, and got a pretty good chunk of change when he sold to billionaire Howard Hughes 145 acres on which to build the North Las Vegas Airport. Ralph reinvested his money in the casino business, launching the Imperial Palace casinos in Las Vegas and Biloxi, and eventually constructed the Las Vegas Motor Speedway for NASCAR races.

It was the birthday parties for Adolph Hitler that made Ralph notorious. Held in a special Nazi memorabilia "war room" in his casino, the parties featured cakes "decorated with a swastika, German food and German marching music." At one party, bartenders wore shirts with a photo of Hitler and the slogan "Adolf Hitler—European Tour 1939-45." The Nevada Gaming Control Board found a plate used to print bumper stickers with the message "Hitler was Right" that were sent out from Engelstad's hotel. Ralph's passion landed him a $1.5 million fine from the Nevada Gaming Control Board in 1988 for damaging the reputation of the state of Nevada—something, I presume, that must be pretty hard to do.[26]

It was about that time that UND dispatched a delegation to meet with its wealthiest alumnus and tour his facilities. At that time, Ralph had pledged a measly $5 million for the hockey stadium, but the fundraising program knew more money was in the cards. Engelstad treated the delegation with the utmost hospitality, but some were concerned. English professor Elizabeth Hampsten was shaken. Paintings of naked women stood next to busts of Hitler wearing Engelstad's hat, and a Nazi propaganda poster depicted children staring out of windows on a train. The caption read "Summer Holiday," but as Hampsten recalls, "I knew the meaning...wasn't a summer holiday."[27]

The university panel came to a rather shameful conclusion: that Ralph was not a Nazi sympathizer but had simply shown "bad taste." That cleared the way for the fundraising program to put a bigger squeeze on Ralph for $100 million, dismissing his interests as idiosyncratic "warts." Although Hampsten objected, she regrets that it was not "loudly enough." It is a clear lesson of how loudly money talks. Meanwhile, down in Las Vegas, Ralph sat cozily in a room filled with busts of Hitler, his 1939 parade car, Heinrich Himmler's Mercedes, and a life-size portrait of Hitler inscribed: "To Ralphie from Adolph."[28] He was a happy man, a smug man.

While Ralphie was building his neo-nazi Las Vegas pleasure palaces, Native students, members of the American Indian Movement, and many others were working to end the use of the Sioux mascot. The university community and most Grand Forks residents and businesses remained staunchly attached to their team tradition. At one point, several businesses in Grand Forks posted signs in their store-fronts that read: "Redskins, go back to the reservations. Leave the name alone."[29]

By the '90s some token progress was being made in the name of multiculturalism. Fraternity and sorority members were ordered to apologize, and to attend multicultural events and educational forums, after they used phrases like "go back to the reservation," "dirty Indians," and "tell your parents to get off welfare" to taunt members of a Native youth traditional dance group, the Seven Feathers Club. Still, when the University Faculty Senate passed a resolution supporting a name change, UND's President William Kupchella responded:

> It is decided that the name will not be changed because of the great feeling of pride and tradition. The real issue is the need for more education about diverse cultures, using the royalties from the sanctioned logo to fund scholarships for Native American students, cultural programming at athletic events and assistance for the various UND Native American organizations.[30]

Sharing the position of the Lakota Tribe on the issue of "blood money," every Native program declined receipt of the logo fund money.[31] Activists kept up their pressure on UND as a growing number of colleges nationally changed their team names. At one point, the Native students and their supporters had even secured an internal memorandum from President Kupchella to the board saying, "I see no choice but to respect the request of Sioux tribe that we quit using their name, because to do otherwise would be to put the university and its president in an untenable position."[32]

Those words were never spoken. Instead, Englestad's words were heard, loud and clear. Englestad sent a letter to President Kupchella threatening to "turn off the building's heat, and take a $35 million loss" on the under-construction hockey arena if the university changed its name. Ralph's threats ended discussion of the logo change. Less than a week after receipt of Englestad's letter, UND announced that the name would remain.[33]

Engelstad built his shrine in the North Country, the most opulent and grandiose shrine to hockey in the world. The immense building resembles Grunewald, the huge German stadium in which Hitler would amass crowds and work them into a frenzy. There are 11,400 leather seats, armrests cut from Valley Forge cherrywood, tiles from India, chandeliers from Italy, escalators from Germany, a $2 million scoreboard, and a 24-person Jacuzzi. Then, of course, there are the 2,400 engraved and painted—*pretty much not moving anywhere*—logos of the Fighting Sioux. As UND professor Lucy Gange observed, Ralph is pretty much "rubbing everyone's noses into that logo."[34]

Engelstad's initial gift was to include $50 million for the hockey arena and $50 million for other programs at the university. In the end, Ralph's arena ate up the entire gift. Faculty members accuse Engelstad of wasting money on the arena as retribution for their opposition to the Fighting Sioux nickname.[35] They point to the arena's many extravagances, including a 400-foot-long hedge that spells out FIGHTING SIOUX for planes flying overhead. "How much was spent on spite?" Gange asked, "How much of what he added was saying 'You will get none of my money.'"[36]

On opening night of the 2001 hockey season, Engelstad walked to center ice of his own Grunewald to a deafening roar of applause. "May this arena keep producing the finest hockey team in the nation…and may the Fighting Sioux and the Fighting Sioux logo stand forever." He earned himself a new name, *Wasichu Canl Wakan,* which in English would mean something like, "Taker of the fat, who is afraid of the sacred, a coward."[37]

Charlene Teeters boils the problem down to an inherent clash of meanings: "Using our names, likeness, or religious symbols to excite a crowd does not feel like an honor or respect. It is hurtful and confusing to our young people. To reduce the victims of genocide to a mascot is callous and unthinking at best, and immoral at worst."[38] Robert Jensen puts it this way:

> If Germany had won World War II, it would be the equivalent of contemporary Germans naming a university team the Jews and using a hook-nosed caricature. I do not mean that hyperbolically. In heated debates, people often compare opponents to Nazis as an insult. This isn't an insult. It's an accurate comparison. The ideology of racial supremacy underneath the genocide of indigenous

people here was not so different from Nazi ideology. Inferior people had to give way so that superior people could make use of land.[39]

Although UND has been castigated by *Sports Illustrated* and the *Chronicle of Higher Education,* other universities have been cautious about criticism within the folds of the family. With increasing private and corporate contributions to the university system, one would hope for a line to be drawn as to when the price exacted on the integrity of an institution is too high and the impact on the students is too difficult to bear.

There are many more positive ways of honoring Native students and Native people, such as putting $100 million toward programs for Native students, faculty, and research programs. In the meantime, UND and other universities should undertake some soul-searching about taking money from various sources, in particular Nazi sympathizers. In November 2002, Ralph Engelstad passed away and moved to the next world. The debate about the Fighting Sioux continues at UND, with the specter of Englestad and his baggage still looming on the edge of the prairie.

In the end, the University of North Dakota cannot truly be the Fighting Sioux because it took $100 million from a neo-nazi. My personal suggestion for an appropriate name for any Grand Rapids sports teams: the Mighty Sandbaggers. After all, that's what a town built on a floodplain must be particularly good at doing.

In the Spirit of Crazy Horse

The purposeful use and appropriation of another ascertainable person's name or likeness in an insulting and disparaging manner, without consent or permission of the lawful owner of said name or his heirs and especially in the commercial exploitation for financial gain in association with a product which has proved so deadly to Indian people, are despicable and disparaging invasions of privacy and are egregious violations of Lakota customary law protecting the spiritual, personal, social and cultural importance of an individual's name to an individual and his family during his life and his spirit and reputation, along with those of his relations, after his life so as to amount to disparagement and defamation of both the individual and the group.

—Lakota Tribal Court complaint against
Crazy Horse Malt Liquor[40]

On April 26, 2001, something rather remarkable happened. A beer company apologized. John W. Stroh III traveled to Mission, South Dakota, the home of the Tasunke Witko (Crazy Horse) *tiosapaye* (the traditional form of extended family and governance in the Lakota Nation) and issued a formal apology for the role his company, Stroh Brewery, had played in the production of Crazy Horse Malt Liquor. In a moving ceremony, Stroh announced the gift of seven thoroughbred horses, 32 Pendleton blankets, 32 braids of sweetgrass, and 32 twists of tobacco, all culturally significant items to the Crazy Horse estate. These, along with desisting in any further misappropriation, were the specific remedies stipulated by the Tasunke Witko estate as "relief" in the case filed in the Rosebud Sioux Tribal Court. The number seven represented the seven facilities where the liquor had been bottled, and the number 32 represented the number of states in which the liquor had been distributed.

With these gifts and its formal letter of apology to the family, the Stroh Brewery Company has made a contribution to the *tiosapaye*'s process of reconciliation with a long history of appropriation of the name of their ancestor. Seth Big Crow, representing the family, called the settlement "a victory for all Native Americans."[41] It's been a long, hard battle to defend the dignity of the dead.

Over 100 years after his murder, the spirit of Crazy Horse is still felt. Considered to have been one of the greatest leaders and military strategists of all time, this charismatic Sicangu Lakota was born around 1842. He lived in a time of great challenge for the Lakota and other tribes of the Great Plains. Encroaching European explorers, Indian agents, and settlements had brought rampant diseases to Indigenous nations, smallpox taking Tasunke Witko's own small daughter and other family members. Whiskey and alcohol had begun to wreak havoc on the communities, causing the deaths of many good people. As the growing settler and Army presence decimated the buffalo and made the situation of the people more desperate, many Lakota came to follow Tasunke Witko. It is also said that his power was the source of envy among some Indians and caused fear in the U.S. military. His assassination was orchestrated on September 5, 1877, at Fort Robinson. As two Oglalas who had turned against Tasunke Witko held him, a soldier bayoneted him in the back.

As he passed on to the spirit world, Tasunke Witko spoke to his family. In his dying instructions, he asked to be buried in a secret location and requested that they never speak of him to non-Native people in the future.[42] For generations the Tasunke Witko *tiosapaye* kept that promise, but in 1993, Seth H. Big Crow, Sr., received permission from his family and from Rosebud Sioux Tribal Court to assume the legal authority to act on behalf of the estate of his great-grandfather. The Rosebud Tribal Court ruled, in the administrative appointment, that the estate had the right to "protect the use of [the] decedent's name particularly with regard to misappropriation and commercial exploitation of said name under the law of the Rosebud Sioux Tribe and any other applicable laws."[43]

It is not as if the name has not been heard in public before. After all, bars, horses, and even a line of clothing (Liz Claiborne) all use the name. "In each case, there is a common thread," explains Gary Brause of the Interfaith Center for Corporate Responsibility. "These companies never discuss the issue with the Native community; there is no consultation, no dialogue with the families."[44] While the lack of consultation was always problematic, the most offensive instance was the use of the name by a beer company.

The liquor naming was the brainchild of John Ferolito and Don Vultaggio, both from Brooklyn, New York. These two businessmen conceptualized a line of beverages they called a "Family of American Originals." The liquors would be brewed under contract by various large national breweries, such as Heileman and Stroh, and marketed under the name of the Hornell Brewing Company. The two men hoped to sell their products to upscale domestic customers of premium liquors and an overseas market.[45]

Hornell's 1986 launch, "Midnight Dragon Malt Liquor," featured a woman clad in a slinky red dress and garter drinking from a beer bottle through a straw, with the tagline, "I could suck on this all night." That beer became a target of protests by women's groups. "PowerMaster," a similar product targeted toward the African American community, was pulled off the market in 1991 after protests by primarily Black churches and social activist groups. In March 1992, that exact same malt liquor was reintroduced as Crazy Horse Malt Liquor.[46] In May of that year, Ferolito and Vultaggio created Arizona Iced Tea, appropriating Native American design elements for the packaging of this product as well.

The insult to the Lakota was not only in the misuse of the name of Crazy Horse but also in the significant negative impact of alcohol on Lakota and other Indigenous cultures. Liquor has been described as "one of the earliest chemical warfare agents used against Indians by Europeans to disable Native intelligence and begin the feeding frenzy on land that the European saw as his innate destiny to possess."[47] Alcoholism continues to affect almost every family on most Lakota and other reservations.

Defense of Spirit

Lakota Wo'ope, or Lakota Customary Law, is the backbone of Lakota culture, dictating how the people must treat one another. Name appropriation violates the custom of *Lakota Wo'ope.* Explains Robert Gough, attorney for the Tasunke Witko *tiosapaye,* "That right to pass on that name is what goes on with the family." This principle was the underlying basis for the lawsuit filed by the estate of Tasunke Witko in August 1993, in the Rosebud Sioux Tribal Court. The estate sued the Hornel Brewing Company and its partners for defamation of the spirit of Crazy Horse.

After 12 years of litigation in over a half-dozen tribal, state, and federal venues, the estate reached a settlement "on the court house steps" with the beer company that ended the manufacturing of the malt liquor under the name of Crazy Horse (now renamed Crazy Stallion), turned over all the intellectual property rights the company claimed to hold, and brought a formal apology and monetary damages to the estate.[48]

It appears that even some large oil companies are acknowledging the sensibilities of cultural property rights. The president of British Petroleum made a 2002 trip to the Rosebud Reservation. The corporation had named its largest oil find in the Gulf of Mexico "Crazy Horse." The leadership of the company got wind of the Lakota concerns, and as Gough explains, "It took a little time to make their official change. They actually brought their commemoration plaque up and presented it along with some sweetgrass and tobacco."[49] So it is that the descendants of Crazy Horse recover his spirit.

To the Rosebud Lakota and the Tasunke Witko *tiosapaye,* "All of these are recognitions of the right of the tribe and the estate to control the use of the name, the intellectual property," Gough says. "And it is also a recognition of tribal law." For the rest of us, there is something to be said for the words "I'm sorry."[50]

In October of 2001, a small but mighty delegation of Minnesota youth attended the Racism in Sports Conference at the University of North Dakota. A demonstration during the conference against the UND mascot was the first such protest for most of the kids from the White Earth Reservation. The Rice Lake boys had signs that read, "Indians Are People, Not Mascots," and "Respect Our Human Rights." A cheeky two-year-old from Round Lake had a sign that read, "Go Home Pilgrims," and another had a sign that read, "Hinkley Honkeys," referring to a Minnesota town near an Ojibwe reservation. Federal marshals, empowered to ensure that our First Amendment rights were protected in a hostile environment, watched over the small demonstration of 100 or so folks who stood in the bitter wind in the shadow of the immense Englestad hockey arena. Our voices were strong; against Englestad's $100 million, the Native students and others stood as bravely as David in the face of Goliath, supporting Native American's self-determination in how their imagery is used.

In the end, it is a question of who gets to decide your identity and how that will be reflected in the dominant society. It is also a question, according to Robert Jensen, of the dignity of white people. In the process of forcing names on other people, Jensen asserts, white people give up our dignity when we evade the truth, and we surrender our humanity when we hold onto illegitimate power over others.... In a very real sense, we cannot steal the dignity and humanity of indigenous people. We can steal their resources, disrespect them, insult them, ignore them, and continue to repress their legitimate aspirations. We can try to distort their own sense of themselves, but in the end, we cannot take their humanity from them. The only dignity and humanity that is truly diminished by the Fighting Sioux is that of white America.[51]

In the new millennium, it is time for the settler to end the process of naming that which he has no right to own, and for us collectively to reclaim our humanity.

Part 3

Seeds and Medicine

Luis Salas
(Photo courtesy of Bad River Gitiganing Project)

Three Sisters

Recovery of Traditional Agriculture at Cayuga, Mohawk, and Oneida Communities

In the late spring we plant the corn and beans and squash. They're not just plants—we call them the three sisters. We plant them together, three kinds of seeds in one hill. They want to be together with each other, just as we Indians want to be together with each other. So as long as the three sisters are with us, we know we will never starve. The creator sends them to us each year. We celebrate them now.

—Chief Louis Farmer, Onondaga[1]

For 300 years, the three sisters of Iroquois agriculture have survived a scorched earth policy, the forced relocation of people, and then, the creation of a monoculture of agriculture—and of the mind. But the Iroquois have begun to return to the land, to restore the three sisters, their relatives, and in that process to strengthen all that they are.

The three sisters—corn, beans, and squash— are the foundation of the Haudenosaunee culture. For at least eight centuries, Haudenosaunee people—those nations we have come to call the Iroquois Confederacy—have grown corn and other plants in what is today known as the New York/Quebec region. Their stories, like those of many other peoples, speak of corn arriving from the spirits and from trade with peoples from the south.[2] Researchers have traced the origins of agriculture in the Finger Lakes regions back to the Owasco period, about 1070 AD.[3]

Cayugas Remember

Signs border both ends of the new Cayuga land in upstate New York, a farm purchased by local non-Indigenous residents for the Cayuga people so that they might be able to return to their heartland, their capital by the Great Gully. The signs read, "No Reservation—No Sovereign Nation," "No to Cayuga Land Claims." The signs underscore two centuries of tension over the beautiful land of the Six Nations, land that today is held in large measure by the state of New York. Over 200 years after they were forced from their land, Mohawk, Cayuga, and Oneida people are returning to their land, to their fields. They bring with them their three sisters: the corn, beans, and squash.

Bernadette Hill, a beautiful Heron clan grandmother, often spurs on her Cayuga people for the return of the land. Bernadette teaches the young, "Our nation was a great nation, a great agricultural nation."[4] As part of the Six Nations Iroquois Confederacy, the Cayugas lived in relative peace until the British and French started warring over access to North American riches. By the time the colonists were fighting for their independence from Britain, Major General John Sullivan of the Continental Army described the Cayuga long houses as "large and elegant," and their communities as "beautifully situated, almost encircled with a cleared flat, which continued for a number of miles, covered by the most extensive fields of corn and every kind of vegetables that can be conceived."[5]

Sullivan came to Cayuga territory in 1779 on orders from General George Washington:

> The immediate objects are the total destruction and devastation of their settlements and the capture of as many prisoners of every age and sex as possible. It will be essential to ruin their crops now in the ground and prevent their planting more.... Our future security will be in their inability to injure us, the distance to which they are driven, and in the terror with which the severity of the chastisement they receive will inspire on them.[6]

The immense quantity of crops destroyed during the Sullivan Campaign provides documentation today of the extent to which Haudenosaunee were flourishing farmers. A subgroup of Sullivan's force destroyed *one million* bushels of corn during one week![7]

The pretext for this scorched earth policy was to punish those members of the Six Nations Confederacy who had sided with the British against the colonists. But according to Jack Rossen, an agricultural archeologist and historian who has studied extensively this period of American and Iroquois history, the real story is that the United States was broke, and it hadn't paid its soldiers for months. The government was looking for a land grab, and that is exactly what happened: The land was taken from the Iroquois and given as a "military tract" to the soldiers. The second lie, maintains Rossen and other scholars, is that there were no casualties. "Although many had fled, those who remained behind were killed in their fields or burned alive in their houses," Rossen explains, having found Sullivan Campaign archeological sites containing human bones.[8]

Elder Bernadette Hill remembers, "There were thousands of us. Now there's around 500 of us in western New York."[9] All that the Cayuga had was destroyed by the Campaign, one of many untold stories of the Revolutionary War. At the center of the destruction was the great Cayuga capital, the heart of their nation, where soldiers burned every home in sight and girdled 1,500 peach and apple trees.

The Cayugas fled the destruction, moving as swiftly as they could from the fires and the cannons. Some hid successfully in the Great Gully, a ravine cut by the west-running Great Gully Creek. Winding through the ravine, the creek drops over limestone ledges and falls; the walls of the ravine rise nearly 300 feet in places. As I walk the Great Gully with Hill, she recalls the voices of ancestors. She reflects on the times she has walked to a great waterfall in the Gully and rested there to "wash my tears away."[10]

Sullivan's terrorism resulted in 3,000 Iroquois refugees walking 120 miles west to British-controlled Fort Niagara. That winter, starvation, scurvy, and other diseases took many of them. The land surveyed during the Sullivan Campaign eventually was given as a bounty of war to colonist veterans of the Revolutionary War. A hundred years after the founding of towns like Elmira and Aurora, the new landowners rejoiced in the history of the Cayugas' banishment, displaying signs reading, "The Wigwam Fell, the Log Cabin Arose," "Scalps in 1779, Brains in 1879."[11]

Monocultures of the Mind and of the Land

Jubilant as those celebrations might have been, 200 years later it is perhaps possible that another change will come and justice may be served. As it turns out, the state of New York took possession of the vast majority of 64,000 acres of Cayuga territory through an agreement known as the Cayuga Ferry Treaty of 1795, five years *after* the federal Non-Intercourse Act of 1790 had barred states from signing treaties with Indian nations. The last of the tribe's land was ceded in 1807. The agreements were "decidedly shady," in the words of the *New York Times* and, it appears, even caused some unease in President Washington.[12] "The state of New York knew exactly how illegal their actions were," surmises Rossen. "They never intended to send them to Congress for ratification. They knew they were illegal. It was really a question of state versus federal power."[13]

The Cayugas are the only Iroquois nation without a reservation, made refugees in their own land. For generations, the Cayuga families who had survived the "ethnic cleansing," in the words of Cayuga leader Clinton Halftone, continued their dream of return to their traditional lands. Halftone, appointed by the clan mothers to forward the political and legal case for the return of the Cayuga land, explains the original goals of the Cayuga's 1980 lawsuit against the state of New York: "When we filed in the 1980s, we sought return of the 64,000 acres that is ours, and $350 million in trespass damages."[14] Four years later, a panel recommended that the Cayugas should be given 8,000 acres in Cayuga and Seneca counties for a reservation and a cash settlement of $15 million. The land to be returned to the Cayugas was publicly owned; no private landholders would have been impacted.

The Cayugas were intent on making some agreement, but the proposed settlement was met with a bitter outcry by a group of non-Native landholders, calling themselves the Upstate Citizens for

Equality. Formed in 1997 specifically as a " voice for those who face displacement," its Seneca-Cayuga chapter has 4,000 members.[15] In a 1984 *New York Times* article, reporter Michael Winerip captured the sentiments of the settlement opponents, reporting that non-Native people complained at public meeting that they didn't want their children going to school with "dirty Indians suffering from dysentery and head lice."[16] When the lawsuit still remained unsettled in 1992, the federal government joined on behalf of the Cayugas. Two years later, Judge Neal McCurn ruled that the tribe indeed had a legal claim to 64,000 acres of land because Congress had never approved the acquisition of the land by the state, as required by the federal law. In 1999, the court-appointed mediator proposed a settlement in the range of $125 million to be split between the federal and state governments. The Cayugas accepted the settlement, but the state, fueled by the Upstate Citizens for Equality and other interests, would not agree, and instead pushed on through the appeals process.

Cayuga claims were acknowledged again in February 2000 when a federal jury in Syracuse returned a verdict awarding the Cayugas $36.9 million for the loss of their ancestral lands, not including interest, and in October 2001, Judge Neal McCurn ordered the state to pay the Cayugas $247.9 million, one of the largest Indian legal settlements in history.[17]

As with all the previous judgements, the state of New York appealed the 2001 decision, prolonging the Cayuga quest for justice. In the meantime, New York Governor Pataki of is "strong arming [the tribes] and forcing them to open casinos as settlement of their land claims," according to journalist Paul DeMain.[18]

Peacemaking among Neighbors

All during this 25-year legal battle, a strange thing was happening. Julie Uticoke's family had mostly not supported the Cayugas' return to their homeland. Julie and her husband, Jim, however, were open to the idea.

When Julie and Jim purchased their land from her father, they needed to have some sort of land claim insurance—that was how it started, how she remembered it as we talked—as the legal battles of the Cayuga, Seneca, and Oneida were already in place. One day, she said, "I started getting information stuck in my mailbox like 'the land claim was coming' and we had better want to get protection."[19] The literature was the organizing work of the Upstate Citizens Alliance, another entity organized to oppose the Cayuga and other Iroquois land settlements. Julie felt uncomfortable about it, and decided to learn more about what the Native issues were. So she took a class with Native American Studies scholar Robert Venables, and then after thinking about it, posted a notice on a local current events listing. The ad said something like, "Anyone interested in a positive, peaceful solution in the Land Claim, meet at Cayuga Lake State Park, Thanksgiving day, 9 a.m. We will share information and opinions, and we will be home in time for dinner. Pumpkin pie and coffee will be served." Julie remembers that 32 people came, including Jeannie Shenandoah, a clan mother from the Onondaga Nation. Julie was a bit nervous at the time. There were some folks driving by and threatening her, but there was a good group and a couple of reporters. So they started talking and meeting.

Brooke Olson, another local resident and professor at Ithaca College, recalls that Julie called for a "peace circle, a peaceful resolution to the land claim."[20] Brooke has the presence of an incredibly earnest, committed woman, and the looks of Meryl Streep. She is amazing to watch as she organizes her meetings, or puts her back to work moving furniture or working the farm. Brooke, her husband Ernie, and Jack Rossen, all local university professors, joined Julie in forming SHARE: Strengthening Haudenosaunee–American Relations through Education. Julie explains the passion that fueled the work of the non-Natives: "We all felt like we were moving to this all of our lives. That we had worked all over the world, but this was something only the white people could do—make an opposition."

Brooke and Ernie's daughter Sierra had a friend at school whose parents owned a 72-acre organic farm. The farm was located just up the hill from the Great Gully, the heartland of the Cayugas. That farm, the boy told Sierra, they were going to sell. To Jack, Julie, Ernie, and Brooke, buying the farm was a perfect, tangible mission for SHARE.

The emerging group talked to the clan mothers and other leaders of the Cayugas and Onondagas, who agreed to work with the group on the condition that the group not get involved in a battle with the anti-Indian organizing groups. "It's an amazing effort on their part," Halftone says as he sits on the couch enjoying a feast at the SHARE farm. "We've seen other nations buy back land, and they've been met with court challenges and attacked. Here are some non-Natives buying land for Native people. It is a great attempt to ease our way back to our homeland."

"We sent Jack to the bank," Brooke remembers with a laugh. "He was the only one who didn't have kids and a family, and could probably get a mortgage." Jack recalls that the bankers "kept saying, 'Why do you want to buy a farm?' "[21] He was a city boy after all, and already had a house. "Jack couldn't exactly tell them that we wanted to buy a farm and give it back to the Indians," Brooke says with another laugh. "They probably wouldn't give him the mortgage then."

For the past two years, the SHARE group and its supporters have cobbled together the money to make the mortgage payments by growing organic produce on the farm to sell at summer farmers markets and holding fundraisers. "For any difficulties we have had, for any challenges in putting together the mortgage payment," Brooke tells me, "there are so many amazing gifts of this farm. We have all grown so much."

The experience has spilled over into the neighborhood. Although the signs of United Citizens for Equality push against the sky on two sides of the farm, telling the Cayugas they are not welcome, another neighbor has helped the SHARE farm plow its fields. The neighbor whose land surrounds the Great Gully, the river canyon that saved the Cayugas from slaughter, has taken legal steps to protect that land from development.

The rooms of the SHARE farmhouse are often filled with Cayugas, the yard filled with festivals and feasts. The Haudenosaunee Resource Center, a regional initiative, has organized gatherings on planting traditions, and is working with the SHARE farm to grow out some Haudenosaunee seed and plant varieties as food for the communities. Rick Hill explains the intent of the Resource Center, "Our plan is simple. Get more people planting a wider diversity of crops. Then work at developing a wider selection of recipes so that our people can eat healthier."[22] So it is that the Cayugas, with their new allies, begin the process of recovering traditional food and culture in the Haudenosaunee Nation.

Kanatiohareke: The Mohawk's Clean Pot

To the east of the Cayuga, the Mohawk Nation of the Iroquois Confederacy made their homes in the Mohawk Valley. The Mohawk call this place *Kanatiohareke,* pronounced "ga-na-jo-ha-lay-gay." "The Place of the Clean Pot" refers to a spot in one of the valley's creeks where tumultuous waters catch small stones in a whirlpool, carving out from the bedrock below what appears to be a pot. Like the Cayuga, the Mohawk have a rich agricultural tradition and cared as well for an ecosystem that supported turkey, deer, and other game. There are fewer animals on the land today, but the land retains its fertility.

"My gramma used to say, you can't be a real traditional Indian if you don't have a garden," Chief Tom Porter, of the Mohawk Bear clan, tells me as we wander by car from one village to the next in the Mohawk Valley.[23] Tom is a rock-solid foundation of the Mohawk Nation. He continues, "The ceremonies are all about our relationship to Mother Earth, from planting to the trees. If you don't work with Mother Earth, they have no meaning." The Indigenous relationship to Mother Earth is the center of a way of life, of a spiritual practice, and of day-to-day living. It is, in the words of Porter, "Almost like your belly button. Your umbilical cord."

War and conflicts in the 1700s, like the Sullivan Campaign, sent the Mohawks, as Tom Porter says "for a rest," up to the north, up to Akwesasne, "Where the Partridge Drums," but they always remembered this place in the Mohawk Valley. Porter recounts the lessons he learned from his ancestors.

> When the white people came—George Washington, Sullivan—they passed out smallpox blankets. We gave up Ohio, Kentucky, they were sort of international hunting grounds. Shared by the Iroquois, the Odawa, Potawatomi, all used to hunt there,

those international hunting grounds. In the treaty with George Washington, we gave them up to keep these lands. They weren't supposed to build Rochester, Albany, any of that. That's why the Mohawks fought for 150 years. Against smallpox, measles, then alcohol and missionaries. Once they broke our spiritual unity [with the missionaries] things changed. That was my great-grandmother's time.

Tom remembered the stories that his grandmother told of the Mohawk Valley. The old people had "always talked about returning to their homeland…. They told us about the return of the people to this area, to rekindle the fire," Tom remembers. "They never stopped talking about it. Ever since I was a little boy." Tom did not realize at the time that "they were talking about us."

In 1716, Mohawk chiefs bestowed part of the Mohawk Valley land on a Harmanus Van Slyck in honor of his grandfather and Mohawk grandmother who had been highly regarded by the Mohawks. Eventually, the farm passed into the hands of Jelles Fonda (an ancestor of Jane Fonda), who cared for the homestead for many years. Then for almost a hundred years, from 1889 till 1991, the Montgomery County Home for the Aged used the majestic tumble of buildings and farm sheds overlooking the Mohawk River. Hard times fell on the nursing home, and through two winters it stood vacant, suffering from vandalism and neglect.

Tom Porter had been visiting the valley for years, making presentations about Mohawks in the past, present, and future at schools and local civic organizations, and, not surprisingly, had made quite a few friends. Tom is more than affable; he is charismatic. Local people heard of the Mohawks' interest in returning and were increasingly supportive. "Then a teacher at the local school points out that this used to be a Bear clan Mohawk village right there," Tom says, referring to the area around the old Fonda farm. When Tom realized that his great-grandmother had lived there, family ties pulled him home. When the property was put up for auction, the Mohawks worked hard to raise money. They sold prepared foods and crafts, and came up with $20,000, far short of the $230,000 needed to pay for the property.

"We came down to the auction, we were running a little late," Tom tells me. "The yard and highway was filled up with all sorts of cars, and some big limousines. We came in and were really worried. They all looked at us as we came in and motioned us over to a table. 'Here, sign the papers,' someone said to us.' " An anonymous donor had purchased the land for the Mohawks.

Porter recalls their moving day fondly. "When we came here [to move in at last], one of the neighbors had painted 'Welcome Home' on the side of the barn." It is fortunate that the Mohawks have a broad array of friends and extremely fortunate that Porter is handy. Much of the building needed refinishing, repairs, and renovation. Jan Swart, a local historian, describes some of the challenges: "It was very hard the first winter. The core families had to fix and fix and fix."[24] Porter also found that the amount of challenging work in the old homeland was a stretch for many Mohawk folks.

Now more than ten years after the Mohawk regained their land in the valley, traditional ways are being revitalized at Kanatiohareke. "It took courage to do it, but family groups are now living and working together plowing with horses and teaching traditional ways of the Mohawk people," Porter explains. Mohawk language programs span the year, bringing in youth from urban areas and reservations alike. The farm continues to grow a wide variety of vegetables: raspberries, tomatoes, strawberries, squash, buckwheat, and corn. And visitors are welcome at the Mohawk Bed and Breakfast, which offers spacious rooms and traditional Mohawk cooking and hospitality. The return to Kanatiohareke is only one part of the Mohawk recovery of the land and the three sisters. Today, Mohawk farmers throughout their territory share seeds, planting, and stories, and continue their feasts and way of life. It is a time of homecoming and renewal.

Not far from the SHARE farm, near Ithaca, the Corn Project was started in 1985, largely to address the need to strengthen the genetic diversity of the Iroquois white flint corn seeds. The Mohawk Nation Agriculture Project began at Akwesasne near the Mohawk Nation Long House in 1998, and continues to grow. The survival of traditional Haudenosaunee seeds is testimony to the continuity of the community. Katsi Cook, a Wolf clan mother at Akwasasne, explains the important role that traditional agriculture plays in retaining other aspects of traditional culture: "The basket makers back at Akwesasne had almost forgotten how to make one [corn-washing basket] because so many people had stopped growing corn. And now, there's really only two serious corn-growing projects up there. But, it's catching on more and more because people love to eat it. That hasn't disappeared."[25]

Today, families continue with communal planting of corn, beans, and squash. Their work is a key component of the Akwesasne Freedom School, where children have a year-round school program, including summer planting and tending the community gardens.[26]

In this new millennium, the traditional seeds and the way of life associated with them are part of the cultural renewal of the Haudenosaunee community.

The Oneida's Tsyunhehkwa: "It Provides Life for Us"

Braids of corn 150 ears long hang from the rafters of a large barn. Greenhouses have been converted to drying rooms for corn cobs, awaiting preparation as fine white flint corn hominy. Jill Nindham moves deftly between the braids of corn, looks over the turkeys that are carrying on in the yard, and scans the land that provides food to the Oneida people—now living in Wisconsin.

They call themselves *Onyota aka,* "People of the Standing Stone." It is said that every 20 years or so, they would move their villages and a large stone would appear outside the gate to their village. Their traditional life has revolved around their agricultural crops, their villages, and the keeping of the Great Law of Peace.

Like other members of the Iroquois Confederacy, Oneida peacekeeping efforts were complicated by the arrival of the fur trade and new military technologies in the 1600s. The Oneidas recognized the pressure of European settlement, and watched as their eastern neighbors, the Mohawks, fled north from their beloved Mohawk Valley to escape the colonists. Oneidas also began to go north, and some converted to Christianity. The Oneida struggled to remain neutral during the Revolutionary War, but were, as Doug-George Kanentiio explains, "drawn into the conflict when their homelands were invaded by both American and British Forces."[27]

One of the Oneidas, Honyere Tehawenkarogwen, "He who Takes up the Snowshoe," became a captain in the American army and a right-hand consultant to George Washington.[28] Paul DeMain, the Oneida editor of *News from Indian Country,* named his youngest son Honyere after this great Oneida military leader. "Oneida women came to our storehouses and took food to George Washington and the starving troops at Valley Forge," Paul DeMain explains.[29]

The Oneida thought that their loyalty to Washinton's army would give them some protection from the land-grabbers, but their solidarity was not returned. As many Oneida fled to Canada and to the West in fear, the remaining tribal members negotiated a treaty in 1788 that relinquished 5.3 million acres of land.

Just west of Green Bay, Wisconsin, some of the Oneida Nation found a refuge on lands of the Menominee Nation. In 1821, the Oneidas negotiated a treaty with the Winnebago and Menominee nations for land west of the Great Lakes. The Oneida then also paid the U.S. government about $25,000 for five million acres in what would become Wisconsin. The 1826 Treaty of Buffalo Creek reduced the Oneida territories to 65,430 acres, and subsequent laws and transactions further whittled down the Oneida territory, until, by 1989 the tribe owned only 2,500 acres of land. Since then the tribe—about 12,000 members strong—has been repurchasing lands and now owns over 4,600 acres in Wisconsin.

The Oneida Community Integrated Food Systems is a community-based 83-acre farm that includes an apple orchard with around 4,500 trees. The farm raises a variety of vegetables, flint corn, and a small herd of cattle, all for the community's consumption. The original intent of the project was to establish a food preservation program to teach canning methods and food preparation to both Oneidas and other local residents. The project also provides herbal remedies to tribal members and works closely with tribal programs and community members to work on issues like diabetes and other prevalent health problems of the Oneida Nation.

At the heart of the Oneida Integrated Food Systems is the Tsyunhehkwa Project and its heirloom white corn. Tsyunhehkwa links retaining biodiversity with strengthening culture. Workshops are held through most of the year, and the annual corn harvest festival is a huge event during which community members harvest the corn by hand and lovingly braid the husks into strands to be hung to dry in the sheds. The festival includes feasting and plenty of youth and children's activities such as making corn husk dolls.

Iroquois biologist Jane Mt. Pleasant describes the centrality of the corn to Oneida continuity:

> I love the corn because it represents accumulated knowledge passed down from farmer to farmer over the millennium. I love the corn because it provides sustenance to my family and community today. I love corn because it represents our promise and commitment to the future. The simple act of planting connects me to the past, roots me in the present, and commits me to the future.[30]

The white flint corn illustrates the beauty of indigenous seeds and crops: Conventional corn has a protein content of around 7%, while the Oneida corn has a protein content of 18%. The corn crop is carefully tended in fields that are rotated annually. Tsyunhehkwa's production staffmembers attend conferences and trainings on organic agriculture to improve their techniques.

Paul "Sugar Bear" Smith, a longtime Tsyunhehkwa staffmember now working at Heifer Project International, understands that there is the thread between a living culture and biodiversity. "We have some 23 bean varieties contained within Iroquois country," he tells me. "When they talk about the breakdown of biodiversity out there, we feel it in here as well, in our own kitchens. We're basically losing out with our foods. That's why you've got nutritional deficiencies."[31]

So the Oneidas, like other Haudenosaunee, have kept their gardens. In their communities there is a revitalization, a remembrance, and a new season coming. The Haudenosaunee Environmental Task Force makes suggestions for its continuity:

Build up seed banks of open pollinated seeds, share seeds with another person and ask them to do the same the following year.
Teach about the three sisters to children and grandchildren. Start a
small garden project in the backyard, and do the same for the community. Sponsor corn husk doll making classes, and gourd rattle
making classes, learn the Iroquois planting songs, plant the three
sisters in a small pot for young people to take home from school.[32]

These projects start with seed banks and seed sharing. As families start growing traditional crops, they often keep half the harvest to
eat and to use for ceremonies, and donate the remainder for seed to
strengthen the genetic diversity of the seed banks.

In the new millennium, the premium cash value for traditional
crops is a part of the new marketing plans for the Haudenosaunee.
The Daybreak Food and Farming Project, founded by John Mohawk
(Seneca) and Yvonne–Dion Buffalo seeks to support the marketing
of Iroquois white corn and other crops. One variety of this corn is
listed as a part of the Slow Food Movement International and has
found more markets regionally and nationally. Launching a traditional foods café at Cattaraugus Seneca Reservation, they serve traditional corn soup, cornbread, and other Haudenosaunee foods. The
market developed through this work is growing, as the café itself purchased 8,000 pounds of white corn in 2003. New market initiatives
are intended to provide financial support to Iroqouis farmers.[33]

The Oneida projects, like other Iroquois projects, celebrate the
corn and the life that the Creator gave their peoples. And somewhere
between the resilience of communities that have survived through it
all, the seeds and the people recover, and biodiversity returns despite
the monoculture of colonialism. The scorched earth once again
brings forth a green life.

Wild Rice

Maps, Genes, and Patents

It is *Manoominike Giizis,* the "wild rice moon," and the lakes teem with a harvest and a way of life. "Ever since I was bitty, I've been ricing," Spud Fineday remembers.[1] He's from Ice Cracking Lake on Minnesota's White Earth Reservation. The wild rice harvest of the Anishinaabeg not only feeds the body, it feeds the soul, continuing a tradition that is generations old for these people of the lakes and rivers of the north. In Spud's childhood, all of the rice lakes teemed with ricers. Laughter punctuated the sounds of boats sliding through rice beds, poles slapping against the water, rice shafts being pulled toward the boat, the gentle "tapping" with cedar sticks, and the rice kernels raining into the boat and back into the water, reseeding for next year.

Each fall, the families would move toward their rice camps on the lakes, beginning in the Crow Wing Lakes to the south and east of the reservation, then moving with the ripening of rice to the northern lakes. The annual finale is at Big Rice Lake, where rice landings still retain names of families and villages—like Big Bear, Bonga, and Ponsford—reminiscent of the long tradition of gathering at lakeside for the annual harvest. The harvest has always been one of the quintessential elements of being Ojibwe. Today, there are fewer ricers. Wage jobs have curtailed the ability of many people to spend days traveling from lake to lake. Ricers are also challenged by the economics of wild rice in the age of globalization, mechanization, and misrepresentative advertising.

Despite globalization, the annual harvest is still met with great anticipation and excitement. The annual Tamarac wild rice permit drawing, the portioning out of ricing rights, commands a huge and restless crowd of determined Anishinaabeg who continue the tradition for sustenance of spirit, food for families, and income.

Scientists suggest that Minnesota wild rice stands "predate by 1,000 years the prehistoric cultures that were known to have used it."[2] Indeed, that knowledge is reflected within the oral history of the Anishinaabeg. *Manoomin* is a gift given to the Anishinaabeg from the Creator. As the story is told, Nanaboozhoo, the cultural hero of the Anishinaabeg, was introduced to rice by fortune and a duck.

> One evening Nanaboozhoo returned from hunting, but he had no game. As he came towards his fire, he saw a duck sitting on the edge of his kettle of boiling water. After the duck flew away, Nanaboozhoo looked into the kettle and found wild rice floating upon the water, but he did not know what it was. He ate his supper from the kettle, and it was the best soup he had ever tasted. So he followed in the direction the duck had taken, and came to a lake full of *manoomin*. He saw all kinds of duck and geese and mudhens, and all the other water birds eating the grain. After that, when Nanaboozhoo did not kill a deer, he knew where to find food to eat.[3]

In the earliest of teachings of Anishinaabeg history, there is a reference to wild rice, known as the food that grows on the water, the food the ancestors were told to find. The presence of this food, we were told, would signal the end of our migration from the eastern seaboard, where we had left our relatives the Wampanoags, the Lenne Lenapi, and the Abenaki. The Anishinaabeg moved over rivers, streams, and lakes to the Great Lakes region, where today a hundred or more reservations and reserves on both sides of the U.S.-Canadian border mark *Anishinaabe Akiing*, the land of the people.

Wild rice is a centerpiece of our community's sustenance. Wild rice offers amino acids, vitamins, fiber, and other essential elements, making it one of the most nutritious grains known to exist. The

her people without toil was wild rice. They could almost defy nature's law that he who will not work shall not eat.[4]

A 1969 report to the Minnesota legislature, commissioned by the Minnesota Resources Commission, disparagingly characterized the Anishinaabeg relationship to wild rice as a "September Santa Claus," a "good berry Mardi Gras," and "the excuse and provision for a spending spree."[5]

Adding to the perception that the Ojibwe had it too easy was the recognition that many Ojibwe lived well from hunting, fishing, and gathering, hence the advent of the state game and fish laws, restricting Ojibwe as well as non-Indian hunters for many years. In many ways, the perception that "civilization" was best served by the Indians removing themselves from the land and, in turn, allowing access to the wealth of the land (i.e., fish, deer, etc.) by sports hunters, seems to underlay much of the colonial philosophy of the state of Minnesota. Not content with securing settlers' access to game, the state also committed itself, in the 1950s, to a program aimed at domestication of the wild rice crop.

Wild rice is incredibly diverse, growing in both lakes and streams throughout the Great Lakes region. Some plants are short, some tall; some kernels are fat, some skinny; varieties have distinct names like "crow foot" or "bottle brush"; the hues range from purple to light brown to greenish. Each rice variety tastes unique. The rice is also subject to the whims of the weather. A strong wind will knock off all the ripe kernels, leaving that which has not yet ripened. Drought or too much water affects both the quantity and quality of the harvest. Let's put it this way: There are a multitude of variables that make wild rice what it is.

Eliminating these variables is an important part of industrializing wild rice. It is about ensuring that all kernels ripen in a timely manner, so there is a small window for harvest. Industrial "wild" rice is grown in diked paddies, which are drained to allow harvest with a combine. Those commercial paddies require a uniform species of wild rice and often a set of chemicals and fertilizers for production. Needless to say, that rice does not taste the same as truly wild rice.

By the 1970s, increased production of wild rice grown on commercial paddies made an inferior imitation of a rare food available to ever-widening circles of consumers. The increase in production, growing public demand, and subsequent interest by the larger corporations (i.e., Uncle Ben's, Jolly Green Giant, and General Foods) permanently altered the market for traditional wild rice. Like other small farmers faced with competition from agribusiness, lake-harvested rice could no longer effectively compete in price with the corporations' mass-manufactured paddy crop. When the Minnesota state legislature designated wild rice as Minnesota's official state grain in 1977, that was perhaps the kiss of death for traditionally harvested wild rice. With an outpouring from the state coffers, the University of Minnesota aggressively began to develop a domesticated version of wild rice. Greed overtook the industry, as prices were fixed by a virtual wild rice monopoly, including, notably, United Wild Rice. The company was later charged by Minnesota's attorney general with violation of the state's antitrust laws, a case that was settled out of court in March 1981.[6]

Ironically, the state of Minnesota lost control over its official state grain to the state of California, which, according to grower Jerry Schochenmaier, offers ample sun, open acreage, and "control over the variables—water is bought, not rained down, no wind, and no hail. You just put it in, tend to it, and harvest it, pretty much like any other grain crop." The rice found in the major markets is quite different from the rice that grows wild in northern Minnesota. Commercially produced wild rice is processed black, parboiled, and scarified, so as "to get its cook time to match that of white rice," explained Schochenmaier. [7]

Today, California growers continue to lead the nation in wild rice production and only 15% of Minnesota's 7 million pound wild rice output is harvested from lakes—machines cull the rest from paddies. A glut of wild rice hit the market in 1986, causing the prices to plummet. Not only was the newly emerging domesticated market affected but the Native wild rice economy was also devastated as lakeside prices crashed. Many Ojibwe lost a major source of their livelihood. To add insult to injury, many of the paddy rice companies were sell-

ing a product as if it were wild rice, even in some cases using Ojibwe images in their advertising.

The Ojibwe decided to fight back, filing in 1988 *Wabizii v. Busch Agricultural Resources,* a lawsuit ostensibly on the issues of false and misleading advertising. Busch Agricultural Resources (a division of the beer conglomerate) marketed a product called "Onamia Wild Rice," which the plaintiffs, Mike Swan and Frank Bibeau, charged was in fact a California-grown paddy product disguised as "authentic" Minnesota lake rice. "They had two Indians on a canoe who appeared to be picking wild rice. They were taking a California-grown product, trucking it to Minnesota where it was packaged and designated as a Minnesota product," Bibeau remembers. Bibeau, a White Earth tribal member, is today an attorney for the Leech Lake tribal government. He has also processed wild rice to supplement his family income. "We had been overly patient and polite with the state of Minnesota, waiting for them to enforce their laws, yet they refused to make even one complaint for false and misleading advertising, and it became obvious that the only recourse for us was to file suit."[8] The case was eventually settled out of court, but it kicked off a public discussion about the difference between paddy-grown wild rice and Native lake-harvested wild rice. Eventually, Minnesota passed a law requiring Minnesota paddy wild rice producers to label their product as such, with the lettering for "paddy rice" no less than half the size of the words "wild rice." A small victory in the age of globalization.

Indian Harvest or Dutch Harvest?

The labeling law, however, has some pretty big loopholes in it, the largest of which is that California-produced wild rice is not subject to Minnesota's labeling laws. Nor, it seems, is there much concern about possibly misleading advertising. The wild rice market today is worth about $20 million. Not the largest of the grains by any measure, but one with a lot of interest for a variety of companies. Companies like Stouffer's, Uncle Ben's, Fall River Wild Rice, and Gibbs Wild Rice are all big names in the industry.

Processing about three-quarters of the national wild rice crop is a company called Indian Harvest Wild Rice. The company has some Minnesota origins, but today processes all of its rice in California. Jerry Schochenmaier, now deceased, was the manager of Indian Harvest for over a decade, and described its origins: "The rice mill was originally designed to be in Bemidji [the footings for the building are still at Bemidji's industrial park], but California was identified as the place to produce rice, if you were going into the business."

Although some lake rice was historically in its program, Indian Harvest is pretty much an operation with few "Indians" today. A truer name for Indian Harvest Wild Rice might be "Dutch Harvest Wild Rice" since it's a subsidiary of a Dutch American family-based Minnesota holding corporation, Duininck. And both present general manager Gene Adding and California plant manager Don Kuken (both of whom are really nice guys) are of Dutch ancestry. Asked about the origins of the name, Adding recalls, "The original wild rice that they sold was hand-harvested, that was the tradition in Minnesota. Once you build up a name and identity with the customers, it's hard to change. I think it was founded on correct principles; whether or not that has followed through, that might be something someone would want to look at some time."[9] In this era of Cherokee jeeps, Crazy Horse beer, and Indian motorcycles, it seems a good question to ask.

In addition to the big companies like Indian Harvest, there are a host of California farmers who rely extensively on chemical inputs, and there are some organic wild rice farmers in Idaho, Oregon, and California. Then there are the seed companies, including Norcal Wild Rice with its patented seeds for wild rice. What they all share, from an Anishinaabeg perspective, is that they are beneficiaries of biopiracy, all having work to do with seeds they were not given by the Creator.

Gene Hunters and the Map of the Wild Rice Genome

We stand to lose everything, That's what we're looking at—the future of our people. If we lose our rice, we won't exist as a people for long. We'll be done too.

—Joe LaGarde, White Earth Reservation ricer and historian[10]

University of Minnesota plant geneticist Ron Phillips and his colleagues have just finished mapping the wild rice genome. Phillips, Regents Professor and McKnight Presidential Chair in Genomics, is an affable guy, who looks at his work as strictly scientific. Yet, the research Phillips is conducting promises benefits beyond abstract science. Phillips writes in his recent study that his work is considered "the reference point for...gene cloning."[11] His genomic data on wild rice is now available for public use courtesy of GenBank, a lab at Cornell University. At a 2005 legislative hearing on a bill to ban genetic engineering of wild rice, Phillips underscored that he had not genetically engineered wild rice, but that he wanted, in true "scientific pursuit," the right to do so.[12]

While the future uses of such scientific data are at present unknown, we can be relatively assured as to who will most likely reap the benefits of this knowledge. Just a few paddy rice firms dominate the $21 million wild rice business. Their interest in genetic work on wild rice stems largely from their own economic interests, not environmental, humanitarian, or tribal interests. More than that, university collaboration with seed companies may be common practice, but some of us take notice when two of the four researchers in the wild rice genome study (Alan W. Grombacher and Wayne C. Kennard) come from little companies like DuPont and Monsanto, the two largest seed companies in the world. Their interests are more likely in terms of gene prospecting: securing DNA material from wild rice to assist in rice crops elsewhere. That would be a start, at least.[13]

One company that has already promised more biotech rice development is Syngenta, an agricultural giant whose largest investments are in the area of rice. In 2002, Syngenta put restrictions on access to its maps of the japonica rice genome and caused a great furor. Dr. Lynn Senior, Syngenta's representative at a national agriculture conference, spelled out Syngenta's biotech growth projections. Referring to North America as "biotech friendly" (as opposed to most of the world, which has expressed significant doubts about genetically modified foods), Senior projected rapid "roll outs" of various biotech crops, including more rice.[14]

The practice of mixing genes of differing plants or other organisms—called "transgenics"—allows geneticists to create new and unique species of plants and animals, species that would never exist without intensive human and technological intervention. When an Australian team applied for a patent for their research combining genes from commercial and wild rice, the Anishinaabeg, along with a host of environmental, food safety, and other organizations, challenged their claim.[15] Watching for patent claims is a bit like looking for a needle in a haystack. Although the Australian patent claim was denied at the U.S. Patent and Trademark Office, the Anishinaabeg anticipate that the researchers will continue their work and their pursuit of patents.

The concerns about transgenics have sparked a worldwide struggle that reaches far beyond the rice of the Great Lakes region. In September 2001, the Mexican government made a public announcement that transgenic sequences of genetically engineered corn had contaminated indigenous corn varieties, in violation of a law banning the importation of genetically modified maize. The Indigenous communities of Oaxaca had wanted to certify that their corn was being produced free of genetic engineering, and instead learned through the certification process that their corn indeed tested positive for transgenic sequences. Fears increased as reports stated that the probable contaminant was a Bt gene.[16] Engineered for its insecticide properties, Bt inadvertently poisons milkweed, the food of monarch butterflies, a migrant species that winters in Mexico.

From the villages of Mexico and India to the villages of northern Minnesota, there is a marked loss in worldwide biodiversity, and a closer hold on who controls the remaining seeds of the world. Monsanto, the creator of Bt, has spent upward of $8 billion in the last couple of years buying up U.S. seed companies, and DuPont recently purchased Pioneer, the second-largest seed company in the world. This concentration of control over world seed stocks is alarming farmers worldwide, especially considering that the closer seeds seem to be held, the fewer there are. In the United States, only 20% of the plant varieties found in a 1904 inventory of crops are still grown commercially or held in collections.[17] Similarly, China has experienced a 90% loss in wheat varieties since World War II. In terms of natural varieties (as opposed to domesticated), the World Conservation Union reported in 1997 that one out of eight plants surveyed internationally is potentially at risk, with extinction rates presently at 1,000 species a year. The highest extinction rates of plants is in the United States.

Of particular concern for millions of poor farmers worldwide who would usually save seed from one crop to the next is the "terminator" seeds, which are genetically bred or engineered to yield plants whose seed will be sterile. With terminator seeds, farmers have to buy seeds they would normally produce themselves. Of course this means more income for the seed companies. As with the unintended consequences of Bt for monarch butterflies, we can't be sure of the future consequences of the wild rice genome studies, but we can be sure that companies like Monsanto don't come to wild rice country without a lot of suitcases.

Patents and Biopiracy

> When we sow seed, we pray: May this seed be exhaustless. Monsanto and the USDA [U.S. Department of Agriculture], on the other hand, are stating: Let this seed be terminated so that our profits and monopoly are exhaustless.
>
> —Vandana Shiva[18]

I'm not sure that Ken Foster has ever seen a northern Minnesota lake as the wild rice softly sways in the warm wind of *Manoominike Giizis*. Nor perhaps has he ever heard a loon, calling a mate across the deep blues of the lake. Perhaps he should. In Woodland, California, 1,500 miles away from Minnesota, Foster and his colleague Zan Hua Zahn of Norcal Wild Rice have successfully patented wild rice.

There was quite a bit of alarm when the Ojibwe heard of the patent. The first sort of inclination was, "How the hell could they do that?" After all, the Creator gave *manoomin* to the Anishinaabeg, not Norcal. For a thousand years or so, the Ojibwe have carefully managed and cared for that wild rice crop. The people have seeded lakes, managed water levels, tied rice heads together in harvest, and held prayers and thanksgiving feasts for each harvest. "I looked through and read the whole 30 pages of the patent," explains John Pershell of the Water Quality Research Department of the Minnesota Chippewa Tribe, and "nowhere did it mention anything about the wild rice being wild or coming from somewhere. That was sort of a problem."[19] Wild rice is about as Ojibwe as it gets, and in that context, Norcal is a biopirate.

The Ojibwe's second major cause for concern is that the version of wild rice described in the patent is sterile. This "cytoplasmic genetic male sterility" is somewhat of a mouthful for the commoner, but it basically has the same meaning as the phrase "terminator seed," and the news sent a shudder through *Anishinaabeg akiing*, the land of the Ojibwe.

This sterility may well prove to be the most controversial aspect of the patent. Wild rice is like corn in that it reproduces a certain way. Many plants, including cultivated rice, have sex cells that co-exist in each flower, and consequently allow the plant to pollinate itself. But corn and wild rice are different. They are cross-pollinators, meaning that their male parts (the stamen in corn and sprigs of tiny petals at the base of the wild rice flower) shed pollen that fertilizes adjacent plants.[20] Of major concern to the Ojibwe is the possibility that some of this sterile variety might eventually diminish the very essence of our sustenance.

Some of the concerns about the sterility in the Norcal seed and patent have historical foundations. After 15% of the hybrid corn crop was wiped out in 1970 by southern leaf blight fungus, scientists discovered that the plants most susceptible to the fungus were those with a genetic trait called the "Texas cytoplasmic male sterility factor, which had been inbred to eliminate expensive corn detasseling."[21] Within that context, there are some spiritual dimensions to this discussion. While our communities for thousands of years have prayed each year for rice fruitfulness and given thanks for the bountiful harvest, genetic manipulations and the introduction of sterile seeds is the spiritual opposite.

Although university researchers like Ron Phillips distance themselves from "genetic engineering," Phillips admits that there is a small possibility of some transference between the two varieties. When asked if the domesticated strain of the stronger paddy rice might possibly overpower the wild strains in the lakes and rivers, Phillips answered, "It's not the kind of thing you could control perfectly."[22] Some University of Minnesota scientists admit that the tribes may have some need for concern. Professor George Spangler asks, "What is the economic outcome of this research?...There's little documentation that the university has ever been overtly concerned about how its research affected this culture....I'm not saying that all the scientists here are arrogant. But it was there in the attitude of the university being surprised that the Native community had any interest in this."[23]

Just a small possibility of any genetic alteration of the rice is enough to concern the Ojibwe. Joe LaGarde from the White Earth Reservation voices the concerns of many: "Man thinks he can improve on something that's been developing over thousands of years. Eventually, he might end up with nothing."[24] The Minnesota Chippewa Tribe echoed this in a letter to the University of Minnesota. "We object to anyone exploiting our treaty wild rice genus for pecuniary gain," then-Tribe President Norman Deschampe wrote in late 1998, referring to the 1837 treaty between the Ojibwe and the U.S. government that recognized Ojibwe rights to harvest wild rice.

> The genetic variants of wild rice found naturally occurring on the waters in the territories ceded by the Minnesota Chippewa Tribe to the State of Minnesota are a unique treasure that has been carefully protected by the people of our tribe for centuries.... We were not promised just any wild rice, that promise could be kept by delivering sacks of grain to our members each year. We were promised the rice that grew in the waters of our people, and all the value that rice holds...a sacred and significant place in our culture.[25]

For the past five years, the Anishinaabeg community has requested that the University of Minnesota stop its genetic work on wild rice. Virtually every tribal government and Native organization in the region has repeatedly called on the university to stop. Finally, after attorneys for the Ojibwe sent a set of Freedom of Information requests, the University of Minnesota began a "dialogue." The re-search in contention, however, continues unabated. What part of "No" is hard to understand?

Academic Freedom and Ethics

It was about a century ago that the University of Minnesota dis-patched its first anthropologists to the reservations in the north. Al-bert Jenks came, joining his colleague from the Smithsonian Institute, Alex Hrdlicka, a physical anthropologist who specialized in comparing Indigenous peoples' heads to those of monkeys. The two came to White Earth, calipers in hand, and measured the heads of the Anishinaabeg. Then university board of regents member and U.S. Representative Knute Nelson introduced an act "for the Relief of the Chippewa Indians of Minnesota." The passage of the act al-lowed for the allotment of the White Earth Reservation and the cre-ation of a blood quantum scandal wherein physical anthropologists turned individuals from full-bloods into mixed-bloods, miraculously allowing them to "sell their land." (See the "Imperial Anthropology" chapter for more material on physical anthropology and genetics, and the "Klamath" chapter for more on allotment.) The consequences of this University of Minnesota research were to cost the White Earth Anishinaabeg most of their reservation lands. So began what would become a rather dysfunctional relationship between the land grant institution, the University of Minnesota, and the Anishinaabeg and other Indigenous people of Minnesota.

The University of Minnesota website once claimed: "University of Minnesota research changes lives and improves communities."[26] Well, sort of. At the International Wild Rice Association meeting in Reno, Nevada, I listen to University of Minnesota extension agent Raymond Porter attempt to dispel some of the criticism levied at the university by tribal representatives. Suggesting that the criticisms have been based in part on "misunderstanding and faulty conclu-sions," Porter contends that most of the issues raised by the tribes have been addressed by research and a number have been cleared up. His essential argument, presented in graphic form, is that the more the Native community understands about modern science and plant genomics, the more that community will be happy with the research.

Porter's turf is the heart of Minnesota cultivated wild rice research: an agricultural extension and experiment station in Grand Rapids, Minnesota, into which hundreds of thousands of dollars of research money for paddy-grown wild rice varieties have poured, and from which new paddy rice varieties have been developed. In 1963, the Bureau of Indian Affairs (sort of keeping with Albert Jenk's better productivity strategy) began providing funds to the agricultural experiment station for work on wild rice. Subsequent federal funding levels kept on rising, with $100,000 a year being allocated to wild rice research largely at the university extension offices. By the late 1990s, the USDA, for instance, allocated more than $200,000 for Porter's research.

And he did produce. Over the years, Porter's extension office was able to "create" several strains of "wild" rice.[27] Now that brings up a question. *Are the varieties developed by the University of Minnesota researchers possibly contaminating the wild rice stands of the Anishinaabeg?* Put it this way: There are around 6,000 bodies of water with significant wild rice beds in Minnesota or around 60,000 acres of rice. Those lakes are within close proximity to around 20,000 acres of cultivated wild rice paddies.

Pollen Drift and Those Ducks

Anishinaabeg advocates have long contended that paddy rice stands are contaminating the natural rice stands. Ron Phillips claims there is little chance of cross-pollination as long as approximately 660 feet separate the two kinds of rice. The university extension office did some research, however, that appears to validate Anishinaabeg concerns. In the summer of 2002, wild rice researchers undertook a study of possible pollen drift from paddy rice stands into wild stands. After a lot of different mathematical formulas, the bottom line is a possibility of between 1% and 5% of the pollen drifting up to *two miles* from the test plots.[28] Last time I checked, there was a whole lot more than 660 feet in two miles.

Then there is the problem of the *zhiishiibig*, the ducks. Surprisingly enough, there have been no systematic studies simulating duck and waterfowl movement in the wild rice area. Ducks and wild rice are a part of traditional Anishinaabeg stories, and will likely be in the future. Ducks and waterfowl do not differentiate between paddy rice plots and natural stands of wild rice, and move freely between them both, carrying the rice and the pollen from one to the other.

There is no security in the answers. "It depends on what you are willing to accept as a threshold of risk," Phillips says.

> The possibility of a trait coming in from one of the bred varieties that would significantly alter the wild type is probably not very great. But it is possible. So you can't guarantee that it won't happen; you can't guarantee that a bird won't pick up a weed and take it 20 miles away. So that's where you have the conflict.... You've got to agree on some threshold, and in our discussions [with the Anishinaabeg], some people said, "Well, one in a million is too great a risk."[29]

Intellectual Property

There is a somewhat similar story of rice that is far away geographically, yet close in implications. Basmati, the "crown jewel" of South Asian rices, is prized for its delicate aroma and taste, and commands a premium price at the market. Hundreds of thousands of small farmers in Pakistan and India have planted innumerable varieties of basmati rice, rice that they have grown for centuries. In September 1997, Rice Tec, a Texas-based company, won a controversial U.S. patent for basmati rice.

The World Trade Organization's Trade-Related Intellectual Property Rights (TRIPs) Agreement provides for some protection where the reputation of a product and its quality are attributable to its geographic origin, such as French champagne and Scotch whiskey. While this provision currently applies only to wine and spirits, a number of countries are seeking to expand and strengthen the protection of their products.[30] The Peruvian government is drafting a law to protect Indigenous intellectual property rights and to ensure the preservation of local biodiversity. "Peru is one of the countries with greatest biodiversity in the world and must begin utilizing the competitive advantage this implies," said Jorge Caillaux, president of the Peruvian Environmental Law Society, "but, it must protect its natural resources as well as the rights of its population."[31]

Increasingly, tribal governments nationally and internationally are looking to enact ordinances preserving their intellectual and cultural property rights, finding that these reservoirs of genetic diversity that lie within their territories should be guarded so that future generations may have some part in their continued relations with the broader ecosystem. The Indigenous Peoples Council on Biocolonialism, in particular the work of executive director Debra Harry, includes new work on tribal ordinances to protect these rights. The Indigenous Research Protection Act (presently under consideration by a number of tribal governments and enacted by the Little Traverse band of Odawa, among others) would potentially protect tribal interests in a broad array of cases, whether biogenetic resources (including plant material, animals, microorganisms, cells, and genes), cultural research (e.g., anthropological studies, medicinal plant research), and traditional Indigenous intellectual property, which may be sounds, knowledge, designs (for instance, northwest coast clan designs), or other elements integral to a community.[32] In early 2005, the White Earth and Fond du Lac bands of Ojibwe in Minnesota both adopted ordinances banning the use of their wild rice for the purpose of genetic modification or the importation onto the reservation of any genetically modified wild rice seed. Also in 2005, the Minnesota legislature began consideration of a law banning the creation or importation of any genetically modified wild rice into the state.

Elsewhere, there have been some successful challenges to patents and other forms of biopiracy. In 1994, two researchers at the University of Colorado were able to secure a patent on quinoa, much to the surprise of Native farmers in the Andes of Bolivia and Ecuador who had raised it for thousands of years. The patent had been awarded on the basis that the individuals were the inventors of the quinoa, and gave them exclusive control over the traditional Bolivian sterile male variety called "Apelawa." The patent also extended to all hybrids developed from breeding of at least 43 traditional varieties of quinoa. In 1998, the Bolivian National Quinoa Producers Association and an international support network successfully forced the researchers to drop the patent. Similarly, a group of Indian organizations and allies successfully challenged a patent at the European patent office secured by the W. R. Grace Company for the neem tree, and in 1999, the Coordinating Body of Indigenous Organizations of the Amazon Basin (COICA) successfully challenged a U.S. biopirate intending to commercialize, after patenting, the use of ayahuasca, a medicinal plant of the Amazon.[33]

Water Levels and Bad Development Projects

While paddy rice continues to flourish in the diked paddies of northern California, native rice stands in the North Country of Minnesota, Wisconsin, Manitoba, and Ontario may be diminishing. One culprit is the water levels, raising questions about who controls them and why. Dale Greene, a traditional leader from the Rice Lake band of Anishinaabeg, tells me that the harvest on Rice Lake itself (near McGregor, Minnesota, as opposed to Rice Lake on the White Earth Reservation) began to decline in 1934 when the U.S. Fish and Wildlife Service dammed the lake and managed it for waterfowl production. Organic material was then trapped in the water. "There's so much sediment on the bottom, the seeds never get to the bottom to germinate," he explains. "There used to be 300 to 500 boats out here. Now...maybe 40...in a good year."[34]

Rice Lake is one of many Anishinaabeg *saagi'aganinan* (lakes) impacted by the U.S. Army Corps of Engineers in its frenzy to alter the flow of water, seemingly everywhere in the country. Under the justification of "stream management," the Corps began massive wetland draining efforts to make room for farms and building sites, and to reduce flood damage to communities along the Mississippi River. This devastated most of the rice beds in the region. The harvest at Lake Winnibigoshish, once a major rice lake, for instance, is at a fraction of its earlier yields. In Canada, the Fort Alexander Indians at Lac DuBois near the mouth of the Winnipeg River must now paddle 50 miles upstream, portaging around hydroelectric dams, to get to rice beds. Stanjigoming Bay on Rainy Lake in Ontario was also a prime

ricing location until the Fort Frances Dam was installed for the benefit of the lumber companies.

In the early 1920s, Northern States Power Company (now
known as the XCEL Corporation) took control over the flowage on
the Chippewa River in Wisconsin. The erection of the Winter Dam
drowned villages, forced resettlement, and submerged the rice beds
on the Lac Courte Orielles Reservation. The damage has neither
been forgotten nor forgiven. In the early 1970s, the Lac Courte
Orielles Ojibwe staged an occupation of the Winter Dam site, and today continue their demands for both compensation and alteration of
the dam structures.[35]

Minnesota's Leech Lake Reservation is today the largest wild
rice producing reservation in the country, with an average of 180,000
pounds of rice processed from their bountiful lakes. (Imagine if Lake
Winnibigoshish was still producing its full potential.) But in 2000,
there was a huge crop failure; only 19,000 pounds ended up getting
processed. The culprit was high water levels due to poor management by the Army Corps of Engineers. "A lot of our major rice beds
are on impoundments managed by the Army Corps of Engineers.
They open these dams and manage this water for recreation and
flood control, not for rice," explains Steve Mortenson, Fish and
Wildlife Biologist for the Leech Lake band. Although the Corps is
presently studying the management of the reservoirs in the Upper
Mississippi region, the Leech Lake band, like others, is pretty much
taking a "wait and see" approach. There is not a lot of historical
goodwill between the tribes and the federal government on the issues
of water.

Of additional concern to many Ojibwe is the toxic contamination of some of the prime rice stands (and subsequently our bodies),
and the lack of state or federal actions to provide redress. The Grassy
Narrows community of Ontario, for instance, was devastated in the
1960s and '70s by mercury contamination (to a level comparable to
the contamination in Japan's notorious Minimata Bay) from the
Dryden paper mill and chemical complex. Anishinaabeg communities for 300 miles were devastated.[36]

The increasing prevalence of both paper mills and wood-processing facilities has meant that wild rice continues to face myriad threats. The Leech Lake Reservation in Minnesota is home to a huge wild rice crop, yet the St. Regis Paper Company, whose operations spanned from the village of Cass Lake to Pike Bay on Leech Lake, was permitted to operate under lax environmental standards. Beginning in 1958, St. Regis produced railroad ties, telephone poles, and bridge supports, all using a soup of chemicals including pentachlorophenol, creosote, and others. Industrial waste was dumped into the city landfill, the fish hatchery, and surface-disposal ponds. Twenty-five years later, the facility is a superfund site owned by International Paper, which has yet to complete the clean-up of the toxic waste. In short, extractive industries leave long-term impacts on a traditional way of life.[37]

To add insult to injury, on numerous occasions Ojibwes were arrested for ricing off reservation or without a permit. Since 1985, when Gordon Henry, Jr., was arrested for "poaching rice" south of the White Earth Reservation, few tribal members have sought to challenge the off-reservation ricing laws.[38] The 1999 U.S. Supreme Court decision in *Minnesota v. Mille Lacs Band of Chippewa Indians,* recognizing tribal rights to harvest off reservation, makes a challenge to state licensing requirements more likely to succeed.

Other threats include invasive plants, pollution, boat traffic, agricultural runoff, and, of course, the beaver. While beavers have obviously coexisted with rice beds for thousands of years, a decline in trapping and a removal of natural predators, especially wolves, means beavers, with all their ambition, rule the northern woodlands. The Minnesota Chippewa Tribe, among many interests, asserts that state funds could be better spent on habitat issues rather than genetic research. John Pershell, director of the Minnesota Chippewa Tribe's research lab, points to the thousands of acres of wild rice that have been destroyed by state development projects, and argues for both state work to protect the natural stands and more state enforcement of labeling laws.

Food on the Water: Rice Lake and the Crandon Mine

In 2003, the Ojibwe of the Mole Lake Reservation in Wisconsin saved their rice beds, and they saved their homeland in the process. For the past two decades, there has been a pitched battle between the Ojibwe and mining companies over the future of these rice beds in the northeastern portion of the state.

"The rice is why we came to Mole Lake hundreds of years ago," notes Fred Ackley, Jr., one of the Sokaogon Ojibwe's elders. "We depend on that rice. Like the rice, we depend on clean water and land. Now, the mining company can buy its way in here, take its profits and go, maybe leaving the land and water ruined. You can understand why we feel under siege here."[39]

The Mole Lake Reservation sits on a tiny 1,900-acre tract of land, a small patch within the 92,000 acres promised the Sokaogon Ojibwe under the 1854 treaty. The Sokaogon Ojibwe people, however, maintain an interest in the larger area, and are concerned about keeping that small bit on which they live. The community has fought off the largest corporation in the world, Exxon, and a succession of mining companies, with amazing tenacity and an incredible ability to ally with a broad range of forces.

The first mining company to set its eyes on the Sokaogon territory was Exxon, which in 1976 announced the "discovery" of a massive copper-zinc formation near the town of Crandon, Wisconsin, just two miles from Mole Lake. Exxon proposed to dig down 2,800 feet, pump an estimated 1,000 gallons of water per minute from the mineshaft (for some 25 years or so), and dig out some 55 million tons of ore. It would leave behind 44 million tons of waste pilings.[40] That proposal sent shudders through the Sokaogon community. The Anishinaabeg "were not reassured when Exxon's biologist mistook their wild rice crop for 'a bunch of weeds.' Exxon's own environmental impact report blandly mentioned that 'the means of subsistence on the reservation' may be 'rendered less than effective.' "[41]

The project, if actualized, would create Wisconsin's largest-ever toxic waste dump. Data from the mining company itself indicated that groundwater contamination would impact the area for more than 200,000 years. The mine's dewatering would impact not only the immediate mine area but Mole Lake, the precious wild rice beds of the Ojibwe, and the Wolf River, one of the most pristine rivers in the nation as well as the centerpiece of the Menominee Nation.[42]

Exxon may have been a bit optimistic when it reported, in a 1980 article in *American Metal Market*, that it "expects to begin serious prospecting of a rich 70 million ton zinc and copper ore body at Crandon, Wisconsin, next year while it works to neutralize objections from environmentalists, residents and Indian tribes in the area."[43] An outpouring of political organizing led to the creation of a statewide coalition opposing this mine as well as more hardrock mining in Wisconsin. Diverse tactics included a successful effort by the Mole Lake tribal community to secure federal status of water quality management, called "treatment as state," through which the tribe opposed the mine's potential detriment to the quality of tribal waters. Finally, in 2003, the mining industry gave the state of Wisconsin the lowest ranking of viability in terms of investment opportunity for potential new mines. Following that, the Mole Lake band joined with the Forest County Potawatomi to purchase the contested mine site and retire the mining operation forever from the horizon. Today, the Mole Lake band is still looking for financing to cover the mortgage for the purchase.

The preservation of wild rice and the biodiversity of the rice crop concerns many far outside the realm of the Mole Lake or Leech Lake reservations. Even Ervin Oelke, a retired University of Minnesota agronomist who has worked with wild rice for more than 20 years and was quite instrumental in its commercialization, worries about maintaining the reservoir of genetic diversity contained within the uncultivated rice stands.

> We should be concerned about losing any kind of plant species, because we never know what they might be useful for.... With wild rice in particular we're concerned because we are now in the process of domesticating the species. It's important we have all the genetics that are available to us to [further] develop this crop.[44]

It is ironic that what *Gichi Manidoo,* the "great" or "loving spirit," gave the Anishinaabeg—wild rice—suffers under public policy until those who forgot it recognize its potential benefit to their own interests. Thus the wild rice of remote Native communities is inevitably linked to worldwide debates on biodiversity, genetic engineering, and, indeed, the future of our foods.

Tribal Laws and Cultural Property Rights

There is, at the center of this, a huge conflict of worldviews—a conflict that has life-transforming implications. "Are plants on this Earth for all people or are they here for just one group?" wonders Oelke. "The issue, I think, boils down to this question of, 'Whose plant is it?' My answer is that I think plants should be used by as many people as possible, for the benefit of humans."[45]

Paul Schultz, a White Earth elder, insists that the conflict

is not about ownership, because that concept implies the right to dispose of or otherwise manipulate "property." And that privilege was never given to science. Scientists have [taken] that right [to manipulate wild rice] for so long that they somehow think 50 to 200 years justifies it for all time. What we are saying is that if you've been making a mistake for 50 to 200 years, that doesn't make it right today.[46]

There may be fewer rice buyers on the White Earth Reservation, but as long as there is rice, there will always be ricers. Back on Round Lake, a pickup truck pulls up at the rice mill. Eugene Davis and Tony Warren bring in around 300 pounds of rice from South Chippewa Lake. They are tired and wet from the recurring rain of morning, but they are happy. "This is the only job we can make $50 an hour at up here," 20-year-old Davis tells me. "I like it when it rains out there. It's nice. You can't hear anything but the rain." It is that peace that brings the ricers back. It is also the memories. I ask Davis what he thinks about the fact that probably five or ten generations of his family have riced on South Chippewa Lake. "I like knowing that they was on the same lake. It makes me feel good," he responds with a smile.[47]

Receiving the rice are Ronnie Chilton, Pat Wichern, Pete Jackson, and a few other men who gather in the new rice mill at Native Harvest on Round Lake. The sweet smell of rice parching wafts through the dusty air, machines shift and creak, and the rice slowly moves through a long chain of events, at the end of which the shiny, dark green, tan, and brown wild rice will glimmer in the September sun. The equipment is old and much of it handmade: a 1940s' Red Clipper fanning mill, a handmade thrasher, a 1980s' set of parching drums made by George Stinson (a regional celebrity), a 1950s' vintage gravity table. Most of the newly produced equipment is for large operations like those in California, not here. The men fiddle around with the machines, fine-tune the gravity table, and then the rice comes pouring out. They are local producers, and this is the quality perfection of the small batch and the simple joy of this life. The air is filled with dust as the husks are blown from the rice. Ronnie, Pat, and Pete look a bit like Anishinaabeg chimney sweeps, covered in rice hulls, but they grin through the dust. They are doing their job, and that rice, like that of their ancestors, is going to feed families and spirits.

This season—the Anishinaabeg wild rice moon *Manoominike Giizis*—is the season of a harvest, a ceremony, and a way of life. "I grew up doing that," reflects Spud Fineday. "You get to visit people you haven't seen for a whole year because just about everyone goes ricing." Far away, a combine is harvesting paddy-grown wild rice somewhere in California, some biopirates are hunting for genes, and consumers are eating a very different food. The Anishinaabeg would not trade. In the end, this rice tastes like a lake, and that taste cannot be replicated.

Food as Medicine

The Recovery of Traditional Foods to Heal the People

Before we can start talking about nutrition, we have to renew the
spiritual connection our people had with food as a gift from the
Creator. It makes sense for us to renew our bodies with that traditional source.

—Lorelei Decora, Winnebago nurse and activist[1]

The work of planting and nurturing seeds—calling forth and
honoring life on the land through an intricate ceremonial cycle—has
been a mainstay of Indigenous cultures. The traditional practices of
gardening, harvesting, fishing, and hunting provided for most Native
American communities not only essential nutrition but also the essential physical activities required for good health. Europeans first
competed with Native Americans for access to game and then destroyed not only the game populations but, in many cases, vast agricultural systems. As colonizers drove Indigenous peoples from our
territories, we were cut off from access to traditional foods.
Starvation and disease became rampant. The forced reliance on in-
adequate government rations, often called "commodity foods,"
only changed the starvation from quick and obvious to hidden and
slow. Today, Indigenous communities are recovering agricultural
traditions linking past to present and future—and, in the process,
restoring spiritual practices related to foods, while strengthening
community health and self-determination.

Traditional Agriculture and Biodiversity

> From the traditional perspective, these seeds encompass more than just characteristics. They are sacred heirlooms, which are "witnesses to the past." These seeds hold cultural value and cultural memory that is a vital part of traditional culture and history. A cultural community that persists in its farming tradition does not simply conserve indigenous seed stock because of economic justifications. The seeds themselves become symbols, reflections of the peoples' own spiritual and aesthetic identity, and of the land that shaped them.
>
> —Rowen White, Mohawk writer and farmer[2]

The Iroquois Confederacy produced at least 60 different corn varieties, not to mention a multitude of other vegetables. In fact, a good portion of the modern world's largest agricultural crops came from Native America: corn, tomatoes, potatoes, chocolate, and a host of other foods. Agricultural diversity and the biodiversity of intact ecosystems feed people. In *Chippewa Customs,* anthropologist Frances Densmore chronicled the traditional diet of the Anishinaabeg:

> The country of the Chippewa abounded in vegetable products, which the women prepared in a variety of ways, and stored for winter use by drying. The principle vegetable goods were wild rice, corn, and maple sugar. Rice was a staple particle of food and was boiled in water, or in broth as well as parched. Corn was roasted in the husk or parched in a hot kettle or dried and boiled. Pumpkins and squash were cultivated in gardens and either eaten fresh or dried for winter use. Maple sugar was prepared in the form of granulated sugar, "hard sugar" and "gum sugar."... Wild potatoes were used and the Chippewa obtained white potatoes at a fairly early date. Acorns were gathered and cooked in several ways.[3]

"Let Them Eat Grass"

Like other Indigenous American nations, the Dakota were able to feed themselves well before the European conquest reached their territory. But as settlers moved in, the buffalo and other game populations started to decline, weapons abounded, and the Dakota entered the treaty-making process. Their primary food source, the buffalo, would last only about another decade. Eventually, 50 million of these huge creatures would be killed by federal military policy. General Phillip Sheridan described this scorched earth policy in this remark to the Texas legislature, "These [buffalo hunters] have done…more to settle the vexed Indian question than the entire regular army has done in the last thirty years. They are destroying the Indians' commissary…. Send them powder and lead if you will, but for the sake of lasting peace, let them kill, skin and sell until the buffalo are exterminated."[4]

At the Great Council at Traverse des Sioux on the Minnesota River in 1851, the Dakota signed away more than 30 million acres of land, for about five cents an acre. The Dakota thought they would actually be paid the 50-year cash annuity as agreed to in the treaty, but instead traders sucked it up in payment for debts allegedly owed by the Dakota.[5] Even the land the Dakota had retained was soon halved: In 1858, the U.S. Senate decreed that the Dakota would keep only the land on the south side of the Minnesota River, as the north side would be turned over to farmers and homesteaders.

In 1862, it got worse. The Dakota had put off their buffalo hunt in anticipation of their annuities and food allocations, but those were caught in national politics. When the food finally arrived, it was cached away in government warehouses. As hunger pangs deepened in the community, sentiments worsened. Finally, on August 4, the Dakota moved in to take the food from the warehouse. As tensions rose, the Dakota requested that the traders be barred from the pay tables, in order that the Native peoples would receive their full annuities. The traders' response was to cut off credit, in effect denying a now-dependent population the ability to feed itself through the trading post. One of the traders, Andrew Myrick, responded infamously to Indigenous concerns, "Let them eat grass."[6]

It is that callous attitude that has resulted in the diabetes epidemic in Native America. "Let them eat grass" turned into "Let them eat garbage," ensuring a long-term decline of health and well-being in our communities.

What We Eat Makes Us Sick

> The Three Sisters are our medicine. When we eat them regularly, we stay in good health. Our bodies are in balance. Our spirit is renewed since we are fulfilling our Creator's instructions. As we drift to western or foreign diets we are no longer in balance and disease develops.
>
> —Brenda LaFrance, Mohawk[7]

The loss of access to traditional foods had a devastating impact. Government rations were meager and of poor quality. Journalist Cate Montana describes the time: "Removed from their accustomed hunting and gathering places, crowded onto often barren reservations, they were handed the staples of the day—refined white flour, white potatoes and white sugar—and told to make the best of it."[8] Each Native family remembers the hard times, with amazing stories of survival, of creating meals from all that could be gathered, boiled, or re-boiled.

"Today, on-reservation and off, tribal members have acquired the habit of eating these foods," writes Montana.

> The government Commodity Food Program hands out cheap, starchy, highly refined foods to reservations. Located in remote areas with healthy whole foods not readily available, tribal members depend on the local convenience stores for their groceries. And what do these convenient and expensive stores carry? More of the same heavily processed, high sugar, high fat, packaged foods.[9]

Each family today has recipes for the creation of meals from government surplus foods like "potted meat," "commodity" cheese, and fry bread or bannock. The food we have eaten, however, has made us ill. McGill University nutrition professor Harriet Kuhnlein writes that it is "widely recognized that the replacement of indigenous foods with a diet composed primarily of modern refined foods is the centerpiece of the [diabetes] problem."[10]

The scorched earth policy and commodity foods program of the 19th century set the stage for a diabetes epidemic in the 20th. The high starch, sugar, and fat content in commodity foods caused high blood sugar levels, which stress the pancreas. If stressed repeatedly, the pancreas essentially becomes poisoned and insulin metabolism becomes permanently impaired. That is where diabetes comes from.

Prior to the 1940s, there is little record of diabetes in most Native communities. In contrast, it is now the second most common diagnosis for Native Americans admitted to the hospital. By the end of the 20th century, one in eight Native Americans had diabetes, a rate that is twice that of the non-Indian population.[11] A full 70% of adult Tohono O'odham suffer from diabetes, the highest rate of adult-onset diabetes anywhere in the world. Other southern Arizona tribes also have rates around 50%. One in every three Cherokees, Zunis, and Senecas has diabetes. Other rates are slightly lower, but the disease remains extremely prevalent in the Native American population.[12]

In addition to the initial diagnosis, a loss of overall health and quality of life is clearly associated with diabetes. For instance, "between 1978 and 1987,…66% of the 377 lower extremity amputations performed at the Navajo-area Indian Health Service (IHS) facilities were associated with diabetes."[13] In Native America, the health costs are astronomical. The Tohono O'odham, with a population of about 12,000, have a $7 million annual budget for diabetes-related costs, "plus another $3 million annually for dialysis charges for diabetics with severe kidney damage."[14]

Diabetes also complicates alcohol consumption. The high levels of sugar in alcohol, the usually sedentary lifestyle of a heavy drinker, and poor diet make a disasterous combination. Alcohol has long been a weapon of choice for the federal government in its goal of destroying Native communities. While some communities had a history of fermented liquors in the Pre-colonial era, alcohol was pushed on Native Americans by traders eager to gain access to land and resources. As the European conquest impoverished and shattered Native communities, alcohol abuse became a way of self-medicating and even suicide.

Today, alcoholism is one of the largest health and social epidemics in Native America. IHS studies indicate that Native American deaths attributable to alcoholic cirrhosis are 18 times higher than the national average. Four alcohol-related causes of death are among the top ten for Native peoples: injuries, chronic liver disease (cirrhosis), suicide, and homicide.[15]

They Can't Even Eat Grass: Navajo Livestock Reduction

The Diné, or Navajo, first learned to adapt to the Nakai, the Mexicans who had come to dominate the Southwest. From Spanish culture, the Navajo adopted livestock raising and rug making, an economy and a way of life that fit with the landscape of the high desert, and the gardens and orchards that the Navajo had traditionally raised. That was not to last as the ambitious Americans came to the Southwest. In June 1863, the U.S. government ordered Colonel Kit Carson into *Diné Bii Kaya*, the Navajo homeland, with a scorched earth plan to destroy all crops and livestock. Carson's troops pillaged the region, killing many Diné, and taking many prisoners.[16] By 1864, Carson's Navajo campaign was able to force 2,400 Diné, with their wagons, horses, and livestock, on "the Long Walk" of 300 miles to Fort Sumner.

Historians Clyde Kluckhohn and Dorothea Leighton refer to the Long Walk as "a major calamity to the People. Its full effects upon their imagination can hardly be conveyed to white readers…. Proud, they saw their properties destroyed and knew what it was to be dependent upon the largess of strangers."[17]

Within a few years, 8,000 Diné were incarcerated at Fort Sumner, where many would perish. Eventually the survivors were allowed to return to their lands, where their sheep, goats, and horses again flourished. But the *Belagonna* ("Americans") would again bring devastation to the Diné, this time in the form of a federal policy known as "livestock reduction." The drought of the early 1930s was used as the justification for the destruction of the Diné subsistence economy. On the premise that the drought had substantially diminished rangeland, Secretary of Indian Affairs John Collier ordered a massive livestock reduction program on the Navajo Reservation. Howard Gorman, past Tribal Vice Chairman of the Navajo Nation, describes how the Navajo viewed this threat to their way of life: "Medicine men…pointed out that the best answer to the drought on our land would be some rain—that decreasing the stock was not the answer. Decreasing our livestock, they said, would only put us in a position of starvation."[18]

The spiritual and ecological connections between the animals, the land, and the drought were clear to the Navajos but not to the U.S. government. According to Navajo author Ruth Roessel:

> They [the Navajo] believed that livestock was a gift from the Holy People. The Holy People watched with pleasure and bestowed their blessings—rain and vegetation—upon the increasing flocks of animals. They were glad to see the Navajos care for these gifts and to see the livestock multiply. Reduction in itself, and particularly when combined with the cruel and inhumane slaughter of these sacred gifts, repelled and shocked all Navajos. To them, stock reduction resulted in the Holy people holding back the rain and moisture. This caused the lack of vegetation, which, in turn, resulted in the erosion of the land and the formation of gullies.[19]

Stock reduction had a huge impact on Navajo nutrition. The initial, so-called "voluntary stock reduction program from 1933 to 1935 resulted in a decline of between 16% and 27% of Navajo livestock. Additional stock reduction initiatives were forced on the Navajo, and by 1952, the Navajo had possibly 36% remaining of their 1936 stock. In percentage terms, Navajos had lost 80% of their per capita holdings."[20]

While the program was initially considered voluntary, most Diné opposed it. Resisting livestock reduction often meant jail time and a slaughter of most of a family's herd by government officials. The Navajo livestock reduction program provides one of the most stark examples federal intervention into Native nutrition in the 20th century, unfortunately mirrored on a lesser scale in other communities, many of which lost control over their livestock industries to encroachment, non-Indian leaseholdings, and denial of access to operating loans. In a more recent example, Native American farmers brought suit in 2001 against the U.S. Department of Agriculture for discrimination and loss of access to funding in a lawsuit similar to a successful proceeding by African American farmers.[21]

Genes or Colonialism?

While many factors—social, spiritual, economic, and physical—have contributed to the loss of our physical health, and particularly to the onset of a diabetes epidemic in Native America, the federal government has primarily focused on the physical aspects of the epidemic. Genetic research has shown that Native Americans have a high prevalence of what is known as the "thrifty gene." This genetic propensity allowed Native communities to adapt to feast or famine conditions, but it did not prove as useful once most Native American people came to rely on government commodities for a good portion of their nutrition. Peter Hanson of the University of Wisconsin writes,

> The descendants of the thrifty gene survivors are now consuming a very different diet loaded with refined carbohydrates, lard, sugar and salt. And they no longer work hard in food gathering and preparation and related daily activities. So their thrifty gene continues to store fat for the anticipated starvation period, and permanent obesity replaces temporary "survival fatness."[22]

The genetic complexity of Native communities has been the subject of many tests and studies (see the "Vampire" chapter), but Native communities have been clear that a holistic approach to restoring Native health is essential to the treatment of diabetes. Contextualizing the importance of genetic potential and actual health conditions, Dr. Louis Montour, a Mohawk physician who sits on the national Canadian Diabetes Advisory Board, urges that the thrifty gene's connection to diabetes should be taken with a grain of salt or maybe a long walk. "You can be born with the genetic trait to develop diabetes, but you will not acquire diabetes unless you expose your body to the wrong lifestyle."[23] In response to this epidemic, many Native communities are attempting to rebuild traditional agriculture while working to diminish the poor nutritional quality of their own food subsidy programs, as well as those of the federal and state governments. Primary targets are the commodity food program and school lunch programs.

The commodity program's influence on Native nutrition is overwhelming. A study of 107 Navajo women found that commodity foods accounted for almost half of their nutritional energy.[24] A 1989 study by the Government Accountability Office reported that the prevalence of obesity, diabetes, heart disease, and hypertension is "likely to continue" unless federal food packages distributed to Native Americans are improved.[25]

Tribes are challenging the program, noting that 82% of their dialysis patients have diabetes, compared to a national average of 25%. The Cheyenne River Sioux of South Dakota declared war on diabetes in 1989, urging the school lunch programs to serve only low-fat lunches to reservation youth, and allowing tribal employees three hours a week to participate in organized fitness programs.

Like other tribes, the Hopi Tribe no longer accepts commodity foods such as butter, whole milk, and cheeses.[26] While the traditional Hopi diet included more than 60 corn dishes, today's diet is primarily beef, mutton, eggs, store-bought bread, potatoes, some canned vegetables, fruits and fruit juices, coffee, sweetened drink mixes, soda, commercial pastries, and sweet and salty snacks, often made with lard.[27]

Food as Medicine

> For the O'odham, and other recently westernized indigenous peoples, a return to a diet similar to their traditional one is no nostalgic notion; it may, in fact, be a nutritional and survival imperative.
>
> —Gary Paul Nabhan, Center for Sustainable Environments, Northern Arizona University, Flagstaff[28]

More than 30,000 members of three O'odham nations live in southern Arizona between Phoenix to the north and the Mexican border to the south, an area larger than Connecticut. These Piman-speaking peoples include the Akimel O'odham or River Pima, the Tohono O'odham (formerly called the Papago), and the Hia c-ed O'odham or Sand People.

O'odham community members have continued to harvest native desert foods like the saguaro and organ-pipe cactus fruit both on their reservation and in the surrounding national parks where they have retained traditional gathering rights. Their territory, the Sonoran Desert, has the highest diversity of food plants and animal pollinators of any desert in the world. For centuries, it supported a healthy, diversified diet rich in plant chemicals known to prevent and control diabetes, high cholesterol, and other nutrition-related diseases. But after a century of land usurpation and irrigation projects removing water from their territories for the creation of urban areas like Phoenix and Tucson, the O'odham capacity to be nutritionally self-sufficient and food secure was dramatically impaired.

Their traditional water-conserving production of native crops has now dropped to less than 1% of what it was in the 1930s, and their wild plant gathering for food and medicine has suffered a parallel decline. With the growth of industrial agriculture on surrounding lands, the U.S. Department of Agriculture and Bureau of Reclamation have subsidized chemical-intensive cropping of alfalfa, sorghum, cotton, and wheat in much of the region, offering only seasonal wages to O'odham farmworkers, who have also leased much of their most arable allotted lands to non-tribal-owned corporations.[29] These agribusinesses have tended to use large doses of toxic pesticides and herbicides on the farmlands they now lease on the Salt River and Gila River reservations of the O'odham, not only killing off insect pollinators required for healthy food yields, but causing respiratory diseases and cancer among the O'odham residents who still live adjacent to sprayed fields.[30]

The loss of traditional harvests, and their replacement with government-donated surplus commodity foods richer in fat and simpler sugars, have left even the O'odham youth suffering from high blood sugar levels formerly found only among adults.

Seeing that nearly all of the government funding to research O'odham diabetes was focused on their genes and not their diet, the nonprofit Native Seeds/SEARCH asked O'odham families if they might donate native food samples to determine their value in controlling diabetes. These samples turned out to be the first Native American foods that nutritionists ever analyzed to determine their impact on blood sugar levels, insulin, and diabetes. When a person eats acorns, mesquite pods, and tepary beans or prickly pear cactus, the special dietary fiber in these foods slows down the release of sugars into the blood stream and extends the period over which nutrients are absorbed into the body, while increasing insulin sensitivity. In short, these "slow-release" native foods protect Native Americans from an imbalance of blood sugar and insulin following a meal. Of several hundred foods sampled from around the world, it appears that mesquite pods and acorns are among the 10% most effective foods for controlling blood sugar levels and diabetes.[31]

Native Seeds/SEARCH co-founder Gary Nabhan has since taken the foods out of the laboratory to see if they can once again make a difference in the health of O'odham families. First, Native Seeds/SEARCH sponsored a ten-day retreat for O'odham diabetics at the National Institute of Fitness, where ten individuals volunteered to eat only native foods and to exercise at the same levels their foraging and farming ancestors would have done. In every case, blood sugar levels and weight dropped dramatically.

Nabhan then assisted the Indian Health Service in obtaining enough native foods to reconstruct a nineteenth-century O'odham diet of the same number of calories, carbohydrates, protein, and fats as in those foods available from convenience stores on the reservations. In the study, 12 O'odham tribal members who were not diabetic volunteered to eat the "traditional diet" of hominy, beans, acorns, and other native foods for two weeks, followed by the "convenience store diet" for two weeks. The results were conclusive: "The traditional high fiber–complex carbohydrate and low-fat diet resulted in a slower release and uptake of sugars from the intestines," while the convenience store diet "soon produced higher blood sugar levels," severe enough to trigger diabetes if that diet had been maintained for very long.[32]

With the results in hand, Nabhan organized the Desert Walk with Tohono O'odham Community Action (TOCA), Native Seeds/SEARCH, and the Seri Indians of Mexico to bring the good news about native foods to more Indigenous communities in the Sonoran Desert. Tribal youth and diabetic elders walked from one tribe's homelands to the next, covering more than 240 miles on foot over 12 days, while eating nothing but traditional foods provided by the 24 host communities along their route. Each night, the youth and elders would explain why they were trying to revive the use of native foods and how diabetes has crippled their communities, and then celebrated the intertribal exchange with traditional dances and songs.[33]

Since the Desert Walk, TOCA has established a farm to cultivate some of these foods and pays tribal members livable wages to gather other wild foods for community use. TOCA and other organizations have now integrated a native foods expo into the annual Intertribal Basketweavers Gathering that brings together artists, chefs, farmers, and foragers from across North America. The benefits of native foods are now returning to Indigenous communities to restore the health and regenerate the wealth that their tribal members deserve.[34]

Dream of Wild Health

When Sally Auger (Abenaki) and Paul Red Elk (Lakota) worked at Peta Wakan Tipi, a Minneapolis/St. Paul transitional housing program for Native men and women in recovery, they realized that recovery required more than simply a physical solution. "One of the things when people go to recovery, they want to take the culture back. A lot of them have been around the urban area for a long time," Sally remembers. "You have to have different ways to teach culture. So, for instance, if you want a woman to put her family back together, the garden was one of the ways."[35]

In 1997, Paul and Sally started a food project that they hoped would aid the whole community. "A lot of our foods and medicines have disappeared," Paul explains. "We wanted to secure both plant knowledge and the seeds."[36] The project was small but urgent. "We had five elders, and we lost three of them," said Sally. The project was designed to involve tribal elders, healers, other community residents, and Native and non-Native ethnobotanists in the cultivation of indigenous plant medicines and foods.

"Once the word got out that we were collecting seeds, they just poured in," Sally noted. She recalls seeds arriving wrapped in newspaper, in envelopes, in old socks, even an amazing dried gourd with the seeds still intact inside it, preserved perhaps for 100 years. "At the beginning, we had about 25 seed [varieties]; we have around 400 now.

Some of them are so old they really need to be taken care of: They are cracked, burned, have been sitting in someone's closet. We set them in the greenhouse to get them a good start," Sally remarks, then pauses. "When we planted 15 to 20 plants in the first Dream of Wild Health Garden in 1998, we weren't sure what would happen. The garden has grown beyond all our dreams and the summer 2001 garden contained over 300 traditional indigenous plants."

In 2000, a wonderful gift arrived. "I had prayed and prayed that someone would take up gardening again. I am very pleased to learn about the project. I feel that the Great Creator has answered my humble prayers," read the letter from Cora Baker, a 94-year-old Potawatomi woman, known as the Indian seed collector. She had farmed in the Wisconsin Dells area, and gifted the Dream of Wild Health her lifetime collection of corn, squash, and bean seeds. Each variety was labeled with the name of the family from whom she had collected the seed and basic growing information. Her letters to Sally are a cherished part of the Dream of Wild Health archives, and also underscore the significance of Cora's actions and memory to the community. "I remember our gardens in Michigan," Cora wrote. "The garden was secluded because my mother always worried the gardens would be raided. She was worried that the government would come and destroy it, and the white man would try and run us back."[37]

There is a pretty immense sense of responsibility and connection that is associated with growing out the ancient seeds. Cached away for a generation or more, many of the seeds are grown not only with potting soil, water, and a greenhouse but also with prayers. Paul remembers planting some 800-year-old corn seeds. He described his feelings as "watching over them like a worried father." After a couple of years of trying, the curled, gray corn kernels grew out to maturity. Safely wrapped in cheesecloth and sealed away, the new seeds will stay potent for at least ten years. The idea is to propagate these and other seeds every five years or so, to maintain the vitality of these species.

The project has a variety of gardens designed to meet different needs in the community. The first was the Women's Medicinal Plant Garden. "We had such a hard time talking about putting a women's medicinal garden together. They had places where they were supposed to get their medicines. My argument was that we needed to work with what we had." Sally talked to the elder women, who deliberated for two years before they felt comfortable with growing all the women's medicinal plants together.

Today, the Women's Medicinal Plant Garden is a 25-by-30-foot plot of land that contains plants from four habitats, and includes echinacea, goldenseal, sage, and, for use in ceremonies, indigo. The second garden is the Children's Diabetes Garden, a mixture of traditional and early harvest foods like lettuces. Sally explains,

> If you are going to keep kids interested, you need immediate results. Early on, the kids also made old original tools from shoulder blade bones and antlers. The kids love to make the tools and use them; then they have ownership and you've got them. Then they get to take the food home. They love that this is Indian food, that they have something others don't. They get excited about that.

It is in the Research Garden that the most endangered seeds are carefully grown out to protect their genetic integrity, and to teach about our nutrition and life. This is where some extraordinary gifts are discovered. Scientific testing reveals astounding differences between native harvests and industrial crops. Hominy corn is high in carbohydrates and protein, while low in fat and with about half the calories of market corn. One serving of hominy yields 47% of the Daily Recommended Value (DRV) for fiber and 33% of the DRV for B vitamin thiamine. Arikara squash has 13% of the DRV for fiber, 64% of the DRV for vitamin A, and half the calories and double the calcium and magnesium of the market equivalent.

It is much the same for the Potawatomi lima beans. They are low in fat, while high in carbohydrates and protein. B vitamins are found in abundance, including thiamine, pantothenic acid, niacin, and B6. Potawatomi lima beans also provide 24 grams of fiber per serving, a full 100% of the DRV. Finally, they have 21 times the antioxidants found in market beans. Antioxidants help protect us from pollutants such as smoke and chemicals, and have been associated with a lower incidence of cancer. These vegetables, rich in so many vitamins and minerals, help fight against heart disease, high blood pressure, cardiovascular disease, and diabetes.[38]

"In the Research Gardens, we are able to find the value in the food is so extreme. Our biggest fear is cross-pollination and that makes it really hard," Sally asserts.

Mino Miijim

Gaawaabaabanikaag is the White Earth Reservation in northern Minnesota, also known as the medicine chest of the Ojibwe people for the plant diversity used by that community. White Earth, like most other Ojibwe reservations, has a food system that is in disarray. Although traditional wild rice harvesting continues to be a large source of both food and income for the community, many of the traditional plants have been destroyed in the draining of wetlands and the move toward industrialized agriculture. Here, a community is doing something about restoring traditional foods, and working also to ensure that those foods get to people who can really benefit the most from them. Margaret Smith, an 87-year-old esteemed elder in the community, is the force behind distributing good food to her elderly peers: "There are a lot of them who are diabetic, and they don't get a chance to get out and get these foods. This is one way to help them out."[39]

This is the challenge that Margaret and the staff at the White Earth Land Recovery Program (WELRP) faced when they launched *Mino Miijim,* the "good food program," in 2001. Each month, 165 or so diabetic elderly people receive good traditional foods like wild rice, maple syrup, buffalo meat, and hominy corn. "We bring them the food at the end of the month when most of them are running short," Margaret explains.

WELRP—focused primarily on restoring the tribal land base, increasing ecological relationships to the land, and strengthening cultural practices—sees the *Mino Miijim* project as part of its overall strategy. Anishinaabeg ancestors selected *Gaawaabaabanikaag* because it had the biodiversity and spiritual significance to provide for the future seven generations of Anishinaabeg people. The land was reserved under the 1867 treaty, which designated 837,000 acres to be the White Earth Reservation. Today, our people, as the White Earth Tribe, hold only about 76,000 acres, about 9% of the original land base.

Much has been accomplished since WELRP's inception in 1989. This includes the acquisition of 1,700 acres of land, held as a land trust. WELRP also created Native Harvest, a project that supports traditional harvesters and artisans. In addition to its advocacy on environmental and economic justice issues, Native Harvest has facilitated the sale of approximately $300,000 worth of traditional foods. In 2005, for instance, with the support of Heifer Project International, WELRP expanded its maple syrup production to around 7,500 taps on 500 or so acres of land. At the center of the project's work is a commitment to protect and restore traditional food systems in the community, whether agricultural or harvesting.

Some of it is by trial and error. Ron Chilton and Bob Shimek came to WELRP from some of the few Native families who still farmed at any scale on the reservation. Cobbling together some old equipment, Chilton and Shimek plowed some fields, sowed some white flint corn from the Oneida Nation, and found some success growing out the statuesque plants. Unusual frost and rain patterns, likely the result of global warming, pushed the Anishinaabeg farmers to find a corn with a shorter growing season. They were pleased to find, at the University of Iowa's seed bank, a 55-day flint corn from Bear Island on Leech Lake—a variety perfectly adapted to their local conditions. Chilton has worked with local organic farmers Curt and Darlene Ballard to grow enough corn so that local folks can once again enjoy eating it. The project also learned from other communities, like the Bad River *Gitigaaning* project, and went into the community to plow gardens and build "grow boxes" as well as some greenhouses. Over the past couple of years, 120 gardens have been plowed annually in villages like White Earth, Naytauwaush, Pine Point, and Rice Lake, with Chilton hoping to get 250 gardens plowed in 2005. The program continues to hold these basic principles: "You cannot determine your destiny if you cannot feed your community" and "food is medicine."

In the years ahead, the WELRP hopes to continue work to restore traditional agricultural systems on the reservation. Growing out heirloom corn varieties is an intricate part of a set of other challenges faced by farmers nationally and internationally: seed theft and genetic contamination. The older Bear Island flint corn and other varieties are at risk of being genetically contaminated by new varieties sold at local feed stores, including Roundup Ready by Monsanto. That corporation in particular has a predatory history of suing farmers whose fields are contaminated with Monsanto's patented varieties through pollen drift—holding farmers responsible for what the wind blows. Tribal work under way today includes initiatives to increase the local food production, move tribal agricultural leases away from genetically modified varieties, and work with tribal school and elderly nutrition programs to provide food to those who need it most. In 2003, WELRP received the International Slow Food Award for its work to protect wild rice from genetic modification and to restore local food systems.

The "food is medicine" teaching has spread nationally and internationally. In Wainaie, a Native Hawaiian community, traditional foods have been replacing store-bought foods, as Hawaiians face similar diabetes epidemics. "In the old days, Hawaii's staple food was taro. Today it's Spam," says Dr. Terry Shintani of Wainaie Coast Comprehensive Health Center. Shintani puts his patients on a diet of taro, seaweed, sweet potatoes, fruit, and small amounts of fish. The results have been amazing. Australian aborigines face similar problems; Koori diabetics experienced similar recovery rates by returning to traditional foods.[40]

The Place of the Gardens

Gitigaaning is the Ojibwe word for "Place of the Gardens." The Bad River Indian Reservation sits perched on the south shore of Lake Superior, near Ashland, Wisconsin. The area's rich soil deposits, created by the annual flooding and spring snow melt, as well as the excellent combination of rain and sunshine, made the place perfect for gardens and farms. It's said that each spring, the Ojibwe would travel from *Moningwanekaning Minis,* or Madeline Island, to the conjunction of the Bad and White rivers to prepare their summer gardens. Old aerial photos of the site, according to tribal organizer Luis Salas and biologist Tom Cogger, show an area as intensively cultivated as California's fertile San Joaquin Valley.

Bad River is not much different from many Ojibwe reservations in the region. Diabetes takes one out of eight people, and all of the challenges associated with it affect each family and the community as a whole. Luis, who has done much of the initial work to create the *Gitigaaning* project, says, "It's based on reciprocity. It's not so much a single garden; it's more individual families expanding. It's more important that individual participants participate in their own households. If we have a big field and that fails, then that's a problem."[41]

For the past few years, the project has been growing steadily, offering classes, plants, and ongoing support to tribal gardeners. In a converted old locker room, the project grows 5,000 plants under grow lights for spring and summer transplanting. They've also planted 400 fruit trees. By the summer of 2003, 117 families had received fruit trees and plants. "If they participate in the class, they get the trees. That way it isn't a giveaway," Luis notes as he takes me on a midsummer drive to see all the gardens, grow boxes, and hoop boxes peeking out from behind trailers and houses, tomatoes and corn boldly showing their faces in the front yards. Almost everywhere there are fruit trees.

Nutritionist Joy Scheibel involved local schoolchildren in the gardening process. At a garden adjoining the Head Start program, Scheibel tells the children, "Let's listen to the plants drink." The kids water the plants and then put a stethoscope on the stalk. "It sounded like thunder," says one of the kids. "We go into these schools, and in the fifth-grade class, three-quarters of the kids are obese. They don't need to know about a food pyramid. They need to know about corporate food and they need to know what to eat," maintains Scheibel.[42]

Luis and his staff believe that the science and history of indigenous agriculture have much to contribute to ongoing debates on the future of the "green revolution" and the purported mandate for genetically modified foods to feed the growing multitudes. Luis argues, "If we can substantiate the agriculture of the Americas, we can defend the oral history of the hundreds of millions of people who lived here." Luis tells the story of Bill Gardener, "the king of raised beds," flying over the Peruvian jungle. Bill asks for a second flyover, then a third. He has seen something: old rows, huge rows. "There were crop fields there, in the jungle, the size of Wisconsin," Luis reports.

Luis has found that there are all sorts of ways to get a garden growing. "We had a Killer Tomato Growing Contest. And now we're going to do a story, a little story, and I am going to make fun of myself. We'll show my fruit tree, and then show the neighbor's fruit tree. All full of apples. And mine, it's all pitiful. Then people will say, there's Luis, head of the gardening program, and he can't even grow. What did that other guy do?... Well, he used nutrient stakes and he watered his trees twice a day, that's how that worked out," Luis says.

"Five to ten years from now, we're going to be looking at a lot of fruit in the community. Then we are going to need a cannery where people can process and dry all of those fruits, along with their meat, the suckers from the sucker run, the venison, all of it."

On the subject of traditional seeds, Luis sobers, reflecting on the challenge of preserving and growing.

> The more I learn, the more I am worried. We need to say, "All of Bad River will only be heirloom seeds." It will have to be a process of bringing in these seeds. The community will need to know why we are growing the Mandan squash and not the Hubbard squash.... The concept is that food is medicine. If we are going to win, we have got to change over our whole lifestyle. But you can't eat what you don't have. So it is a long-term change. We are talking and working on the answer to that question.

Luis Salas and Indigenous leaders like him in many other places know that they are taking the first steps of what will be many years, even generations, of effort to renew the connection between healthy foods and healthy communities. In this generation, around 20,000

Native families in the United States continue farming, and probably only a small percentage of these grow the traditional foods grown by their ancestors.[43]

The recovery of the people is tied to the recovery of food, since food itself is medicine: not only for the body, but for the soul, for the spiritual connection to history, ancestors, and the land. The sustainability of land-based life rests on the biodiversity of traditional agriculture, the life stuff for pollinator diversity, and the web of life itself.

Part 4

Relatives

Pat Spears and Bob Gough with the Rosebud windmill
(Photo courtesy of Bob Gough)

Return of the Horse Nation

The Earth is turning,
So there will be a new day.

—Horace Axtell, quoting traditional Nez Perce (*Niimiipu*) song[1]

Rudy Shebala ambles through the stable in Lapwai, Idaho. He looks in on his babies, Yellow Jacket, Halhelooya, and Nez Perce Glory, the new generation of Nez Perce horses, a cherished result of careful thought, breeding, prayer, and ceremony. Not far to the west, in Washington state, the descendants of the people who followed Nez Perce leader Joseph are also continuing their horse-breeding traditions in the communities that grew in exile after the Nez Perce surrendered their ancestral home in Oregon. It is a new millennium, and the Nez Perce or *Niimiipu* people are finding their way home. They are recovering the river valleys in which they have lived for millennia and, with their horses, are finding allies in those who once were their enemies.

The people once called themselves *Cupnitpelu*, meaning the "Emerging" or "Walking Out" people. It is said that this name came from their ancestors' origins in the high mountains in the Bitterroot Country. They are a people who speak Sahaptin, a language that binds them together with many people of the northwestern plateau, including the Umatilla, Yakama, Cayuse, Palous, and Walla Walla peoples. Their traditional lands span some 13.5 million acres of what is today known, in the white man's lines and boundaries, as Washington, Oregon, and Idaho, from the Eagle Cap Wilderness in northeastern Oregon's Wallowa Valley, east to the Bitterroot Range in central Idaho, and north to the Blue Mountains. Historically, their traditional bands were named for the river watersheds that they inhabited, in 300 or so villages throughout the region. More recently, the *Niimiipu* have come to be known as the Whitebird band, Looking Glass band, Joseph band, Snake River band, and others—names denoting the last leader in the village, or the village's location, prior to their displacement. The name Nez Perce was given to them by French trappers who took stylistic note of a dentalium shell nose ring, an ornamentation that was not actually common to the tribe.

Jaime Pinkham, of the Nez Perce Tribal Environmental Program, describes how the people saw themselves as only a small part of a land rich with salmon, deer, elk, berries, and edible roots:

> We didn't make the skies bring rain, we didn't make the roots and berries grow, we didn't make the salmon run. When it was time for the salmon to run, we moved down to the rivers, and when it was time for the foods and medicines to grow, we turned to the mountains. We moved in reference to the landscape and to the resources that nature provided to us.[2]

The Wallowa Valley, in what is now known as northeastern Oregon, is a land of rivers, meadows, and mountains. Geographically isolated for many years from early colonization (whether from the eastern seaboard or through California), the Nez Perce embroidered a culture rich with songs and spiritual traditions. While they became skillful at acquiring trade goods they admired, especially horses, they avoided full participation in the fur trade, which the Nez Perce viewed as "generally unappealing."[3] In retrospect, this was probably a strategic decision. By the 1830s, among their most prized possessions were their horse herds, which they had begun to carefully breed for coloring, gait, and endurance. These gifts would eventually be passed to the horses we now call Appaloosa.

When Lewis and Clark's party, half-famished and sick with dysentery, came upon Nez Perce territory in September 1805, Meriwether Lewis noted their remarkable animal husbandry. "Their horses appear to be of an excellence, they are lofty, elegantly formed, active and durable, in short many of them look like fine English coursers and would make a figure in any country."[4]

The Nez Perce welcomed the explorers, supplied them with food, and stabled their horses while the legendary delegation canoed to the mouth of the Columbia. Following in the wake of Lewis and Clark, a smallpox epidemic spread along the Columbia River and up into Nez Perce territory in 1810, wiping out many of the lower Columbia River bands. The epidemic not only destroyed peoples, it also caused spiritual and social disruption in the communities, with some people believing that these "diseases [were] supernatural retribution for having violated Mother Earth by plowing fields. Others saw the arrival of the diseases as the fulfillment of prophecies that foretold the turning of the earth and the coming of the white people."[5]

It is hard to imagine the immense changes that lay in store for the Native peoples. For any people who had lived in one way for millennia, the rapid technological, ecological, spiritual, and economic transformations that would come with European contact would be daunting. What had come after the traders and the explorers (aside from diseases and more laws) were the settlers, whose numbers increased from 20 or 30 annually to thousands each year by 1843.[6] Those settlers saw the lush river valleys of the Nez Perce and other Indian nations and pushed for the creation of the Oregon Territory Organic Act in 1848. The discovery of gold in southern Oregon in 1851 greatly expanded the flow of settlers into the territory.

The policy of Manifest Destiny and the greed for gold drove settlers north along the coastal valleys and east along the rivers. As the Nez Perce saw the numbers of immigrants increasing, as well as their boldness, they sought to forestall violence by signing a treaty in 1855. The Nez Perce retell the scene on that May 24th:

> members of the Nez Perce nation (numbering at least 2,500 people) made their entrance [to the treaty council grounds]. As the Nez Perce chiefs rode to be formally introduced to the [territorial] governor [Issac Stevens], a thousand Nez Perce warriors riding two abreast and mounted on fine horses circled the flagpole. They put on a show of horsemanship and dancing that was spectacular. Stevens was impressed by the show, but he failed to recognize the

significance of the Nez Perce entrance. Our Nez Perce ancestors were not only honoring him as an important person; they were demonstrating that the Nez Perce were a strong and important people who expect to be treated as equals.[7]

The primary goal for the Nez Perce was the exclusion of settlers from the core of their territory and the maintenance of hunting, pasturing, and fishing rights to their traditional homelands. The settler government promised to deliver "conveniences such as blacksmith shops, tinsmith shops, hospitals, sawmills, fences, schools and money" and to protect the Nez Perce Reservation from trespassers.[8] When gold was discovered in eastern Oregon, the federal government stood by as 15,000 miners trespassed on Nez Perce lands and began to take the gold from the people's land, and with it the land itself.[9] As pressure from the gold rush intensified, white officials proposed a new treaty in 1863 that would take away three-fourths of the Nez Perce land and leave them a small reservation at Lapwai, Idaho.[10]

In the 72 years since Lewis and Clark's arrival into Nez Perce territory, at least 50 Nez Perce had been murdered by white men—their murders unpunished. Some 50,000 gold prospectors had by now invaded Nez Perce territory, digging for the wealth that should rightfully belong to the Nez Perce. The federal government had done nothing, and treaties had been broken. The new treaty was the federal government's answer to its lack of action; rather than upholding the 1855 treaty and prosecuting trespassers and murderers, it chose to push the Nez Perce onto a smaller reservation. While some Nez Perce signed the new treaty and moved to Idaho, Chief Old Joseph and his descendants, including his son Joseph, disputed the treaty and continued living in the Wallowa Valley. For a short two years, President Grant upheld their claim, but pressure from settlers and gold seekers finally brought the threat of forced removal and outright war.[11]

Old Joseph died in 1871, and in 1877, Grant sent the Army to force the Nez Perce from Oregon. So began a long and heartbreaking nightmare for the Nez Perce. From June through October 1877, Joseph and other chiefs led approximately 750 Nez Perce, predominantly women, children, and elders, along with 2,000 horses, on a 1,700-mile odyssey, seeking to escape the Cavalry.

Nez Perce elder Horace Axtell remembers the oral history of that trek as he returns to the places traversed by his ancestors. At the bottom of a place known as Hell's Canyon, the Nez Perce were forced to cross the snowmelt-swollen Snake River, losing many of their prized livestock in the process. "I imagine people yelling, telling each other which way to swim," Axtell tells a reporter.[12]

They were forced to fight the soldiers at Clearwater, and their families were ambushed in Big Hole Valley, Montana, where more than 60 people, mostly women and children, were killed and many more wounded. Axtell recalls his grandmother Peweyatamililpt, who was six years old in 1877, describing the terror she felt as soldiers assaulted the sleeping Nez Perce at Big Hole. "She remembers gunshots, people crying, people lying on the ground, tipis burning. I guess you would say she was glad to be alive. So many her age got killed."[13]

The Nez Perce continued their arduous path through what today is Glacier, Montana, and finally into the Bear Paw Mountains where, just 30 miles south of the Canadian border, the Cavalry caught up with them. After five days of fighting in bitterly cold weather and snow, some 80 Nez Perce men and 350 women and children surrendered. Chief Joseph's surrender speech is probably one of the most quoted Native oratories in U.S. history. Recorded by C.E.S. Wood for General Oliver Howard, Joseph's words testify to the desperate conditions that finally forced the Nez Perce to stop fighting: "The little children are freezing to death…. My heart is sick and sad. From where the sun now stands, I will fight no more forever."[14] Those words remain a testimony to the Nez Perce saga today.

Only a small band of the Nez Perce, under the leadership of White Bird, escaped and found sanctuary in Canada under the protection of Sitting Bull. The Nez Perce were scattered like leaves from trees in the autumn—many were sent to prison at Fort Leavenworth, Kansas, and then to the death camps in Oklahoma, where thousands of Native people from across Turtle Island had been relocated, many of them perishing due to the poor conditions and lack of food. Some

Nez Perce were allowed to return to their reservation at Lapwai, but Joseph and his band were considered too dangerous, and were sent, eventually, to live in exile on the Colville Reservation in Nespelem, in northwestern Washington.

Indian agents would boast to Washington, D.C., that they had taken seven million acres of Nez Perce land through a treaty process that would cost Washington less than eight cents an acre. Ninety percent of traditional Nez Perce landholdings were taken in the 1863 treaty, including the Wallowa, Imnaha, and Grand Ronde valleys near the Salmon and Snake rivers and trails to the Bitterroot Valley, Asotin, and Camas Prairie. The federal government, however, was not content with what it had already taken from the Nez Perce. With the passage of the General Allotment Act in 1887, individual parcels inside the Lapwai reservation were allocated to Nez Perce people, with remaining lots declared surplus and put up for sale. This process opened the reservation to non-Indian landholders who established 13 towns and 20 post offices by 1902. By the end of the 20th century, less than 11% of the Nez Perce Reservation itself was still owned by tribal members.[15]

The Horse Nation

When Joseph's band of the Nez Perce was captured in 1877, hundreds of its horses were shot by the U.S. Calvary. Some were taken home as war bounty by the soldiers or given to the settlers in the same valleys the Nez Perce had cherished. The settlers came to call these distinctive dappled horses "Appaloosas" after the Palouse Valley where the Nez Perce were known as horse breeders. While today's Appaloosa horse has its origins with the Nez Perce, more than a century passed from the decimation of the tribe in 1877 until the late 1900s when the Nez Perce would begin to be known again for their skills as horse breeders.

In the years following Joseph's surrender, C.E.S. Wood was troubled by his memories of the war against the Nez Perce, calling the Army's actions "morally reprehensible and unjust."[16] Wood left the military, settled in Portland, and became a lawyer who advocated for the Nez Perce survivors. Through this effort, he formed a relationship with Chief Joseph and, in 1892, began sending his son Erskine Wood to summer with Joseph on the Colville Reservation. It was at the end of the second summer with the Nez Perce that the young Erskine, under instruction from his father, asked Joseph if there was, in the words of Erskine's granddaughter Mary Wood, "a gift he could offer Joseph in return for the hospitality he had extended to young Erskine."[17]

Mary recalls, "Joseph replied that he would like a fine stallion to improve his herd but Erskine never conveyed that message back to his father. He looked upon Joseph as such a great man that he thought he deserved much more than a horse, and thought it was too small of a request. As a young boy, he lacked judgement."[18] Mary Wood, a law professor at the University of Oregon, says that her grandfather Erskine lived to be 104 years old and over the years felt a great regret that he had not passed Joseph's words on to his father. This memory spurred the Wood family to action in the 1990s, a time when the Nez Perce had successfully litigated for their land and fishing rights, and an increased recognition of Nez Perce and other Native sovereignty movements had emerged in the region.

Mary Wood and her twin sister, Becky Wood Hardesty, wanted to honor Joseph's request, a hundred years later. Their view was that of their grandfather: that honor was between families and would extend between generations. Together, the sisters researched the pedigrees of over 500 Appaloosa stallions, narrowed the choices down to a dozen and presented the information to the Nez Perce. After much deliberation and consultation, the Nez Perce selected a handsome black and white stallion named Zip's Wild Man.

In 1997, the Wood family descendants presented a stallion to Keith Soy Red Thunder, the closest living descendant of Joseph, and other Nez Perce at Wallowa Lake, Oregon, the homeland of Joseph's band before its forced exile. Nez Perce elder Horace Axtell led the ceremony to honor the relationship and the gift of the horse. Nez Perce journalist Beth Hege Piatote recalls his words: "It was a great feeling, especially when that beautiful horse was introduced. In our time, we had a lot of these beautiful horses, and now they can revive and grow among our people again. It was touching to my heart to see this with my own eyes and to hear the words spoken by the Wood family and by the Nez Perce people."[19]

So the descendants of Joseph are finally able to enjoy the gift that Joseph knew would be treasured by the Nez Perce community in Nespelum, Washington. Zippy, as he is now called, has sired many new Appaloosas.[20] At Lapwai, Idaho, Nez Perce relations with the Horse Nation are also being strengthened—in the process, a new breed of horse is being created or, perhaps, re-created.

The Lapwai program was begun in 1994 by Rudy Shebala, a Navajo married to a Nez Perce woman. Shebala hoped to work with the Nez Perce and create a new breed by crossing the Appaloosa and the Akhal-Teke, a rare breed renowned for swiftness. The Akhal-Teke horse is thought to be the most ancient horse in the world and an important ancestor of the horses that the Nez Perce would have started their herds with in the 1700s. There is evidence of their existence since 3000 BC. The horses are said to have originated in the region of Nissa, now called Turkmenistan. The horses are from the Akhal oasis in the Turkmenistan desert, home of the Teke people.

To start the new breed, Shebala took in four types of mares: the Arabian/Appaloosa, the Thoroughbred/Appaloosa, the Quarterhorse/Appaloosa, and the Appaloosa/Appaloosa. The Akhal-Teke came to the tribe through Hans Sprandtel, a German immigrant to Minnesota who had raised Akhal-Teke horses with his brother. "We were looking to buy a horse and we got in contact with him," Shebala remembers. "He says, 'Come and see me,' and he makes us an offer."[21]

Shebala was amazed when Sprandtel offered to donate four stallions, two mares, and three geldings to the Nez Perce. "I couldn't believe our fortune. I remained composed and sat there. I called the tribal council and we got those horses."

Akhal-Teke horses are incredibly rare, with less than 300 of them in the United States and a registry of only some 3,600 internationally. Journalist Ike Boone describes how dear these horses are to the Turkmen. "In 1999, in Ashgabat, the only Akhal-Teke auction in the world, over 80 horses were offered for sale. Only two were actually sold—a four-year-old stallion named Karar for $100,000 and a weanling for $25,000. It is not easy for a Turk to part with one of these horses."[22] That is part of why it is so amazing that the Nez Perce found these horses and began the new breeding program with them.

"Pretty soon everybody started to come around to see them," says Shebala. "We offered an introductory breeding for $90. Some of our people went for it right away." Others were more concerned about the new horse and wondered if it would damage the Nez Perce reputation for breeding Appaloosas.

"We want a breed of horse that people will remember us for," asserts Shebala. "We are known internationally and historically as horsemen and horse breeders. Now that we are in the modern day and age, this is one way we can contribute to this modern horse industry, while helping ourselves and keeping our ancestors' horse-breeding tradition alive."

Teaching history, culture, and horsemanship, the Nez Perce Young Horseman's Program is considered a national model, with a number of other reservations today looking to start similar programs. Since the late 1990s, the White Earth band of Anishinaabeg has sent their young people to see what the Nez Perce are doing with their horses and have sponsored programs bringing Shebala's sons to White Earth for a month-long youth program including week-long trail rides and cultural practice in addition to more academic learning about horses.

The Nez Perce are working tirelessly to recover the spirit of the Horse Nation and to honor the ancestors who lost their lives in the long struggle to maintain and recover their community's vitality. The horses have played and will continue to play a big role in that recovery.

In the late 1990s, the National Park Service approached the Nez Perce to begin a commemoration at the battlefields of the Nez Perce war, including White Bird Creek and the Big Hole National Battlefield. Shebala remembers the conversation:

> There was an annual event hosted by the National Park Service on the anniversary of the battle. They had Army reenactments and the Park Service wanted to know if we would bring horses out to the

Big Hole Field. Some 60 to 90 Nez Perce lost their lives there and ultimately this was a turning point for the Nez Perce. I didn't think it was right to parade there. I asked our elders what to do.

One elder woman remembered a ceremony they used to have at Umatilla. It was a longhouse memorial on horses called an Empty Saddle Ceremony. They would bring the horses into the longhouse and a well-known speaker would talk for the family. It's an old ceremony. They led their horses back after the battle, and then led them around. It became a custom a year after the warriors died, to bring the riderless horse out, with the war bonnet, leggings, and have a ceremony.

After much deliberation and prayer, Shebala and the elders came up with a plan. Shebala made a staff of 90 eagle feathers to commemorate those lost in the battle at Big Hole, then,

I said to the kids, "I want to have young guys paint the horses." They painted them with hail designs and lightning marks on the legs. Then we dressed the horses up and put trappings on them. Jessica Red Heart had most of the trappings. We brought five stallions there for that ceremony. We had pipe ceremonies since 1997. A veteran walked out in front, Allan Moody. We followed him around three times, and then we traveled around one more time and led the horses up the hill. These horses had blankets on them. Then we called out the names of those present and the blankets were given away.

In that way, the Nez Perce remember their ancestors, and honor both the horse and the people.

The Wallowa Valley Homecoming

In 1887, when Chief Joseph was forced to surrender his claim to his beloved Wallowa Valley, he spoke eloquently about the spiritual and political principles that bound him and his people to the land.

The Earth was created by the assistance of the sun, and it should be left as it was.... The country was made without lines of demarcation, and it is no man's business to divide it.... The Earth and myself are of one mind. The measure of the land and the measure of our bodies are the same. Understand me fully with reference to my affection for the land. I never said the land was mine to do with as I choose. The one who has the right to dispose of it is the one who has created it.[23]

General Howard was evidently less than comfortable with considering Joseph's perspective. "We do not wish to interfere with your religion, but you must talk about practical things. Twenty times over you have repeated the Earth is your mother, and that chieftainship is from the earth. Let us hear it no more, but come to business at once."[24] Those two worldviews were in stark conflict for a hundred years in the land of the Nez Perce. Now, a century later, there is the beginning of a change.

It is 1997 and a ceremony is being held in the Wallowa Valley in Oregon. Thirty-one Nez Perce Appaloosas and riders in traditional regalia move across the broad hillside as 300 people watch. They are gathered to commemorate the return of Chief Joseph's homeland to the Nez Perce people. "The spirit of the Nez Perce people and the spirit of the horse have missed this place," Carla HighEagle, a past Tribal Council Secretary, tells a reporter. "It is good we are coming back."[25]

Despite the mythology of America's creation, the centennial celebrations of states, the commemorations of "explorers" like Lewis and Clark, Native people remain vigilant and never give up hope for their land and their people, nor the work that is a part of that process. So it is that 120 years after Chief Joseph was driven from his beloved Wallowa Valley in Oregon, the Nez Perce would return to claim this land.

Much occurred in the intervening century between the Nez Perce banishment from Oregon and their return. Towns like Enterprise and Joseph grew from the land of the Nez Perce and the work of the descendants of settlers. The Nez Perce continued to petition Washington, D.C. for the return of their lands. Even though a good portion of the lands taken from the Nez Perce in the Wallowa Valley itself were "public lands"—the government holds 64% of Wallowa County—Washington would not return that which it had stolen, and white settlers refused to sell the Nez Perce any land.[26] That has changed.

Gary Fletcher's ancestors homesteaded in the Wallowa Valley. He was one of those who worked to return land to the Nez Perce. Acknowledging that he had never seen a Nez Perce for 50 years, he says, "I grew up very ignorant about the Nez Perce even though I occupied the very land that was theirs," echoing the sentiments of, frankly, most Americans. E.H. Van Blaircom, another local resident who was a part of the dialogue on recovery, spoke about his conflicting feelings: "It creates a certain amount of shame to think that our government treated them that way. They were here, they had their culture, and boy, I can see why they didn't want to give up this land."[27]

Hans Magden, a rancher in Joseph County, began the process of returning the land to the Nez Perce by "optioning" his family's land to the Trust for Public Lands to be held for sale to the tribe. "It was the perfect circle, the perfect endpoint for the ranch," Magden said. "It was just and fitting that the land go back to the Indians."[28]

So it was that the Trust for Public Lands, a national land trust conservancy, began to recover Wallowa Valley land for the Nez Perce. The proposal met with some opposition by local landholders, including individuals like Judy Wortman, whose family had homesteaded the lands right after the Nez Perce had been driven out. "We sure have a lot of empathy for the Nez Perce because now we understand exactly what happened to those people who loved this Wallowa Valley.... But it's one of those injustices that happened and we have to move forward. We can't go back and fix it. I'm sorry, but we can't." Judy's husband, County Commissioner Pat Wortman, however, disagreed with his wife, and was instrumental in pushing through the Nez Perce land deal.[29]

Through a complicated series of negotiations and transactions, the Trust for Public Lands was able to negotiate the purchase of the land for the tribe, and in September 1996, the Nez Perce tribe signed an agreement designating $2.5 million for the purchase of the Chief Joseph Ranch and an additional $1.5 million to buy 6,200 acres more.[30] Although the land is priceless to the Nez Perce, it is worth noting that they have paid a good deal more for it than those who originally stole it more than a century ago. At the ceremony returning the land, Horace Axtell rises to pray for the land and pronounces the new name, *Hetewisniix Wetes,* or "Precious Land."

In the lives of the Nez Perce and the lives of their horses, there is a relationship to land and place that has always remained. The reconciliation of loss is only through vigilance and a long-term vision. Ceremony and prayer weave together the continuity of people on their land and a way of life.

In memory of the ancestors and the long road home, each fall the Nez Perce hold the Empty Saddle Ceremony. There is no recipe for healing your hearts or your community from a great loss. Today the Nez Perce remember all that has happened to them, and they nurture their lives with new growth, precious land, new foals, and healing.

Namewag

Sturgeon and People in the Great Lakes Region

"River connectivity" is a phrase that is lived by the lake sturgeon of central North America. Ancient beings whose presence graced the stories, songs, and memories of countless generations of people, these large freshwater fish, called *namewag* in Ojibwe, were banished by greed. Today, with the dreams and hands of fisheries biologists, tribal members, and some luck, they are returning to the rivers and lakes of the forest country just west of the Great Lakes, returning in their own glory. *Bi azhi-giiwewag omaa;* "they are returning here." And as they return, they teach us all a lesson—the lesson of river connectivity and our own relationships with each other. That lesson, I believe, is that we can begin the process of undoing some of what we have done to each other, and that all of us, ultimately, are connected to each other.

The sturgeon are in many ways an image of how we have mistreated our ecosystem everywhere—we've dammed rivers, clearcut forests, drained wetlands, divided the land, and put our own signs of management on it. We have told ourselves that we could live in isolation from other species, not perceiving our connections to the larger world, thinking that we do not have responsibilities, and that we are not connected to each other. In the end, time tells us that we cannot escape from our past, that indeed we must use our knowledge to reconcile ourselves with our history and with each other. We are not going anywhere. Generation after generation, we look each other in the eyes—our ancestors in the past, we ourselves today, and tomorrow our descendants. Will we look to create isolation, or will we look to create relationship?

Before the Rocky Mountains began to rise, before the dinosaurs were in their glory, the lake sturgeon was swimming the inland waters of North America. That was 136 million years ago or so. *Name,* pronounced "na-may," is our word for sturgeon, the word in Ojibwe. To the Anishinaabeg, the sturgeon is almost a mythological creature. Numerous stories—including those like "The Great Sturgeon" and "The Chief's Son Who Was Taken by the Sturgeon"—testify to the relationship between the Anishinaabeg and the sturgeon. The animal has been the source of sustenance for generations, and we recognize it as a relative, one of the clans of the Anishinaabeg.

There is a story told about Darky Lake, north of my reservation a hundred or so miles. It is said that one spring a family went out to net the namewag in a small waterfall. One of the young girls had just reached her puberty, so the grandmother made the girl a sort of "moon lodge" for her stay in for her eight-day vigil to honor her new maturity.

Four days and nights later, the girl noticed that the camp had become very quiet. Even the smell of the fire was gone. The girl felt very curious, but she was afraid to stop her vigil. For two more days she waited, but finally she could stand it no more and went to check on her family.

The camp was completely quiet, except for an odd noise from her grandmother's wigwam. When she looked inside, she was shocked to see her grandmother turning into a very large fish, a sturgeon. "I am so glad that you have finally come," said the grandmother. "Look at my belly. Do you see the red stripe here? From now on, our family will be living here as part of the sturgeon clan. Please carry me to the lake, so I can live."

The girl worked hard to carry her grandmother over the rocks and gently lowered her into the river. As she watched, the old woman finished her transformation into a fish and swam into the dark waters.[1]

The relatives are a part of us. So it is that a community related to a fish by its history of lakes, habitat, and continuous survival realizes that its recovery as a community is tied to the recovery of the sturgeon themselves.

Sturgeon were once bountiful in our region's lakes. It was the sad, too often repeated story of greed and dams that brought the end of the sturgeon. Tim Holzkamm is a historian and a keeper of sturgeon lore and fisheries data. As the crow flies, he lives about five miles from my house, at Bad Medicine Lake, but it was actually the First Nations of Canada that referred me to him. Holzkamm has done a great deal of research for Canadian First Nations on historical fisheries. The era of the great fish was almost ended in this region, according to Holzkamm, as a result of waste and over-fishing.

"We have a record of sturgeon harvest from Rainy River [Ontario] that goes back to 1835," Holzkamm explains. "Very few fisheries records go back that far. One of the things that the record shows is a fairly stable period of sustainable harvest by the Anishinaabeg until the advent of the white community's commercial fishing and resource exploitation, dams, and, finally, the incredible pollution from the pulp mills."[2]

The waste was astonishing. They literally used the fish only for its swim bladder and the isinglass produced, which was an important ingredient for alcohol distilling. Sturgeon were stacked up like cordwood on steamboats, used as fuel for the boilers. Minnesota's Department of Natural Resources regional fisheries director Gary Huberty echoes Holzkamm's words with an emphasis on dams. "The major reason the sturgeon went down the tubes was the dams. They are a real wide-ranging fish species, and they need all that habitat and range."[3]

Holzkamm recorded much of the decline of the sturgeon in a series of papers and as an expert witness in a number of legal cases in Canada. According to his research, Rainy River's traditional Anishinaabeg-managed sturgeon harvest averaged 275,000 pounds annually between 1823 and 1884, providing an essential part of the Anishinaabeg diet. With the advent of the commercial non-Native harvest and the drive for increasing amounts of isinglass, in 1886 the sturgeon harvest exceeded one million pounds and caused a collapse of the population. By 1925, the fish had declined to about 1% of their original population. "It was not until the 1970s," Holzkamm continues, "with the Clean Air Act and its subsequent enforcement, that rivers formerly choked with silt, logs, and pollution began to recover, and with them, the sturgeon themselves began to recover."

Their destruction was so intense, you could think of the sturgeon as the buffalo of the aquatic ecosystem. Both species need large ranges and both were plentiful before the settlers' greed overtook the animals' capacity to reproduce. The last sturgeon recorded on the White Earth Reservation was a big one taken by Frank Laquier on White Earth Lake in the '40s. "He killed it at White Earth Lake, there where they got a sandbar," White Earth elder Paul Bellecourt remembers.[4] "The sandbar it runs to shore, and the sturgeon was stuck on that sandbar. That Frank Laquier, he took a pitchfork, that's what he did. It weighed over 175 pounds, that sturgeon did." Then they stuffed it and put it into the Coast to Coast store in downtown Detroit Lakes for a few decades.

It was the northern cousins of the White Earth Anishinaabeg who became instrumental in ending the roughly 50-year absence of the sturgeon from the watersheds south of the 49th Parallel. In the boundary waters between Minnesota, Manitoba, and Ontario, the Rainy River bands of Ojibwe have kept their sturgeon population strong through one of the few Native-run hatcheries on the continent, the only one in Canada. The Rainy River First Nations is a group of seven bands of Anishinaabeg situated near Fort Frances, Ontario. The community established a sturgeon hatchery in 1993, drawing from one of the last sturgeon populations in the region.

Joe Hunter has been the hatchery manager since it was started. "Our elders said that we should be doing what we could for those fish to restore and enhance the population," Joe tells me.[5] The elders knew that strengthening the sturgeon would also be strengthening the people, as the fishery was always an important part of the traditional economy of the region. That hatchery has used wild fish from Rainy River as its base. The fish are returned to the river after they spawn, and fingerlings are returned to the watershed once they are mature enough to survive.

Few viable sturgeon populations remain on the continent. Only seven Canadian rivers still have sturgeon populations.[6] In the United States, two lake sturgeon populations remain in the Great Lakes watershed: Michigan's Sturgeon River and the Bad River in northern Wisconsin. Smaller populations remain on the Menominee Reservation's Wolf River. As they are doing with the buffalo, tribal biologists and Native communities are now working hard toward restoration of this great fish to the culture and the ecosystem.[7]

It is 1999, and my family is fortunate enough to attend the Rainy River Fish Fry, along with some 10,000 other fans of the sturgeon, the Rainy River, and the Anishinaabeg. Even luckier is our visit to the hatchery, where it just so happens that Joe Hunter, his colleague Lorraine Cupp, and a Hungarian sturgeon reproduction specialist named Tomas Gulyas are making sure that all of the big fish are in the mood to spawn. Joe and Lorraine's outfit have captured about 50 of the big sturgeon (which weigh in at around 50 pounds each) for this important breeding season. The little hands of Ashley and John Martin from White Earth's Rice Lake and Waseyabin and Ajuawak Kapashesit from Round Lake reach in to pet the big fish. "The sturgeon are pretty docile fish," explains Joe, who is also fondly known as the Sturgeon General of Canada. "They aren't predator fish like northerns and walleyes," he tells us. "They pretty much have no one that bothers them, so they don't bother anyone either."

Dr. Gulyas has come to "midwife" the big breeding at Rainy River. Gulyas, the world's most renowned expert on sturgeon reproduction, works for the International Union for the Conservation of Nature, which is a United Nations affiliate. He spends most of his time trying to protect and restore sturgeon populations worldwide. "They are very close to extinction in the Danube, in the Black Sea," he tells us.[8] "They usually call me in when there's only a few fish left," he says, marveling at the privilege of working with a population that isn't threatened. Loss of habitat is one of the main causes of the extinction internationally. Then there is greed. Gulyas explains that since one sturgeon produces a good chunk of caviar, and some of that caviar can be worth up to $3,000 in a delicacy market, "poachers kill a lot of fish." They are almost gone in much of the world. That is perhaps why Gulyas, "Sturgeon General" Joe Hunter, and those children from the White Earth Reservation are so excited about these fish. The strongest and most viable population of sturgeon in the world is in the Rainy River system.

So taken were the Ojibwe from White Earth with the sturgeon of the Rainy River that they decided to make a return trip to bring some home. Armed with Coleman coolers, a bubbly thing that hooked up to a car lighter, and some determination, a small delegation traveled 200 miles from White Earth to visit Hunter and bring some sturgeon back to the southern part of the sturgeon habitat.

The White Earth Reservation embraces the headwaters of two river systems: the Mississippi, which drains to the south, and the Red River, which drains to the north. This makes the community ecologically rather unique: connecting ecosytems from Hudson Bay to the Gulf of Mexico. Five fish returned in the Coleman coolers across the U.S.-Canadian border to White Earth and were then ceremonially released into the depths of Round Lake at the headwaters of the Ottertail River system, a tributary to the Red River.

The White Earth tribal government followed this lead, multiplying those first five mature sturgeon with 50,000 sturgeon fry. Randy Zortman, Fisheries Director for the White Earth band of Chippewa, and other tribal biologists crossed the U.S.-Canadian border with the fry on Memorial Day, 1999. "We stopped at the customs office in Baudette," Randy recalls. "They asked us if we had any fish with us and Matt Heisler said, 'Yeah, around 50,000.' They pulled us over, but we had all the paperwork and permits."[9] It is with that casual air that Randy makes history. It is the first time in 50 years that sturgeon fry have graced the waters of White Earth, and that is an amazing thing in itself.

Deconstructionism at Its Best

Taking down dams is sort of the antithesis of American notions of progress. When the U.S. Bureau of Reclamation celebrated its 75th anniversary a few years ago, we realized that the United States had created the world's largest water distribution and obstruction system in history. The Bureau of Reclamation, busy as beavers, had put in 322 reservoirs, 345 diversion dams, 14,490 miles of canals, 34,990 miles of laterals, 930 miles of pipelines, 218 miles of tunnels, and some 15,000 miles of drains. We are a damming bunch. In the end, there may be some questions about whether that was the smartest thing to do. Removing dams is a key part of sturgeon restoration; the fish like to move, and need to range hundreds of miles through lakes, rivers, and streams. And they take no notice of borders, legal jurisdictions, or water management districts.

So far, the relatives of the fish have worked together to take down the Mid-Town Dam in Fargo, North Dakota, altering it to a sort of sloping rapids, which is much more fish friendly. Similarly, the Heiberg Dam on the White Earth Reservation is going and a small dam is already out at Frazee, Minnesota. The White Earth band plans on modifying structures at the head of the Ottertail (Round Lake), White Earth Lake, and on the Wild Rice River. Dams in Grand Forks and the Christine and Hickson dams may also be removed or modified so that the fish will have room to roam.

The ability of sturgeon to move a great distance disregarding political boundaries is humbling. One of the first crop of fingerlings reintroduced in Minnesota's Pelican River by the state's Department of Natural Resources found its way up to Manitoba's Lake Winnipeg, a distance of some 500 miles. The department's Gary Huberty expressed some surprise at the distance those sturgeon moved in a short period of time. "I have a record here of at least four or five that have been captured and released in Manitoba, and others that have been captured and released all along the way. One I think is even in the Sheyenne River," which is, as the crow flies, 100 miles west of the Ottertail and Pelican rivers.

At the Red Cliff Fish Hatchery on the north shore of Lake Superior, tribal biologists learned how tough a sturgeon was when a broken pipe sent fingerlings splashing onto the cement floor of the hatchery. "They just swam around on the floor until we were able to pick them up," explained Hatchery Manager Greg Fischer of the mishap. "We did not lose a single fish. Now if that had happened to a walleye or trout, we probably would have lost them all."[10] Fisheries managers for a number of Ojibwe tribes in the Great Lakes region have been working together over the past few years to restore the sturgeon to their ecosystems. Both the Bad River and Red Cliff bands of Ojibwe in northern Wisconsin have been stocking the fish in the Bad River, where 23,000 sturgeon fry have been stocked in the past few years. Those fry were joined by several thousand six- to eight-inch fingerlings, which were micro-tagged on their fins for easy tracking and monitoring. While those fish grow and travel the Bad River watershed, they will surely pass aptly named Sturgeon Falls, where sturgeon traditionally spawn. They have no guarantee of long-term access to the Falls since the site is presently owned by the XCEL Energy Corporation of Minneapolis—a corporation prone to large dam projects.

A sturgeon can live up to 150 years and it travels through many watersheds during that long life. It is a great teacher of interconnectivity, showing us connections not only over distance but also over time. Burn some toxins in an incinerator in Perham, Minnesota, and they will end up in the body of a fish in Round Lake, in the seeds of a rice plant growing in far more distant lakes and rivers, or even in the breast milk of women living in the Arctic Circle. Many a lake in northern Minnesota has been papered with increasingly stringent fish consumption advisories. Most of the toxins that we are being warned about, particularly heavy metals and mercury, come from two sources: coal-fired power plants and waste incinerators. The state of Minnesota's reliance on fossil fuels has compromised water quality in most of the state's 10,000 lakes; upwind in North Dakota, with its huge lignite coal reserves and massive coal-fired power plant complexes, emissions from those plants blow directly east with the prevailing winds, over and into Anishinaabeg lakes.

A sturgeon, with its long life, has a good deal of time to suck up toxins, a process that is more formally known as bioaccumulation. To the Anishinaabeg, bioaccumulation means that whatever toxins the fish has swallowed and stored in its flesh will come to be stored in our flesh as we participate in our traditional way of life based on harvesting from our lakes and streams. The disaster of mercury contamination has already impacted tribal communities throughout North America (see the "Wild Rice" chapter). Increasingly, Native communities are speaking out and challenging energy development plans in the region.

In the end, we are interconnected; the dams we have constructed need to be more permeable, the garbage cleaned away, and our long-lost plant and animal relatives need to be nourished in places protected from chemical and social destruction. So it is that the sturgeon teach us the same about our relatives with two legs, how little we know, and how long-term survival depends, even *among* relatives with two legs, on not damming and contaminating all that surrounds us. Teach your kids intolerance of others, and they will end up living that intolerance as adults, face-to-face with Native people, African immigrants, and a world that, by and large, does not look anything like them.

For years now, the Anishinaabeg have been working to strengthen and restore their relatives. At a sturgeon release ceremony, White Earth elder Joe Bush prayed as the small fish were carefully poured from pails into the lakes of their ancestors. "I feel good about them coming back. I hope that they survive and really multiply in our lakes up here. That is what I hope. They've been extinct.... It's good to have them back."[11]

Recovering Power to Slow Climate Change

> Just as the human body adapts itself to the regular intake of "hard" drugs, its systems coming to depend on them to such an extent that the user goes through a period of acute distress if they are suddenly withdrawn, so the use of "hard" fossil energy alters the economic metabolism and is so highly addictive that in a crisis, a user community or country will be prepared to export almost any proportion of its annual output to buy its regular fix.
>
> —Richard Douthwaite, *Short Circuit*[1]

Let's face it, we are energy junkies. The United States consumes a third of the world's energy resources with only a twentieth of the population. We own more major appliances, televisions, cars, and computers than we have people to use them. We even slather oil-based fertilizers and herbicides on our food crops. We have allowed our addictions to overtake common sense and a good portion of our decency. We live in a country with the largest disparity of wealth between rich and poor of any industrialized nation in the world. And, we live where economic power is clearly translated into political power. A good portion of that power is held in the hands of energy corporations. That is the story of the United States, and that is what we must change.

Oklahoma, the first "Indian Territory," was a preview of the role Native Americans would play in the attempt to slake the settler society's seemingly insatiable thirst for oil. Edward Byrd, under a contract issued by the Cherokee Nation, was the first to discover oil in Indian Territory in the late 19th century.[2] Within just a few short years, oil development raged across Indian Territory and stripped Native communities of control over the resources on their land. As historian Angie Debo writes, "The Department [of the Interior] was given complete control of mineral leasing by the ratification of the Creek Supplemental and the Cherokee agreements. Detailed regulations were adopted in 1903, and leasing developed rapidly. By 1907 there were 4,366 oil and gas leases in effect, covering about 363,000 acres."[3] That was the foundation of most major oil companies in the United States.

A little over 100 years after Byrd's discovery, we can now begin to see the end of the world's oil reserves, the "peak" after which it will become increasingly difficult—and expensive—to uncover new oil fields. George Monbiot has reported that "every year we use four times as much [oil] as we find." Monbiot and others predict that the peak year for global oil extraction will arrive before 2038.[4] In any case, the price of fossil fuels is likely to rise exponentially once peak production is past.

The Economics of Energy

"Energy is the biggest business in the world; there just isn't any other industry that begins to compare." Well-spoken by someone who should know. Lee Raymond is the chair of ExxonMobil, the largest energy corporation and probably the largest corporation in the world.[5] The world's energy markets turn over a whopping $1.7 to $2 trillion a year. It is an immense business. And it will keep on growing as more and more countries and communities become electrified (a third of the world's population currently has no access to the world's power grid).

Tribes have historically played a large role in energy production, although they have received a pittance for their resources. Conservatively, 10% of U.S. reserves and energy markets are on tribal lands, yet tribes receive less than 1% of the value of those resources—far below their market value. Tribal energy revenues do, however, represent a significant part of many tribal treasuries. The Navajo Nation, for instance, receives the majority of its annual $100 million operating budget from the royalties and taxes generated from coal, oil, and gas leases.[6]

Fossil fuels, fortunately, are far from the only natural energy resource to be found on tribal lands. In summer 2000, Energy Secretary Bill Richardson announced the release of a new report, "Energy Consumption and Renewable Energy Development Potential on Indian Lands." The study noted that "sixty-one Indian reservations appear to have renewable resources that might be developed for power generation at a cost of less than two cents per kilowatt-hour above regional wholesale prices."[7] About half of the reservation-based American Indian community lives on these 61 reservations.

In the past few years, the work of Native Americans and their allies has created some significant changes. For instance, Great Plains tribes, largely members of the Mni Sose Intertribal Water Rights Coalition, have successfully negotiated for some of the electrical power from the very dams that flooded their lands half a century ago. The Western Area Power Administration (WAPA) and the Bonneville Power Administration are participating in these agreements, and a number of Native nations in the Missouri Basin are receiving 25% of their electricity from these dams at considerable savings over what they had been paying. The Rosebud Lakota, for instance, anticipate hundreds of thousands of dollars in savings from their WAPA allocation. Tribes in the Southwest have negotiated similar arrangements. This type of thinking, combined with energy efficiency and alternative energy in Indian Country, makes immense economic sense.

Taté: The Wind is Wakan

I am standing on Porcupine Butte, near a village with the same name on the Pine Ridge Reservation in South Dakota. The KILI radio station stands next to me, blasting 50,000 watts of power across the prairie, with everything from Lakota talk shows to almost any imaginable kind of music. KILI is an amplifier for the heartbeat of the Lakota Nation. The winds, or Taté (pronounced "taa-tay"), are blasting as well; my hair heads out in all directions in sort of an Albert Einstein 'do.

It is February, and the wind speed at KILI Radio clocks in at around 17 miles per hour, strong and prime for a wind generator. That is why I am here. A consortium of KILI Radio, Honor the Earth, the Intertribal Council on Utility Policy, *Native*Energy, and the Midwest Renewable Energy Association is putting up a wind turbine. We plan on having the turbine operational by 2006. A couple of bluffs over, a second wind turbine should be up and running in 2005 on the land of the White Plume *tiosapaye* ("extended family") along the banks of Wounded Knee Creek.

From Porcupine Butte, the rest of the world seems distant—the politics of Washington, D.C., and the seats of state governments—but it is here that some of the most dramatic potential for transforming America's energy policy is emerging. The Lakota are looking to harness *Taté* and play their part in moving us from combusting the finite leftovers of the Paleozoic into an era of renewable energy. It is all part of a strategy by Native people across the Great Plains to power their communities in an environmentally sound manner and to, over time, build an export economy based on green power. In the case of Pine Ridge, the wind energy potential is immense, with the possibility of tapping 4,500 times more power than all the reservation's electrical consumers use. In the fall of 2004, Pine Ridge signed a $300 million wind development contract with a Chicago-based wind company. In other words, things are changing, and rapidly.

I'm waiting to go on the air with Tom Casey, the station manager for KILI Radio; Debbie White Plume; and Stone Gossard, the bass player for Pearl Jam. The band estimates that it produces around 5,700 tons of carbon on a six-month tour and is interested in doing something to make up for that in ecological terms.[8] Pearl Jam figures that renewable wind energy at Pine Ridge is a good place to start. (The Indigo Girls have also raised money for the wind turbines and have been to KILI a couple of times.) Today, we plan on talking about wind energy and energy politics, the war in Iraq, and of course music.

We watch as Bob Gough pulls up in his vintage blue Honda Accord with Zoe "the rez dog" in tow. Bob is a brilliant and funny jack-of-all-trades: lawyer for the Rosebud Sioux Tribe, erstwhile handy guy, and secretary for the Intertribal Council on Utility Policy (COUP). Comprised of 28 different tribes, Intertribal COUP is committed to restructuring energy production in the Great Plains. Bob's vision and commitment are playing a key role in advancing an agenda of wind generation in tribal communities across the country.

That process is, in itself, more than a little convoluted. We are working in some of the windiest communities on the planet, with very little infrastructure. Tribal governments and communities have seen more than their share of lemon projects and been ripped off by a long list of unscrupulous and shady Indian agents, corporations, and *wasichus,* "those who take the fat," the Lakota word for white people. Starting with that history, think about convincing a community that change is possible and that we can do something amazing. After you get the commitment to move ahead, then you have to leverage the resources and buck federal energy policy. There is only a pittance of money out there for wind turbines, and there are only a handful of manufacturers. Add to that the tendency of most of the folks who want to invest in wind energy (whether private interests or foundations) to spend money near urban areas, and that most of the wind technicians live in nice cosmopolitan cities pretty damn far away from Pine Ridge, or any other reservation.

Multiply all those challenges with bad policy. While a federal law requires that rural electric cooperatives and utilities "buy back" power produced locally, the "buy-back" rate is rock bottom, little more than stealing. In other words, most utilities would rather bilk their customers with the sporadic high rates of "spot" purchases of power (as Enron did during the 2001 California energy crisis) than encourage local power production and a just price for power. So you've got to be really creative, clever, and committed. That would be an apt description of Indian Country.

"We believe the wind is *wakan,* a holy or great power," explains Pat Spears, from his home on the Lower Brule Reservation in South Dakota. Pat is a big guy with a broad smile, the president of Intertribal COUP, and a member of the Lower Brule Tribe. "Our grandmothers and grandfathers have always talked about it, and we recognize that this is sacred and this is the future."[9] Indeed, the Lakota, like other Native peoples, have made peace with the wind, recognizing its power in change, historically and perhaps today.

Alex White Plume echoes Spears's words, talking about *Taté* as the power of motion and transformation, a "messenger for the prayers of the Lakota people."[10] The power of the transformation is growing stronger these days and tribal nations want a return to, as Debbie White Plume puts it, "the power the Creator gave us," not the power doled out by electric utilities and energy corporations.[11] The wind is as constant on the Pine Ridge Reservation as anything, bringing the remembrances of ancestors, the smell of new seasons, and a constant reminder of human insignificance in the face of the immensity of Creation.

Spitting or Pissing in the Wind?

"While we've figured out that you don't pollute upstream from yourself, we now are just figuring out that you don't pollute upwind from yourself," Bob Gough tells me.[12] Such is the idea of the "windshed," a term coined by COUP to talk about why anyone east of the Great Plains might want to support the idea of a bit more wind power and a bit less coal.

Already, on the many Minnesota Ojibwe reservations and essentially anywhere in the Great Lakes and Northeast regions, advisories put limits on the number of fish considered safe to eat. The culprit contaminants are mercury and heavy metals. Their origin: coal-fired power plants and incinerators. A number of New England states filed suit against power producers in the Midwest, hoping to hold them accountable for acid rain and air pollution as well as for noncompliance with the Federal Clean Air Act. Some of that pollution, however, may be coming from further west, since the prevailing winds sweep eastward from the Great Plains.

"They are burning dirt," explains Pat Spears, as he talks about the North Dakota lignite that ends up being burned in Basin Electric Power's coal-fired plants in the Dakotas. Basin Electric, according to a recent study by the Natural Resources Defense Council, produces the most CO_2 per megawatt-hour of electricity of any utility nationally.[13] "That is pretty much the dirtiest coal in the country," says Pat Spears. A couple of these power plants are located just upwind from the Fort Berthold Reservation, and they spew poisons directly onto some Mandan, Hidatsa, and Arikara communities. In Montana, the Colstrip complex at the Crow Reservation contributes a heavy dosage of CO_2 into the skyline, and then, of course, it blows east.

Further south, the situation is similar. Of the top ten emitters of air pollution in New Mexico, most are on the Navajo Reservation. The Environmental Protection Agency reported in 2000 that two power plants and their coal mines in San Juan County released 13 million pounds of chemical toxins into the Four Corners air in one year alone—toxins breathed in locally by largely Native communities.[14] All in all, Native nations, according to Joseph Kalt at Harvard University, hold the third-greatest coal reserves in the world. The Bureau of Indian Affairs leases those coal deposits to big corporations that make sure the coal gets to market, usually returning to the tribes only a pittance.

"We can either give you coal or we can give you wind," Bob Gough quips. The theory of Intertribal COUP and its partners is that if we put up more wind power, those utility companies won't have to buy coal or other fossil fuels or nuclear power. That's the larger strategy. To get there is a bit more of a challenge; the power lines are literally clogged with coal, so we continue to work on decommissioning coal plants. One strategy that's been put into place in several states is the establishment of state laws that require local energy companies to purchase a set amount of energy from renewable or efficient sources.[15]

Ironically, climate change has actually augmented utility company CO_2 output in the Great Plains. As the average temperature rises, the Rockies' snowpack evaporates before the snowmelt reaches the rivers. As the water flow into the Missouri is reduced, the hydroelectric commitments of the region are not met, and so electrical contracts must be fulfilled with coal power, releasing more global climate change gases. It's a really dysfunctional economic and ecological feedback loop, which is one big reason why a move toward wind power is important: We're combusting ourselves to oblivion.

Global Warming and the Quality of Ice

Our community has seen real dramatic effects as a result of the warming that is occurring in the Arctic Ocean and the Arctic environment. In the springtime, we are seeing the ice disappearing faster, which reduces our hunting time for walrus, seals, and whales. The ice freezes later. Ice is a supporter of life. It brings the sea animals from the north into our area and in the fall it also becomes an extension of our land. When it freezes along the shore, we go out there to fish on the ice, to hunt marine mammals, and to travel. Ice is a very important element in our lives. We see ice in different ways. When the quality of ice—in other words, its hardness, its durability, and our ability to walk on it, hunt on it—changes, then it affects our life. It affects the animals too. They depend on the ice for breeding, for pupping, denning, lying, and having their young. They molt on it; they migrate on it. So ice is a very important element to us. When it starts disintegrating and disappearing faster, it effects our lives dramatically....

There is no doubt that the ice disintegrating and the changes that we see in the Arctic are caused by global warming.... While the effects we're seeing today are dramatic on our people in the present, the effects for our future generations are going to be much greater.

—Caleb Pungowiyi, Savoonga, Alaska[16]

On a worldwide scale, global warming is daunting in its scope and implications. In the past 200 years, we have caused the amount of carbon dioxide gases in the atmosphere to grow by almost a third. That's more than we have seen in the past 20 million years. The Earth's snow cover has decreased by 10% since the late 1960s, and since 1990, the thickness of Arctic sea ice from late summer to early autumn has decreased by 40%. Antarctica has lost ice sheets the size of Rhode Island. As a consequence of the ice melt, the sea level is on the rise, low-lying land is being flooded, and the prevalence of waterborne and airborne diseases is exploding. Insect reproduction has also increased exponentially. The spruce beetle is now able to reproduce twice annually and has laid to waste at least 4.2 million acres of the Alaskan spruce forests, and many more acres in other states and Canada. New vector-borne diseases are increasing. West Nile virus is a sign of those viruses and diseases to come.

In terms of money, we meet with another worrisome problem. Munich Reinsurance, the world's largest reinsurer, has reported a record number of natural disasters affecting its clients in recent years. The increase in the number of forest fires and hurricanes in North America illustrates the early consequences of a changing environment. Munich Re expects that $300 billion annually will be lost through weather-generated disasters by the year 2050.[17] Journalist Ross Gelbspan reports that "Britain's biggest insurer [has] projected that, unchecked, climate change could bankrupt the global economy by 2065."[18]

Power, Inequality, and Environmental Injustice

The year is 2003, 14 years after the Exxon Valdez spill in Alaska. The oil industry still drives the state's politics and much of the policy on the environment. Senator Frank Murkowski has just been elected governor, and he has appointed his daughter to fill out his term. Linda Murkowski is proposing a bill that would exempt most new oil exploitation from any environmental impact statements, and Prince William Sound, devastated by the Exxon Valdez spill, is still not cleaned up. Out of the 28 most impacted species by the spill, only two are recovering. "It will be a long time till we know the damages to our way of life," explains Dune Lankard, an Eyak Native from Cordova.[19] And still, ExxonMobil tries to keep reducing the fines it should pay in punitive damages.

Originally, a $5 billion award was approved by an Alaskan jury, but it was deemed "excessive" in 2001 by the U.S. Ninth Circuit Court of Appeals in San Francisco. The legal battle continues to go back and forth. Not surprisingly, ExxonMobil argues for reduced damages despite record profits for the corporation. In 2002, it was the richest corporation in the world. In that same year, *Forbes* reported that CEO Lee Raymond received $32.6 million in compensation, almost 10 times the energy industry median.[20]

Dune Lankard, Evon Peter, Chief of the Gwich'in Nation from Arctic Village, and Violet Yeaton, from the Port Graham Village on Lower Cook Inlet, have joined with hundreds of other Native Alaskans to form the Alaskan Native Oil and Gas Working Group to challenge the "sacred cow" of Alaskan politics: the oil industry. They are also challenging the Alaskan Native Corporations, which the community members charge were created largely to exploit resources and continue to be one of the largest problems for Native peoples.

The new coalition also seeks to challenge the state of Alaska to look at diversifying the economy of the region and to address the pollutants now within the state. The challenge is immense. Alaska, although stunning, is also amazingly polluted. It ranks number four of the most polluted states in the country with over 535 million pounds of toxic releases into the environment in 2000 alone. Much of that is either military or oil industry pollution. The oil industry, like the military, has exemptions from reporting its toxic releases. The fact that federal law exempts exploration and production facilities—such as Prudhoe Bay and Cook Inlet, pipelines such as the TransAlaska Pipeline, and natural gas refineries such as Phillips Petroleum at Nikiski—from Toxics Release Inventory reports would, it seems, call into question the point of even having an inventory.

The industry justifies the reporting exemption by saying that the facilities are located "too far from communities to have an impact."[21] Lankard, whose Indian name refers to "a little bird who screams really loud and won't shut up," makes clear that his concerns are not only aimed at the big corporations like British Petroleum, ExxonMobil, and Chevron but also the Alaskan Native Corporations. "The Chugach Alaska Corporation has decided it wants to drill for oil near Katalla, on the Copper River Delta and an ancestral village site of the Eyak," Lankard says. "We've never been asked for our opinion. The Copper River Delta is the world's finest salmon habitat and fishery, and we do not want to lose this way of life. If the development happens at Katalla, it will affect everything we know about the Copper River Delta."

Violet Yeaton of Port Graham Village echoes Dune's concerns: "Our traditional use in an uncontaminated state is crucial to the sustainability of our culture." A 1997 EPA draft study documented heavy metal contaminants in the traditional resources. Yeaton tells me, "Before the final report was completed, the EPA renewed permits for oil and gas development to the companies. It is unacceptable that Cook Inlet oil activities be allowed to continue based on exemptions from the law, which are illegal elsewhere. We require zero discharge."[22]

Robert Thompson is an Inupiat from Kaktovik, a village that has historically been involved in oil development. Acknowledging that many people are "in support of oil development in his area," he also points out that "the smoke from Prudhoe has reached Kaktovik at times."[23] The debate over opening the Arctic National Wildlife Refuge has also been used to pit Native communities against each other. Some Inuit, for instance, hope to avert oil development in the offshore region that would impact their traditional areas and instead support oil development in Gwich'in territory. The oil interests, and subsequently the state government, have driven a complex, untenable wedge into the heart of Alaskan Native territory.

Alaska is a snapshot of how colonialism and neocolonialism are repeated. "The discovery of oil on the North Slope pushed Congress to enact the Alaskan Native Claims Settlement Act (ANCSA) in 1971, which took nearly all the land from Indigenous control, and allowed the industry and state to gain access to the resources. It set up a tool to divide and exploit the Alaskan Native tribal nations and our traditional lands and resources," explains Chief Evon Peter of Arctic Village. When Alaska entered the United States in 1959, approximately 85,000 Native people lived throughout the state. The discovery of oil one year later drove a federal mandate to redress aboriginal title questions in the region and, in particular, to find a tenable legal loophole through which to secure an 800-mile pipeline through the heart of Alaska from the North Slope to the oil companies.

In 1971, the government, with an estimated $562 million dangled by oil companies, finally figured out how to address the problem of Alaskan Native jurisdiction. As Clayton Thomas-Muller of the Indigenous Environmental Network explains, "President Nixon convinced Wally Hickel to retire as governor of Alaska in order to be immediately appointed as the new Secretary of Interior, making him instrumental in brokering the Alaskan Native Claims Settlement Act."[24] Evon Peter notes that ANCSA was passed with little input from the affected Native nations. "With the passage of the ANCSA legislation, all aboriginal land claims were extinguished. The law passed without a voice or vote by Alaskan Native people or the general public."

Under the new system, tribal control of Native lands was replaced by a for-profit corporate structure, the Alaskan Native Corporations, and the Indigenous people were made shareholders. The situation in Alaska, then, was not so different from the "termination era" in the lower 48 states that liquidated the assets of many Native communities. There is widespread concern that ANCSA has wreaked social havoc on Alaskan Native communities.

Today, Alaskan Native Corporations, like the Arctic Slope Regional Corporation, hold land entitlements to 5.1 million acres of land. Many of the corporations have entered into joint ventures or partnerships with mining and oil development companies. Although 9% of the jobs on Corporation projects are held by Indigenous shareholders, the Corporations' obligations to their out-of-state partners are far more sizable than their payrolls.

Restructuring the Energy Industry

The new power plants of choice the world over are using either natural gas or renewable energy and are smaller, nimbler, cleaner and closer to the end user than the giants of yesteryear. That means, power no longer depends on the vagaries of the [electric power distribution] grid and is more responsive to the needs of the consumer. This is a compelling advantage in rich countries, where the digital revolution is filling the thirst for high quality, reliable power that the antiquated grid seems unable to deliver. California provides the best evidence: although the utilities have not built a single power plant over the past decade, individuals and companies have added a whopping 6 GW of non-utility micro power over that period, roughly the equivalent of the state's installed nuclear capacity. The argument in favor of micro power is even more persuasive in developing countries, where the grid has largely failed the poor.[25]

Some of us will be in the forefront of the micropower program and others will not. ExxonMobil is pretty much the Wal-Mart of the energy business and will not be supporting the development of many alternatives. It will instead be ensuring that its production and exploration continue almost exponentially. ExxonMobil must find 1.6 billion barrels of oil a year just to stay even with its present production.

The output of "mature fields" diminishes at the rate of 6% to 7% per year. A shrinking resource base creates a drive for constant exploration and development. If the Bush administration succeeds in opening up the Arctic National Wildlife Refuge, ExxonMobil will be right in the forefront. But ExxonMobil will also not be investing much into alternative energy. In fact, the company spent "not a penny" in 2001 on renewable energy. Company boss Lee Raymond considers it "a waste of money," according to a report in *The Economist*. He says, "Oil and gas will continue to be the dominant energy for the next 25 years."[26]

We can either be about getting some control over our consumption and production of power, or we can continue to relinquish that control to large corporations. Unlike ExxonMobil, which is only thinking forward a couple of decades, more and more Native communities, as well as others, are looking toward the alternatives that will endure into the future. Localizing power production, increasing the production of power for the grid as an alternative source of economic development, and having a vision for the future are only a few avenues by which communities are regaining local control over their power.

Democratizing Power Production

The United States is the wealthiest and most dominant country in the world, yet it can't keep the lights on in New York City nor can it provide power in "liberated" Baghdad. Centralized power production based on fossil fuel and nuclear resources has served to centralize political power, to disconnect communities from responsibility and control over energy, and to create a vast, wasteful system. We need to recover democracy. And one key element is democratizing power production.

Alternative energy represents an amazing social and political reconstruction opportunity, one that has the potential for peace, justice, equity, and some recovery of our national dignity. Right now, we are missing the canoe. While renewable energy is the fastest-growing market in the world, the United States is dropping way back in the race to develop new energy technologies. Heck, the Rosebud Sioux had to import turbine parts from Denmark, and that's a long way away.

Investing in alternative energy is investing in jobs since the fuel supply is itself free, courtesy of the Creator. Alternative energy investment averages 60 times more high-paying jobs than those created by the fossil fuel and nuclear power industries. It is our choice. We can either create jobs and economic stability in Indian Country, or we can continue to line the pockets of utility and energy companies.

Conservation and alternative energy make huge economic sense. The Starwood Hotel group (which includes the Sheraton) recently invested in energy-smart solutions for 748 properties. The investments saved the corporation $6.1 million in one year, the equivalent of 9,400 hotel-room bookings. Those energy savings also represent the equivalent of taking 1,800 automobiles off our roads, planting 2,400 trees, or disconnecting 1,200 homes from the electric grid.

We stand on the cusp of something important. By democratizing power production, we are investing in "homeland security." After all, who's going to fly an airplane into a wind tower? Some of us believe that instead of contaminating Newe Segobia (at Yucca Mountain) with nuclear waste storage, we should be investing in solar panels. We know that the wind blows endlessly on Pine Ridge, the poorest county in the country, and we believe there should be wind turbines here. We must be about democracy and justice. We must put the power back into the hands of the people. That is why what is happening on Pine Ridge and a host of other reservations is so significant. It is tribal self-determination, and it is visionary.

The tribal wind program is also an opportunity to bring the wealthiest Native communities (those on the east and west coasts) into a partnership with some of the largest landholding, wind-rich tribes in the country. This is not only about sharing wealth, it is about restoring trade relations between Indigenous nations, and, in some ways, allowing Native people an opportunity to recover land and culturally based traditions in the context of a new set of technologies and a new millennium. Speaking with some of the largest casino tribes at the United Southern and Eastern Tribes meeting in February 2003, Bob Gough laid out the potential for tribal investment, income, and environmental protection through new partnerships. "We don't just want to be there when the blue-haired ladies put quarters into the machines. We want to be there any time a light switch goes on."[27]

The Mohegans of Connecticut have taken some of the first steps in adopting alternative energy. The tribe recently purchased a collection of hydrogen fuel cells to power its casino complex. While traditional generating systems create as much as 25 pounds of pollutants to generate 1,000 kilowatt-hours of power, the same energy produced by fuel cells equates to less than one ounce of pollutants. The Mohegans have been among the first to show an interest in investing in tribal wind power with the cash-strapped, wind-rich tribes in the West. A number of us hope this interest develops further.

The Lakota are also taking advantage of a new sort of politics on the wind. In March 2004, the mayors of 150 cities joined with Intertribal COUP, Honor the Earth, and other organizations in pledging to voluntarily meet the provisions of the Kyoto Accord, which the United States refused to sign. Taking things a step further, mayors of cities ranging from Denver and Duluth to Santa Monica and Dallas reiterated their commitment to make changes by issuing a Declaration of Energy Independence: "In the course of human events it has now become necessary for all people to face the threat of catastrophic global climate change and so we do hereby declare our commitment to a renewable energy future."[28] The mayors, joining with tribes, urged a commitment to renewable energy and called on Washington to support the transition.

In summer 2004, a coalition of churches joined in the effort, specifically supporting tribal wind generation as a centerpiece of energy justice and part of these churches' calling to be "stewards of God's creation."[29] Michigan Interfaith Power and Light, a collection of 100 congregations working to both mitigate global climate change and look toward energy and environmental justice, signed an agreement with *Native*Energy to buy "green tags," a market mechanism to reward green power producers, from the Rosebud expansion project and, over time, from other Native wind turbines. As with *Native*Energy's support of the first Rosebud turbine, the green tags will be purchased on an up-front basis to help finance new projects.[30]

Intertribal COUP and groups such as the Apollo Alliance, representing a host of environmental groups and 12 labor unions, are looking toward renewable energy component manufacturing as a way to create jobs here in the United States while mitigating climate change. The Apollo Project has called for a $300 billion federal investment into renewable energy. That investment, according to the Project, would add 3.3 million new jobs and stimulate an estimated $1.4 trillion in new Gross Domestic Product.[31] The tribes' goal is to turn some of these investments into jobs in Indian Country.

So it is that new wind projects are planned for the reservations at Fort Berthold, Northern Cheyenne (Montana), Makah (Washington), and White Earth (northern Minnesota). The economics makes sense to tribes like the Assiniboine and Sioux of Fort Peck that hope to bring on-line a 660-kilowatt turbine. The Poplar, Montana, wind turbine would produce enough energy to reduce the tribal electric bill by $134,000 annually and help finance other programs through savings.

While remote tribal communities on the Great Plains and elsewhere wrangle through the "white tape" created by the fossil fuel industry, they are clear about their commitment to ending the unsustainable exploitation of their natural resources. It is as if they were saying, "That was then; this is now. We will not be cheated or stolen from."

The fossil fuel century has been incredibly destructive to the ecological structures—the air, earth, water, and plant and animal life—that keep planet Earth habitable for humans. Whether human populations will continue to flourish 100 years from now will depend on the choices we make today. Oliver Red Cloud, a traditional Oglala headman, reminds us of our spiritual agreements with the Creator when he says, "The *Takoche* [grandchild] generation is coming. We've got to take care of all of this for them."[32] Native American communities are creating momentum for change and providing some critical leadership in the face of global climate change and the energy crisis to come. By democratizing power production, Native nations are providing the solutions that all of us will need in order to survive into the next millennium.

Endnotes

What is Sacred?

1 Bradley and Jennifer Soule, "Death at the Hiawatha Asylum for Insane Indians," *Native Voice* (Rapid City, SD) Vol. 2, No. 3 (Feb. 2003), p. B3. Indian agents, appointed as U.S. governors over local Indian tribes, often identified Native individuals who adhered to their traditions as "malcontents," thus consigning them to the asylum. From there very few would ever return.

2 For more on this topic, see Vina Deloria, Jr., *God is Red: A Native View of Religion, 30th Anniversary Edition* (Golden, CO: Fulcrum Publishing, 2003).

3 Chris Peters, author's interview, June 8, 1992.

4 Vine Deloria, Jr., "Sacredness among Native Americans," in *Native American Sacred Sites and the Department of Defense,* Vine Deloria, Jr., and Richard W. Stoffle, eds. (U.S. Department of Defense, The Legacy Resource Management Program, 1998), available at: https://www.denix.osd.mil/denix/Public/ES-Programs/Conservation/Legacy/Sacred/ch2.html.

5 Public Law 95-341, 42 U.S.C. 1996 and 1996a, "Protection and Preservation of Traditional Religions of Native Americans," Aug. 11, 1978.

6 Executive Order 13007, "Protection and Accommodation of Access to 'Indian Sacred Sites,'" May 24, 1996, available at: http://www.gsa.gov/gsa/ep/contentView.do?noc=T&contentType=GSA_BASIC&contentId=16912.

8 http://resourcescommittee.house.gov/democrats/pr2002/20020718NativeAmericanSacredLandsActIntro.html.

9 Valerie Taliman, "Sacred Landscapes," *Sierra Magazine,* Nov./Dec. 2002, p. 3.

10 Taliman.

God, Squirrels, and the Universe

1 Mt. Graham Coalition, "Permit to Pray?" (press release) Aug 13, 1998.

2 Steve Yozwiak, "UA Requires Prayer Permits for Indians on Mt. Graham," and Jim Erickson, "Mt. Graham 'Prayer Permit' Angers Apaches," *Arizona Republic*, Aug. 15, 1995, p. A1.

3 John Dougherty, "Special Report: Star Whores—The Ruthless Pursuits of Astronomical Sums of Cash and Scientific Excellence," *Phoenix New Times*, Vol. 24, No. 25 (June 16-22, 1993).

4 David Webster, "Apaches Protest 'Project Columbus' on Arizona Mountain," *Catholic New Times* (Toronto), Sept. 22, 1991.

5 Dee Alexander Brown, "Bury My Heart at Wounded Knee" (New York: Henry Holt, 1970), p. 205-6.

6 The Apaches specialized in raiding for horses, and are, in the historical context, some of the major purveyors of fine horses, and the impetus, along with the Comanches and Navajos, for the initial distribution of the fine creatures on the North American continent.

7 Carl Waldman, *Atlas of the North American Indian* (New York: Facts on File, 1995), pp. 140-41.

8 Brown, pp. 204-5.

9 Elizabeth A. Brandt, "The Fight for Dzil Nchaa Si An, Mt. Graham," *Cultural Survival Quarterly*, Vol. 19, No. 4 (Winter 1996), p. 55.

10 Waldman, p. 143.

11 Brandt, p. 56.

12 Brandt.

13 John Dougherty, "Star Gate," *Phoenix New Times*, Vol. 24, No. 25 (June 16-22, 1993), p. 4, available at: http://www.phoenixnewtimes.com/issues/1993-06-16/news/feature.html

14 Robert Nelson, "Lab Rats," *Phoenix New Times*, Vol. 32, No. 51 (Dec. 20-26, 2001), p. 18

15 McCain and DeConcini qualified their support for the telescope by not supporting the Mt. Graham exemption from the Endangered Species Act.

16 Sabino Maffeo, S.J., (G.V. Coyne, S.J., trans.) *In the Service of Nine Popes, One Hundred Years of the Vatican Observatory* (Vatican City State: Vatican Observatory Publications, 1991), p. 207.

17 Steve Goldstein, "The Pope's Telescope," *Philadelphia Inquirer*, Sept. 7, 2002, p. 1.

18 Bruce Johnston, "Vatican sets evangelical sights on outer space," *London Daily Telegraph*, Oct. 28, 1992.

19 Brandt, p. 53.

20 George V. Coyne, S.J., "Statement of the Vatican Observatory on the Mount Graham International Observatory and American Indian Peoples," University

of Arizona, Exhibit B, *Apache Survival Coalition et al. v. U.S. et al.,* University of Arizona, intervenor, CIV, NO 91-1350 PHX-WBC, April 6, 1992.

21 Brandt, p. 54.

22 Coyne, "Statement of the Vatican Observatory."

23 Coyne, "Statement of the Vatican Observatory."

24 San Carlos Apache Tribe, resolution JN-01-04, June 5, 2001, available at: http://www.mountgraham.org/pdf/RecordofApacheOppositiontoMtGraham observatory1989to2001.pdf, p. 50.

25 Steve Yozwiak, "Priest Calls Telescope Foes Part of 'Jewish Conspiracy,' " *Arizona Republic,* Aug. 14, 1992.

26 Yozwiak.

27 "Affidavit of Father Charles W. Polzer, S.J.," University of Arizona, Exhibit C, *Apache Survival Coalition et al. v. U.S. et al.,* University of Arizona, intervenor, CIV NO 91-1350-PHX-=WPC, April 2, 1992.

28 Dougherty, "Star Gate."

29 Dougherty, "Star Gate," and John Dougherty, "Making a mountain into a starbase: The long, bitter battle over Mount Graham," *High Country News,* Vol. 27 No. 13 (July 24, 1995), available at: http://www.hcn.org/servlets/hcn.PrintableArticle?article_id=1149

30 Guy Lopez, author's interview, May 12, 2003.

31 Steve Yozwiak, "Worst Spot Chosen for UA telescope," *Arizona Republic,* June 15, 1993, and Student Environmental Action Coalition, "Mt. Graham, Sacred Mountain, Sacred Ecosystem," available at : http://www.seac.org/seac-sw/mtg.htm

32 Dan Haugen, "Astronomers See a Clearer Future with Arizona Telescope," *Minnesota Daily,* Oct. 23, 2002.

33 Letter to the Editor, *Minnesota Daily,* Oct. 23, 2002, available at: http://www.mndaily.com/articles/2002/10/23/36727. The worst of what might come is evidenced at Mauna Kea, a sacred site for Hawaiian people, where traditionally only the most reverent could ascend. Today, 1000 astronomers annually visit, paying a pittance for use to the National Park Service. They leave behind some 500,000 gallons of human waste annually, and introduce a host of chemicals ranging from ethylene glycol and liquid mercury into the environment (Joel Helfrich, Dwight Metzger, and Michael Nixon, "Native Tribes Struggle to Reclaim Sacred Sites," *The* [Minneapolis]*Pulse,* June 5, 2005, p. 7).

34 Brandt, p. 53.

35 George V. Coyne, S.J., "Personal Reflections upon the Nature of Sacred in the Context of Mt. Graham International Observatory," May 1992 (unpublished), p. 2, and Sacred Land Film Project website http://www.sacredland.org/endangered_sites_pages/mt_graham.html.

36 Brandt, p. 56.

37 Jack Hitt, "Would You Baptize an Extraterrestial?" *New York Times Magazine,* May 29, 1994, p. 36.

Salt, Water, Blood, and Coal

1   Laurie Weahkee, author's interview, Oct. 10, 2004.

2   Jim Enote, author's interview, Oct. 21, 2001

3   Rene Kimball, "Salt of The Earth: Tribes Fear Mine Will Disturb Cultural Sites, Damage Sacred Salt Lake," *Albuquerque Journal,* Feb. 27, 1994, available at: http://www.native-net.org/archive/nl/9403/0223.html.

4   This and other quotes from Vernon Masayesva, unless otherwise noted, are from author's interview, Sept. 20, 2002.

5   Natural Resources Defense Council, "Water Life: An Interview with Vernon Masayesva," available at: http://www.nrdc.org/water/conservation/ivmblmesa.asp.

6   Charles F. Wilkinson, author's interview, Oct. 9, 2001.

7   For more information, see Emily Benedek, *The Wind Won't Know Me: A History of the Navajo-Hopi Land Dispute* (New York: Alfred A. Knopf, 1920).

8   David Beckman, Michael Jasny, Lissa Wadewitz, and Andrew Wetzler, "Drawdown: Groundwater Mining on Black Mesa," (Los Angeles: Natural Resources Defense Council Environmental Justice Program, 2000), p. vii, available at: http://www.nrdc.org/water/conservation/draw/drawinx.asp.

9   Beckman, et al., "Drawdown, " p. 23.

10 Vernon Masayesva "Hopi Must Rely on Their Own Observation and Reason for Water Use" *Navajo Hopi Observer,* May 9, 2001, p. 4, available at: www.blackmesais.org/hopi_must_rely.html.

11 Alvin Honyumptewa, author's interview, Sept. 2002.

12 Leonard Selestewa, author's interview, Sept. 20, 2002.

13 Beckman, et al., "Drawdown, " p. vi-vii.

14 Judd Slivka, "Hopi Runners Deliver Plea on Aquifer," *Arizona Republic*, Aug. 15, 2001, p. B4.

15 Brenda Norrell, "Hopi and Navajo Protest Peabody's Coal Slurry Pipeline," *Indian Country Today,* June 27, 2001, available at: http://www.blackmesais.org/Hopi_and_Navajo_protest.html.

16 Slivka.

17 Tim Folger, "A Thirsty Nation," *OnEarth* (Natural Resources Defense Council), Fall 2004, available at: http://www.nrdc.org/onearth/04fal/blackmesa1.asp, and Fred Mayes, "Energy Consumption and Renewable Energy Development Potential on Indian Lands," U.S. Dept. of Energy, National Energy Information Center, March 2000, available at: http://wire0.ises.org/wire/Publications/Research.nsf/0/2573209718d564d1c125690e004c6df2?OpenDocument.

18 Starlie Lomayktewa, et al., "Statement by Hopi Religious Leaders," *N- Aquifer Threatened by Industrial Overpumping,* (report) (Flagstaff, AZ: Black Mesa Trust, April 20, 2001).

19 National Academy of Sciences, *Rehabilitation Potential of Western Coal Lands: A Report to the Energy Policy Project of the Ford Foundation,* (New York: Ford Foundation, 1974), available at: http://www.fordfound.org/elibrary/documents/0301/toc.cfm.

20 Edward Wemytewa, author's interview, Sept. 20, 2002.

21 Ben Neary, "Sacred Land Under Seige," *Santa Fe New Mexican,* Jan. 7, 2001.

22 Paul Bloom, "Brief Chronology of the Administrative Failure to Protect Zuni Salt Lake," (unpublished paper), p. 1.

23 Bloom, p. 2.

24 Wemytewa interview.

25 Wemytewa interview.

26 Zuni Salt Lake Coalition, "Zuni Salt Lake and Sanctuary Zone Protected," press release, Aug. 7, 2003. available at: www.minesandcommunities.org/Action/press181.htm

27 Zuni Salt Lake Coalition.

Klamath Land and Life

1 Jeff Barnard, "Karuk Tribe Seeks Removal of Dams to Restore Healthy Salmon Diet," *News from Indian Country,* April 4, 2005, p. 23.

2 Erika Zavaleta, "A Recent History of the Klamath Tribe: Termination, Restoration and the Struggle to Retrieve Homelands," (unpublished paper), 1993, p. 25.

3 Klamath Tribe website, http://www.Klamathtribes.org/history.

4 Dee Brown, *Bury My Heart at Wounded Knee* (New York: Henry Holt, 1970), p. 215

5 Brown, p. 220.

6 Brown, p. 225.

7 Brown, p. 223.

8   Jeff Zucker, *Oregon Indians: Culture, History and Current Affairs* (Portland: Western Imprints, the Press of the Oregon Historical Society, 1983), p. 107.

9   Zucker.

10 Theodore Stern, *The Klamath Tribe: A People and their Reservation* (Seattle: University of Washington Press, 1965), p. 145.

11 American Indian Policy Review Commission, *Final Report to Congress* (Washington: General Accounting Office, 1976), pp. 447-8.

12 Carolyn M. Buan and Richard Lewis, eds., *The First Oregonians*, (Portland: Oregon Council on Humanities, 1991), pp. 51-2.

13 The Menominee were restored after a pitched battle in 1973. James Wilson, *The Earth Shall Weep,: A History of Native Ameirca*, (New York: Atlantic Monthly Press, 1999) p. 362.

14 Zavaleta, p. 12.

15 Zavaleta, p. 27.

16 Wilson, p. 366.

17 Zavaleta, p. 22.

18 *Behold a Nation is Coming: The Story of Chief Edison Chiloquin and the Termination of the Klamath Tribe of Oregon* (Klamath Falls, Oregon: The Chiloquin Fund, 1975).

19 Chuck Kimbol, interviewed by Erika Zavaleta, March 26, 1992.

20 Wilson, p. 367.

21 *Return of the Raven: The Edison Chiloquin Story,* (video) Televideos, PO Box 1118, Cottage Grove, Oregon 97424.

22 Jean Johnson, "Klamath Tribes Closer to Settlement," *Indian Country Today,* Jan. 16, 2004, available at: http://www.indiancountry.com/content.cfm?id=1096409721.

23 Johnson.

24 Johnson.

25 Jay Ward, author's interview, Feb. 10, 2005.

26 Johnson.

27 Jean Johnson, "Water in the West: Klamath Tribes Know its Worth," *Indian Country Today,* Aug. 10, 2004, available at http://www.indiancountry.com/content.cfm?id=1092142810.

28 Jim McCarthy, "The War on the River, Native Voices in the Contested Klamath Basin," *Terrain,* Winter 2001, p. 21, available at: http://www.terrainmagazine.org/article.php?id=13043.

29 McCarthy, p. 23

30 This and other quotes from Bud Ullman, are from author's interview, Oct. 17, 2001.

31 McCarthy, p.20.

32 Troy Fletcher, author's interview, June 16, 2005.

33 Oren Lyons, author's interview, Sept. 16, 2000.

34 Ross Anderson, "Fighting an Upstream Battle Massive Salmon Kill Stokes Water Management Conflict in California," *Washington Post,* Oct. 7, 2003, p. A3.

35 Orna Izakson, "Death in the Klamath," *E Magazine,* Vol. 14, No. 1 (Jan./Feb. 2003), p 12.

36 James May, "Klamath Tribes Believe a River Should Run Through It," *Indian Country Today,* Nov. 4, 2003, available at: http://www.indiancountry.com/content.cfm?id=1067960386

37 Richard Manning, *Grassland: The History, Biology, Politics, and Promise of the American Prairie* (New York: Penguin books, 1995), p.161.

38 Johnson, "Klamath Tribes Closer to Settlement."

39 Johnson, "Klamath Tribes Closer to Settlement."

40 Johnson, "Water in the West."

41 Gerard Seenan, "US Tribes Dance to Shame Scottish Power," *The Guardian,* July 24, 2004, available at: http://www.kwua.org/power/tribesscotland-2articles072404.htm.

42 Judith Johansen, the chief executive of PacifiCorp, earned just under $1million in 2003; see http://www.opinion.telegraph.co.uk/money/main.jhtml?xml=/money/2004/06/20/ccscot20.xml&sSheet=/opinion/2004/06/20/ixopright.html

43 Jeff Barnard, "Karuk Tribe Seeks Removal of Dams to Restore Healthy Salmon Diet," *News from Indian Country,* April 4, 2005, p. 23.

Imperial Anthropology

1 This and other quotes from Mickey Gemmill are from author's interview, Oct. 12, 2004.

2 Theodora Kroeber, *Ishi in Two Worlds* (Berkeley: University of California Press, 1961, 1989 edition), p. 15.

3 Kroeber, p. 30.

4 Kroeber, p. 65.

5 David E. Stannard, *The Conquest of the New World: American Holocaust* (New York: Oxford University Press, 1992), p. xii.

6 Kroeber, p. 46.

7 Kroeber, p. 22.

8 Kroeber, p. 234.

9 Melissa L. Meyer, *The White Earth Tragedy Ethnicity and Dispossession at a Minnesota Anishinaabe Reservation* (Lincoln: University of Nebraska Press, 1994), p. 168–70.

10 Ales Hrdlicka, "Physical Anthropology of the Lenape or Delawares and of the Eastern Indians in General," *Bureau of American Ethnology,* Bulletin 62 (Washington, D.C.: Government Printing Office, 1916).

11 Mary Curtius, "Academic Detectives Find the Long Lost Brain of Ishi: Anthropology Trail Leads to a Smithsonian Warehouse; Tribes want to rebury remains of the last Yahi Indian," *Los Angeles Times,* Feb. 20, 1999.

12 Devon A. Mihesuah, ed. *Repatriation Reader: Who Owns American Indian Remains* (Lincoln: University of Nebraska Press, 2000), p. 2.

13 Robert Eugene Bieder, "League of the Ho de sau ne or Iroquois in 1851," *Science Encounters the Indian, 1820–1880: The Early Years of American Ethnology* (Norman: University of Oklahoma Press, 1989), p. 30.

14 Bieder, p. 31.

15 Bieder, p. 32.

16 Roger Echo-Hawk and Walter Echo-Hawk, *Battlefields and Burial Grounds: The Indian Struggle to Protect Ancestral Graves in the U.S.* (Minneapolis: Lerner Publications, 1994), p. 48.

17 James Riding In, "Repatriation: A Pawnee's Perspective," in Mihesuah, p. 111.

18 Robert Eugene Bieder, "The Representations of Indian Bodies in Nineteenth-Century American Anthropology," in Mihesuah, p. 29

19 Mihesuah, p. 3.

20 Mihesuah, p. 1.

21 Echo-Hawk and Echo-Hawk, p. 52.

22 Echo-Hawk and Echo-Hawk, p. 32.

23 Devon A. Mihesuah, "American Indians, Anthropologists, Pothunters, and Repatriation: Ethical, Religious, and Political Differences," in Mihesuah, p. 97.

24 Mihesuah, in Mihesuah, p. 102.

25 Echo-Hawk and Echo-Hawk, p. 34.

26 The National Museum of the American Indian opened on the National Mall in Washington, D.C. in Sept. 2004.

27 Jack F. Trope and Walter L. Echo-Hawk, "The Native American Graves Protection and Repatriation Act: Background and Legislative History," in Mihesuah, p. 138.

28 Trope and Echo-Hawk, in Mihesuah, p. 135.

29 Michael Kan, " 'U' to Return Burial Remains to Tribe," *Michigan Daily,* March 18, 2005.

30 Suzanne J. Crawford, "(Re)Constructing Bodies: Semiotic Sovereignty and the Debate over Kennewick Man," in Mihesuah, p. 216.

31 Michelle Locke, "Thousands Remain on Museum Shelves, Ishi's remains were finally returned to his homeland, but this case is an exception," *Grand Rapids* (Michigan) *Press,* Sept. 3, 2000, p. A9.

32 Alex White Plume, author's interview, June 22, 2001.

33 Matt Palmquist "Poisoned Gods," *San Francisco Weekly,* Sept. 4–10, 2002, p. 20.

34 Palmquist p. 20.

35 Palmquist. Note that the Wounded Knee collection (see related chapter) did not have any preservation chemicals on it. According to Audrey Stevens, curator, it was placed in the case 100 years ago and was not removed. That collection is in "wearable condition."

36 Palmquist.

37 Palmquist.

38 Palmquist, p. 21. The Hoopa regalia were contaminated with thymol, p-dichlorobenzene, naphthalene, lindane and DDT, all of which can be carcinogens.

39 Palmquist, p. 25.

40 Palmquist.

41 Palmquist, p. 27.

42 Weisbaden Manifesto, Nov. 7, 1945, quoted in Elizabeth Sackler, "The Spoils of War/Conquest: A Call for a Code of Ethics in the Indian Art Market," *Native Peoples Magazine,* Vol. 9, No. 3 (Spring 1996), pp. 18-19. See also http://www.repatriationfoundation.org/spoils.html#ret4.

43 Sackler.

44 Gerald Vizenor, *Crossbloods : Bone Courts, Bingo, and Other Reports* (Minneapolis: University of Minnesota Press, 1990), pp. 70, 73.

45 James Riding In, in Mihesuah, p.106.

46 Eddie Benton Benais, author's interview, Oct. 2, 1990.

Quilled Cradleboard Covers, Cultural Patrimony, and Wounded Knee

1 Mario Gonzales and Elizabeth Cook–Lynn, *The Politics of Hallowed Ground: Wounded Knee and the Struggle for Indian Sovereignty* (Urbana: University of Illinois Press, 1999), p. 26.

2 Among other things that the Hearsts did with their gold, they built the Phoebe Apperson Hearst Museum, discussed further in the "Imperial Anthropology" chapter.

3   Jeffery St. Clair, "Daschle's Deal Dooms the Sacred Land of the Sioux," *Counter Punch,* Aug. 1, 2002.

4   Edward Lazarus, "Same Black Hills, More White Justice: Senator Daschle's Provision Granting Barrick Gold Company Immunity from Liability," *Find Law Legal Community,* Jan. 24, 2002.

5   Gonzales and Cook–Lynn, p. 332.

6   Ward Churchill, *Struggle for the Land* (Albuquerque: University of New Mexico Press, 1985), p. 120.

7   Churchill, p. 121.

8   Lazarus.

9   Oliver Red Cloud, author's interview, March 8, 2003.

10 Greg Bourland, Cheyenne River Sioux Tribal Chairman for 12 years beginning in 1988, was assigned by the other tribal chairman of the Lakota reservations to watch over the Black Hills settlement money. "The Department of the Interior took that money and drew money out for themselves. They put it into ready cash securities such as overnight deposits, bonds, and short-term treasury bills. It drew as little as 1.5% interest," Bourland explains (in Tim Giago, "Black Hills Claims Settlement Revisited" *Lakota Journal,* Aug. 2-9, 2002, p.1). The mismanagement of the Lakota funds was a microcosm of the overall mismanagement of federal Indian trust funds, the subject of the *Cobell v. Norton* lawsuit that remains in federal court. By 2002, the federal government's settlement offer to the Lakota Nation stood at $623 million for docket 74B and $88 million for docket 74A, a total of around $712 million.

11 James Abourezk, author's interview. March 7, 2003.

12 St. Clair.

13 Abourezk.

14 Jon Lurie, "Who Would Do Such a Thing?" *The Circle,* April 1995, p. 15. For a 2002 update on Costner's plans, see Els Herten, *KOLA News,* "Kevin Costner Has a Change of Heart!" available at: http://www.homestead.com/arvollookinghorse/Articles_On_Chief_Arvol_A pr2002.html

15 St. Clair.

16 St. Clair.

17 St. Clair.

18 Indianz.com, "Plans for shooting range near sacred site scrapped," Jan. 12, 2004, available at: http://www.indianz.com/News/2004/000075.asp.

19 Gonzales and Cook-Lynn, p. 23.

20 William S. E. Coleman, *Voices of Wounded Knee* (Lincoln: University of Nebraska Press, 2000), pp. 15-17.

21 Coleman, p. 19.

22 Coleman, p. 56.

23 Coleman, pp. 89-90.

24 Dee Brown, *Bury My Heart at Wounded Knee* (New York: Henry Holt, 1970), pp. 435-38.

25 Gonzales and Cook–Lynn, pp. 17-18.

26 R. Eli Paul, "Wounded Knee and the 'Collector of Curios,' " *Nebraska History Magazine,* Vol. 75, No. 2 (Summer 1994), pp. 214-215.

27 Coleman, p. 342.

28 Jerry Green, "The Medals at Wounded Knee," available at: http://www.dickshovel.com/GreenIntro.html. Among those who received the Army Medal of Honor were: John E. Clancy, Marvin C. Hillock, Harry L. Hawthorne, James Ward, Mosheim Feaster, Ernest A. Garlington, John C. Gresham, Joshua B. Hartzog, George Lloyd, Albert W. McMillan, William G. Austin, Herman Ziegner, Thomas Sullivan, Mathew H. Hamilton, Frederick E. Toy, Jacob Trautman, Bernard Jetter, and George Hobday.

29 Green.

30 Green.

31 Avis Little Eagle, "Stolen Massacre Items Found," *Indian Country Today,* Vol. 12, No. 16, (Oct. 15, 1992), p. A1.

32 Paul, p. 214.

33 Audrey Stevens, author's interview, Dec. 9, 2002.

34 Audrey Stevens, author's interview, May 2, 2001.

35 Stevens interview, Dec. 9, 2002.

36 This and other quotes from Bill Billeck are taken from author's interview, Jan. 9, 2003.

37 Mario Gonzales, letter to John Cirelli, Dec. 4, 1993.

38 This and other quotes from Alex White Plume are taken from author's interview, Feb. 19, 2003.

39 Kim Ann Gronberg, "Indian Finds Spirits Still Lingering in Barre Museum" *Ware River News,* Vol. 106, No. 18 (Feb. 4, 1993), p. 1.

40 Dan L. Monroe, personal letter to John Cirelli. March 23, 1993.

41 "Museum Set to Lose Indian Treasure," *New York Times,* Feb. 19, 1993, p. A12.

42 Little Eagle.

43 "Museum Set to Lose Indian Treasure."

44 Little Eagle.

45 Stevens interview, Dec. 9, 2002.

46 Gonzales and Cook-Lynn, p. 26

47 Abourezk.

48 Gonzales and Cook-Lynn.

49 M.Y.H. Brave Heart–Jordan, "The Return to the Sacred Path: Healing from Historical Trauma and Historical Unresolved Grief Among the Lakota," (Ph.D. diss., Smith College School for Social Work, 1995). *Abstracts International,* A 56/09, 3742. Copies available from The Takini Network, P.O. Box 4138, Rapid City, SD 57709-4138.

Vampires in the New World

1 Paul Rubin, "Indian Givers," *Phoenix New Times,* May 27, 2004, p. 29.

2 Rubin, p. 27.

3 Rubin, p. 29.

4 Article 29 of the Declaration of the Rights of Indigenous Peoples, Aug. 1994.

5 Victoria Tauli-Corpuz, author's interview, July 11, 2001.

6 Debra Harry, author's interview, July 11, 2001.

7 Monsanto won the award in the "Worst Corporate Offender" category for its European patent on soft-milling, low-gluten wheat that is derived from a traditional Indian wheat variety. Monsanto's patent (European Patent No. EP0445929B1) claims not only the low-gluten wheat, but also the flour, dough, and edible products (biscuits, cake, etc.) produced from it! Greenpeace, the Research Foundation for Science, Technology and Ecology, and the Indian farmers' organization Bharat Krishak Samaj are opposing Monsanto's patent at the European Patent Office. See http://www.captainhookawards.org

8 Debra Harry, "The Human Genome Diversity Project and Its Implications for Indigenous Peoples," available at: http://www.ipcb.org/publications/briefing_papers/files/hgdp.html

9 L.L. Cavalli-Sforza, A.C. Wilson, C.R. Cantor, R.M. Cook-Deegan and M.C. King, "Call for a Worldwide Survey of Human Genetic Diverstiy: A Vanishing Opportunity for the Human Genome Project," *Genomics,* Vol. 11, No. 2 (Oct. 1991), p. 490.

10 Harry interview.

11 Victoria Tauli-Corpuz, "Biotechnology and Indigenous Peoples," *Indigenous Perspectives,* (Baguio City, Philippines: Tebtebba Foundation), Vol.4, No. 1 (June 2001), p. 56.

12 Robert Engelman, Brian Halweil, and Danielle Nierenberg, "Rethinking Population, Improving Lives," in Linda Starke, ed., *State of the World 2002,* (New York: Norton, 2002), p. 134.

13 J. T. Houghton, et al., eds., *Climate Change 2001: the Scientific Basis, contribution of Working Group I to the Third Assessment Report for the Intergovernmental Panel on Climate Change,* (Cambridge: Cambridge University Press, 2001).

14 Tauli-Corpuz interview.

15 Patrice Trouiller and Pierre L. Olliaro, "Drug Development Output from 1975 to 1996: What Proportion for Tropical Diseases?" *International Journal of Infectious Diseases,* Winter 1998-99, p. 61.

16 Tauli-Corpuz, "Biotechnology and Indigenous Peoples," p. 57.

17 Terence Turner, "The Yanomami and the Ethics of Anthropological Practice," Occasional Paper Series, Vol. 6, Cornell University, Department of Latin American Studies, Nov. 2001, p. 7.

18 Turner, p. 9.

19 Turner, pp. 1, 39.

20 Rubin, pp. 22-24.

21 Harry interview.

22 National Congress of American Indians, Resolution NV-93-118, Dec. 3, 1993, excerpted at:
http://www.ipcb.org/resolutions/htmls/summary_indig_opp.html.

23 Indigenous Peoples Council on Biocolonialism, "Indegenous Peoples Opposition to the HGDP," available at:
http://www.ipcb.org/resolutions/htmls/summary_indig_opp.html.

24 Tauli-Corpuz, "Biotechnology and Indigenous Peoples," p. 56.

25 Sandra Awang, "Indigenous Nations and the Human Genome Diversity Project," in *Indigenous Knowledges in Global Contexts,* George D. Sefa Dei, Budd L. Hall and Dorothy Goldin Rosenberg, eds., (Toronto: University of Toronto Press, 2000).

26 This and other quotes from Audie Huber are from author's interview, Nov. 14, 2003.

27 Mathew Daly, "Scientists Fear Bill Would Halt Study," *Charlotte* (North Carolina) *Observer,* April 9, 2005, p. 6A.

28 Debra Harry, Stephanie Howard, and Brett Lee Shelton, "Indigenous People, Genes and Genetics, What Indigenous People Should Know about Biocolonialism," (Nixon, NV: Indigenous Peoples Council on Biocolonialism, 2000), p. 22.

29 Rubin, p. 29.

30 Rubin.

31 Harry, et al., p. 22.

32 Genetic markers linked to Indigenous American ancestry include the haplotypes A, B, C, D, and X, and the haplogroups M3 and M45.

33 Brett Lee Shelton and Jonathan Marks, "Gene Markers Not a Valid Test of Native Identity," *GeneWatch,* Vol 14, No. 5 (Sept. 2001).

34 Harry interview.

35 Department of Defense, Directive No. 6420.1, Oct. 9, 2004, available at: http://www.dtic.mil/whs/directives/corres/html2/d64201x.htm.

36 Rural Advancement Foundation International, "Human Genome Research—Human Genetic Diversity Enters the Commercial Mainstream," (communiqué), Jan./Feb. 2000, available at: http://etcgroup.org/documents/com_phase2.pdf; see also Global Exchange, "Biopiracy: A New Threat to Indigenous Rights and Culture in Mexico," (pamphlet) April 2001, available at: http://www.globalexchange.org/countries/americas/mexico/biopiracyReport.html.

37 Rural Advancement Foundation International, "The Patenting of Human Genetic Material" (communiqué), Jan. 30, 1994, available at: http://www.etcgroup.org/article.asp?newsid=218.

38 Rural Advancement Foundation International, "US Government Dumps the Hagahai Patent," (press release) Dec. 3, 1996, available at: http://www.etcgroup.org/article.asp?newsid=149.

39 Harry interview.

40 Harry interview.

41 Harry interview.

42 Harry, et al., pp. 32-3.

43 Indigenous Peoples Council on Biocolonialism, "IPCB Action Alert to Oppose the Genographic Project," available at: http://www.ipcb.org/issues/human_genetics/htmls/action_geno.html, and Indigenous Peoples Council on Biocolonialism, "Petition to Oppose the Genographic Project," available at: http://www.ipcb.org/issues/human_genetics/petition.php.

44 Harry interview.

Masks in the New Millennium

1 Crazy Horse Defense Project, http://crazyhorsedefense.org.

2 "In Whose Honor?"is a film on the subject of mascots depicting the story of the University of Illinois' Fighting Illini.

3 Robert Jensen, "The Past and Human Dignity: What the Fighting Sioux Tells Us about Whites," *CounterPunch,* Oct. 10, 2003, available at: http://www.counterpunch.org/jensen10142003.html.

4 Carol Spindel, *Dancing at Halftime: Sports and the Controversy over American Indian Mascots* (New York: New York University Press, 2002), p. 29. See also Geneva Smitherman, *Black Talk: Words and Phrases from the Hood to the Amen Corner* (New York: Houghton Mifflin Co., 1994), pp. 87-88.

5 Arlene B. Hirschfelder, Paulette Fairbanks Molin, Yvonne Beamer, Yvonne Wakim, *American Indian Stereotypes in the World of Children*, (Lanham, MD: Scarecrow Press, 1999), p. 3.

6 I first heard Reverend Stephen Chapman (Cherokee) say this at Metropolitan State University, Minneapolis, Minnesota, Nov. 15, 1992.

7 Scott Ostler, "Insensitivity Training in Colorado," *San Francisco Chronicle*, March 14, 2002, available at: http://www.sfgate.com/cgi-bin/article.cgi?file=/chronicle/archive/2002/03/14/SP193744.DTL.

8 www.fightingwhites.org/aboutus.aspx.

9 Ostler.

10 Foster Stangell, "Fighting for a Good Name," *The Circle*, Dec. 2000, p. 10.

11 C. Richard King and Charles Fruehling Springwood, *Team Spirits: The Native American Mascots Controversy* (Lincoln: University of Nebraska Press, 2001), p. 2.

12 Dean Schabner, "Demeaned and Victimized, Indians Say Sports Mascots, Ads Create Subhuman Image," *ABC News*, March 20, 2001.

13 Cornel Pewewardy, "American Indian Imagery and the Mis-education of America," (unpublished paper presented at Educating Tomorrow's Leaders: Through Awareness, Acceptance, and Appreciation, Florida State University, Tallahassee, March 20, 2001), available at: www.racismagainstindians.org/STARArticle/IndianImagery.htm.

14 Schabner.

15 Helena Norberg Hodge, "Shifting Direction, from Global Dependence to Local Interdependence," in Jerry Mander and Edward Goldsmith, eds., *The Case against the Global Economy* (San Francisco: Sierra Club Books, 1996), pp. 393-95. Hodge writes about Ladakah in the Himalayas.

16 Spindel, p. 32-33.

17 Serle L. Chapman, ed., *We, the People: Of Earth and Elders* (Missoula: Mountain Press, 2001), p. 223.

18 Carl Waldman, *Atlas of the North American Indian* (New York: Facts on File, 1995), p. 155.

19 Ralph K. Andrist, *The Long Death: The Last Days of the Plains Indians* (New York, Collier Books, 1964), pp. 343-44.

20 Robert Gough, author's interview, Sept. 3, 2002.

21 Martina Greywind was a Spirit Lake woman who was extensively covered on the front pages of the *Fargo Forum* for almost two weeks in 1993. Her problems of substance abuse and pregnancy became a spectacle of the antiabortion movement and the city of Fargo's law enforcement. See, for example, Tom Pantera, "Drug Addict Offered Thousands to Keep Her Baby," *Fargo Forum,* Jan. 19, 2003.

22 Andrew Brownstein, "A Battle Over a Name in the Land of the Sioux," *The Chronicle of Higher Education,* Feb. 23, 2001, p. A46.

23 Spindel, p. 28.

24 Holly Annis, "Fighting the 'Fighting Sioux' Tradition," *Native Directions,* Vol. 6, No. 2, (Spring 1999), p.2.

25 Annis.

26 Itancan'Win, "Looking A Gift Horse In The Mouth," *Native Directions,* Vol. 7, No. 2 (Spring 2000), p. 2.

27 Brownstein.

28 Brownstein.

29 Annis.

30 Annis, p. 3.

31 Annis.

32 Brownstein.

33 Doug Grow, "Do As I Say, Donor Says, Or the Puck Stops Here," *Minneapolis Star Tribune,* Jan. 17, 2001, p. 2B.

34 Lucy Gange, author's interview, Oct. 12, 2001.

35 Gange.

36 Gange.

37 Alex and Debbie White Plume, author's interview, Feb. 18, 2003.

38 Mark Anthony Rolo, ed., *The American Indian and the Media,* (New York: National Conference for Community and Justice, 2000), pp. 27-28.

39 Jensen.

40 Robert Gough, "Application of Lakota Customary Law in the Protection of Culturally Based Property Rights: The Case of Crazy Horse Malt Liquor," (unpublished paper) p. 5.

41 Heidi Bell Gease, "Stroh Apologizes for Crazy Horse Brew," *Rapid City Journal,* April 26, 2001, available at: http://www.rapidcityjournal.com/articles/2001/04/26/news01.txt.

42 Gough interview. For more on Crazy Horse's death, see Edward Kadlecek and Mabell Kadlecek, *To Kill an Eagle: Indian Views on the Last Days of Crazy Horse* (Boulder: Johnson Books,1982).

43 Gough, "Application of Lakota Customary Law."

44 Gary Brause, author's interview, Oct. 29, 2001.

45 Gough, "Application of Lakota Customary Law," p. 17.

46 Seth H. Big Crow, Crazy Horse Defense Project,
    http://www.crazyhorsedefense.org/menu3a.html.

47 Patricia D. Mail and Saundra Johnson, "Boozing, Sniffing, and Toking: An
    Overview of Past, Present, and Future of Substance Abuse by American
    Indians," *American Indian and Alaskan Native Mental Health Research,* Vol. 5, No.
    2 (1993), p. 16.

48 Robert Gough, personal correspondence with author, April 15, 2005.

49 Gough interview.

50 Gough interview.

51 Jensen.

Three Sisters

1   Rowen White "Haudenosaunee Native Seed Conservation," (master's thesis,
    Hampshire College, 2001), chapter 1, p. 1.

2   White, chapter 6, p. 1.

3   Stephen Lewandowski, "Diohe'ko, The Three Sisters in Seneca life:
    implications for a native agriculture in the Finger Lakes region of New York
    State," *Agriculture and Human Values,* Vol. 4, No. 2/3 (Spring/Summer 1987), p.
    76-93.

4   Bernadette Hill, author's interview, Feb. 7, 2002.

5   Frederick Cook, ed., *Journals of the Military Expedition of Major General John
    Sullivan against the Six Nations of Indians in 1779* (1887; repr., Bowie MD:
    Heritage Books, 2000), pp. 296-303.

6   Timothy T. Shaw, "Refugees of Niagara 1779-1780: The Winter of Hunger,
    Sullivan-Clinton Campaign: 1779-2005," available at:
    http://www.sullivanclinton.com/texts/articles/archives/000072.php

7   F.W. Waugh, *Iroquois Foods and Food Preparation,* (1913; repr., Honolulu:
    University Press of the Pacific, 2003), p. 5.

8   Jack Rossen, author's interview, Feb. 6, 2002.

9   Dave Tobin, "George Washington's Campaign of Terror," *Syracuse Post
    Standard,* Aug. 20, 2002, page B1.

10 Tobin.

11 Cook, p. 567.

12 Bob Herbert, "In America; Justice, 200 Years Later," *New York Times,* Nov. 26,
    2001, pg. A17.

13 Jack Rossen, author's interview, Feb. 6, 2002.

14 Clint Halftone, author's interview, Feb. 7, 2002.

15 Meghan McCune, "From Monocrop to Monoculture: The Cultural Famine of Monocropping in Cayuga County," (senior thesis, Wells College, 2003), p. 33.

16 Michael Winerip, "Perennial Hope of New York's Scattered Cayuga Tribe - Land," *New York Times,* Aug. 10, 1984, p. B1.

17 Herbert.

18 Paul DeMain, author's interview, Nov. 25, 2002; See also William Kates, "Pataki puts land claim settlements on hold," Associated Press State and Local Wire, Syracuse NY, April 15, 2005.

19 This and other quotes from Julie Uticoke are from author's interview, Dec. 27, 2002.

20 This and other quotes from Brooke Olson are from author's interview, Feb. 6, 2002.

21 Jack Rossen.

22 White, chapter 7, p. 15.

23 This and other quotes from Tom Porter are from author's interview, Feb. 5, 2002.

24 Jan Swart, author's interview, Feb. 5, 2002.

25 Carol Cornelius, *Iroquois Corn in a Culture-Based Curriculum: A Framework for Respectfully Teaching about Cultures,* (Albany: State University of New York Press, 1998), p. 194.

26 White, chapter 7, p. 16.

27 Doug George-Kanentiio, "History of the Onyota'aka Oneida," Oneidas for Democracy, available at: www.oneidasfordemocracy.org/history.htm.

28 Oneida Indian Nation, "Culture and History, Notes from the Past" website: http://www.oneida-nation.net/notes.html

29 DeMain.

30 White, chapter 7, p. 14.

31 Paul Smith, author's interview, March 30, 2001.

32 Haudenosaunee Enviromental Task Force, "Words That Come before All Else, Environmental Philosophies of the Haudenosaunee," (Rooseveltown, NY: Haudenosaunee Enviromental Task Force, 1999), p. 75.

33 White, chapter 9, pp. 9, 19.

Wild Rice

1 This and other quotes from Spud Fineday are from author's interview, Sept. 17, 1997.

2   Greg Breining, "The Puzzling Loss of Wild Rice," *Minnesota Volunteer,* July-Aug. 1992.

3   Albert Jenks, "The Wild Rice Gatherers of the Upper Lakes: A Study in American Primitive Economics," *Nineteenth Annual Report of the Bureau of American Ethnology,* (Washington: Government Printing Office, 1900), p. 1094, available at: http://content.wisconsinhistory.org/cgi-bin/docviewer.exe?CISOROOT=/tp &CISOPTR=5447.

4   Jenks, pp. 1073-74 (quoting a letter from Pelican Lake, WI, settler J. Motzfeldt, Dec. 3, 1898) and pp. 1112-13.

5   Quoted in Frank Clancy, "Wild Rice Case Study" (unpublished paper, University of Minnesota), 2001.

6   Elizabeth H. Winchell and Reynold P. Dahl, *Wild Rice: Production, Prices and Marketing,* (University of Minnesota: Agricultural Experiment Station, 1984) p.6.

7   This and other quotes from Jerry Schochenmaier are from author's interview, Aug. 1, 2001.

8   Frank Bibeau, author's interview, Aug. 10, 2001.

9   Gene Adding, author's interview, June 27, 2001.

10 Joe LaGarde, author's interview, June 11, 2001.

11 W. C. Kennard, R.C. Phillips, R.A. Porter, A.W. Grombacher, "A Comparative Map of Wild Rice," *Theoretical Applied Genetics,* Vol. 101 (2000), pp. 677-684.

12 Minnesota Senate, Agriculture, Veterans and Gaming Committee, March 16, 2005.

13 Sharon Schmickle, "Genomics May Give Wild Rice a Legitimate Claim to its Name," *Star Tribune,* Nov. 27, 2000, p. 4.

14 Lynn Senior, "The New Biotechnology Frontier," (paper presented at the seventh Farm Journal Forum, Washington D.C., Dec. 3-4, 2002.

15 The Australian research team was led by M. Abedinia, R.J. Henry, A.B. Blakeney, and L.G. Lewin at Southern Cross University.

16 Doreen Stabinsky, "Transgenic Maize in Mexico: Two Updates," *GeneWatch* Vol. 15, No. 4 (July 2002), available at: http://www.gene-watch.org/genewatch/volume15.html.

17 This number shrinks to 5% in some crops.

18 Vandana Shiva, "Golden Rice and Neem: Biopatents and the Appropriation of Women's Environmental Knowledge," *Women's Studies Quarterly,* Vol. 29, Nos. 1-2 (Spring/Summer 2001), p. 14.

19 John Pershell, author's interview, Dec. 28, 2001.

20 Schmickle, p. 3.

21 Breining, p. 12.

22 Richard Phillips, author's interview, June 7, 2001.

23 Peter Ritter, "A Rice by Any Other Name," *Minneapolis/St. Paul City Pages,* Sept. 27, 2000, p. 6, available at: http://citypages.com/databank/21/1034/article9005.asp.

24 LaGarde.

25 Norman W. Deschampe, letter to Mark G. Yudof on behalf of the Minnesota Chippewa tribe, Sept. 8, 1998.

26 www1.umn.edu/systemwide/research2.html, accessed on Feb. 26, 2002.

27 University-generated rice varieties include: 1968 Johnson, 1970 Ml, 1972 M2, 1974 M3, 1978 Netum, 1983 Voyager, 1986 Meter, 1992 Franklin, and 2000 Petrowske Purple.

28 A 2004 study of genetically modified creeping bentgrass, used on golf courses, found that the GMO version (produced by Monsanto) outcrossed into wild varieties. Lidia S. Watrud, E. Henry Lee, Anne Fairbrother, Connie Burdick, Jay R. Reichman, Mike Bollman, Marjorie Storm, George King, and Peter K. Van de Water., "Evidence for landscape-level, pollen-mediated gene flow from genetically modified creeping bentgrass with CP4 EPSPS as a marker," *Proceedings of the National Academy of Science,* Vol. 101, No. 40, (Oct. 5, 2004).

29 Clancy.

30 Abraham Lama, "Law to Protect Native Intellectual Property," *IPS News Bulletin,* Jan. 12, 2000, available at: http//www.ips.org.

31 Lama.

32 Indigenous Peoples Council on Biocolonialism, "Indigenous Research Protection Act," available at: http://www.ipcb.org/pdf_files/irpa.doc.

33 Stephanie Howard, "Life, Lineage and Sustenance/Indigenous Peoples and Genetic Engineering: Threats to Food, Agriculture, and the Environment," Indigenous People's Council on Biocolonialism, Sept. 2001, p. 14, available at: http://www.ipcb.org/pdf_files/LifeLineageandSustenance.pdf

34 Breining, p. 9.

35 Thomas Vennum, *Wild Rice and the Ojibway People* (Saint Paul: Minnesota Historical Society Press, 1988), p. 290.

36 Anastasia M. Shkilnyk, *A Poison Stronger than Love: The Destruction of an Ojibwe Community* (New Haven: Yale University Press, 1985), p. 189.

37 For an update on Cass Lake, see St. Regis Paper Community Reuse Planning Project, Land Use Committee Meeting, March 22, 2005, available at: http://www.epa.gov/Region5/sites/stregis/pdfs/stregis-reuse-planning-20050 322b.pdf.

38 Vennum, p. 292.

39 Kevin Brewster, "Where the Food Grows upon the Water," *Ojibwe Akiing* (Hayward, WI: Indian Country Communications, 2001), p. 7.

40 Al Gedicks, "What You Should Know about Exxon/Rio Algom's Proposed Mine at Crandon/Mole Lake," Wisconsin Resources Protection Council briefing paper, 1999, available at: http://www.wrpc.net/reports.html.

41 Gedicks, *New Resource Wars* (Boston: South End Press, 1993), p. 61.

42 Gedicks, "What You Should Know"

43 Gedicks, *New Resource Wars*, p. 67.

44 Ervin Oelke, author's interview, March 20, 2001.

45 Oelke interview.

46 Paul Schultz, in meeting with Charles Muscoplat, UM vice president of agricultural policy, at University of Minnesota, Black Bear Crossing, St. Paul, MN, Sept. 22, 2003.

47 Eugene Davis, author's interview, Sept. 29, 2001.

Food As Medicine

1 Lorelei Decora., author's interview, June 18, 1998.

2 Rowen White, "Haudenosaunee Native Seed Conservation," (master's thesis, Hampshire College, 2001), chapter 1, p. 3.

3 Frances Densmore, *Chippewa Customs* (St. Paul: Minnesota Historical Society Press, 1929), p. 39.

4 Valerius Geist, *Buffalo Nation: History and Legend of the North American Bison* (Stillwater, MN: Voyageur Press, l996), p. 91.

5 Ralph Andrist, *The Long Death: The Last Days of the Plains Indians* (New York: Collier Books, 1964), p. 30.

6 Andrist, pp. 30-31.

7 White, chapter 8, p. 2.

8 Cate Montana, "Project develops Native American food systems models," *Indian Country Today,* Aug. 30, 2000, available at: http://www.indiancountry.com/content.cfm?id=2482.

9 Montana.

10 Harriet Kuhnlein, "Culture and Ecology in Dietetics and Nutrition," *Journal of the American Dietetic Association,* Vol. 89, No. 8 (1989), pp. 1059-60.

11 Gitigaaning Project Proposal to the VISTA Program, 2003.

12 Micheal Higgins, "Native People Take on Diabetes," *East West Magazine,* Vol. 21, No. 4 (April 1991), p. 94.

13 Amy C. Brown and Barrett Brenton, "Dietary Survey of Hopi Native American Elementary Children," *Journal of the American Dietetic Association,* Vol. 94, No. 5 (May 1994), p. 518.

14 Higgins.

15 Higgins.

16 Dee Brown, in *Bury My Heart at Wounded Knee* (New York: Henry Holt, 1970), writes: "Before returning to Fort Canby, Carson ordered complete destruction of Navaho properties within [Canyon de Chelly]—including their fine peach orchards, more than five thousand trees. The Navahos could forgive the Rope Thrower [Carson] for fighting them as a soldier, for making prisoners of them, even for destroying their food supplies, but the one act they never forgave him for was cutting down their beloved peach trees" (p. 27).

17 Clyde Kluckhohn and Dorothea Leighton, *The Navajo* (Garden City, NY: Anchor Books, 1942), p. 41.

18 Ruth Roessel, *Navajo Livestock Reduction: A National Disgrace* (Chinle, AZ: Navajo Community College Press, 1974), p. 39-50.

19 Roessel, p. 224.

20 Roessel, p. 221.

21 *Keepseagle v. Veneman,* D.C. District Court, Civil Action 99-03119 (2001).

22 Peter Hanson, "The Traditional Diet and American Indian Health," *Masinai'gan* (Great Lakes Indian Fish and Wildlife newsletter), Sept. 2003, p. 4.

23 Higgins.

24 W.S. Wolfe and Diva Sanjur, "Contemporary diet and body weight of Navajo women receiving food assistance: an ethnographic and nutritional investigation," *Journal of the American Dietetic Association*, Vol. 88, No. 7 (July 1988), pp. 822-27.

25 U.S. Government Accountability Office, "Audits of the Commodity Food Area," TRCED-90-15, Nov. 15, 1989, p. 11.

26 Brown and Brenton, p. 520.

27 Brown and Brenton, p. 521.

28 Gary Paul Nabhan, personal correspondence with author, April 6, 2005.

29 David Fazzino, "Traditional Foods: Revitalization of Health and Culture amongst the Tohoho O'odham Via NGO Interventions," National Science Foundation grant proposal, p. 1.

30 Nabhan, personal correspondence.

31 Higgins.

32 Hanson, p. 22.

33 The walk was covered on the internet day by day, and was featured in the *New York Times* and *Boston Globe,* and on *Scientific American Frontiers* television and *Living on Earth* radio.

34 The Renewing America's Food Traditions Campaign, co-sponsored by the Cultural Conservancy, Slow Food USA, and Native Seeds/SEARCH, is now reviving the use of many more of these foods, promoting them through Slow Foods Ark of Taste.

35 This and other quotes from Sally Auger are from an interview conducted by the author, June 18, 2003.

36 This and other quotes from Paul Red Elk are from an interview conducted by the author, June 18, 2003.

37 Cora Baker, letter to Dream of Wild Health, Feb. 1997.

38 Craig Hassel, "Good Nutrition at Harvest Time," Dream of Wild Health newsletter (St. Paul, MN), Vol. 3 (Nov. 2003).

39 Margaret Smith, author's interview, March 2, 2003.

40 Laura Shapiro, "Do Our Genes Determine Which Foods We Should Eat?" *Newsweek,* Vol. 122, No. 6 (Aug. 9, 1993) p. 64.

41 This and other quotes from Luis Salas are from author's interview, July 23, 2003.

42 Joy Scheibel, author's interview, March 13, 2002.

43 Nabhan, personal correspondence.

Return of the Horse Nation

1 Nez Perce Tribe, Environmental Restoration and Waste Management Department, *Treaties: Nez Perce Perspecives* (Lewiston, ID: Confluence Press, 2003), p. 16.

2 Nez Perce Tribe, p. 70.

3 Nez Perce Tribe, p. 20.

4 Ike Boone, "The Nez Perce Horse," Emerald Racing Fan Zone–Horse Tales web site: http://www.emeraldracing.com/boone120699.html.

5 Nez Perce Tribe, p. 21.

6 Nez Perce Tribe, p. 23.

7 Nez Perce Tribe, p. 38.

8 Nez Perce Tribe, p. 40.

9 Nez Perce Tribe, p. 37.

10 Carl Waldman, *Atlas of the North American Indian* (New York: Facts on File, 1995), p. 133.

11 Waldman.

12 Vicki Monks, "The Long Ride Home, After 120 Years the Nez Perce Return to the Land of Chief Joseph," *Land and People*, (Trust for Public Lands), Fall 1997, p. 5.

13 Monks.

14 Dee Brown, *Bury My Heart at Wounded Knee* (New York: Henry Holt, 1970), p. 328-9.

15 Nez Perce Tribe, p. 55.

16 Beth Hege Piatote, "A Circle of Words, Two Families Honor a Gesture to Chief Joseph," *Native Americas,* Vol. 15, No. 1 (Spring 1998), p. 41.

17 Piatote, p. 41.

18 Piatote, p. 41.

19 Piatote, p. 44.

20 Keith Soy Red Thunder, author's interview, Nov. 11, 2000.

21 This and other quotes from Rudy Shebala are from the author's interview, Nov. 17, 2000.

22 Boone.

23 Nez Perce Tribe, p. 22.

24 Nez Perce Tribe, p. 9.

25 Monks, p. 8.

26 Monks, p. 6.

27 Monks, p. 4.

28 Monks.

29 Monks, p. 6.

30 Monks.

Namewag

1 A good source of Anishinaabeg folk tales is Basil Johnson, *Ojibwe Heritage* (Lincoln: University of Nebraska Press, 1990).

2 Tim Holzkamm, author's interview, June 23, 1998.

3 Gary Huberty, author's interview, June 23, 1998.

4 Paul Bellecourt, author's interview, June 29, 1998.

5 Joe Hunter, author's interview, May 12, 1998.

6 Sue Erickson, "Joint Effort Pumps Lake Sturgeon into Bad River System," *Masina'igan: A Chronicle of Lake Superior Ojibwe,* (Odenah, WI: Great Lakes Indian Fish and Wildlife Commision), Summer 2000.

7   Charlie Otto Rasmussen, "Lake Superior Sturgeon Population Gets Boost from Red Cliff Hatchery," *Masina'igan: A Chronicle of Lake Superior Ojibwe,* (Odenah, WI: Great Lakes Indian Fish and Wildlife Commision), Fall 2001.

8   Tomas Gulyas, author's interview, May 12, 1998.

9   Randy Zortman, author's interview, May 20 1998.

10 Greg Fischer, author's interview, May 20, 1998.

11 Joe Bush, author's interview, May 15, 2001.

Recovering Power to Slow Climate Change

1   Richard Douthwaite, *Short Circuit* (Dublin: Lilliput Press, 1996), p. 179.

2   Angie Debo, *And Still the Waters Run* (Princeton: Princeton University Press, 1940), p. 86.

3   Debo, p. 67.

4   George Monbiot, "Bottom of the Barrel," *The Guardian,* Dec. 2, 2003. The 2004 estimate is from geologist Kenneth Deffeyes and the 2037 projection is from the U.S. Department of Energy.

5   "The Slumbering Giants Awake," *The Economist,* Feb. 8, 2001, available at: http://www.economist.com/surveys/displayStory.cfm?Story_id=497418.

6   Brenda Norrell, "Four Corner Power Plant Fouling Navajo Air," *Indian Country Today,* June 14, 2000.

7   Energy Information Administration, "Energy Consumption and Renewable Energy Development Potential on Indian Lands," U.S. Department of Energy, available at: http://www.eia.doe.gov/cneaf/solar.renewables/ilands/ilands.pdf.

8   "Pearl Jam Hug the Trees," ChartAttack.com, April 28, 2003, available at: www.chartattack.com/damn/2003/04/2807.cfm. To estimate your own carbon footprint, go to www.nativeenergy.com/carbon_calculator_both.htm.

9   Pat Spears, author's interview, Dec. 10, 2002.

10 Alex White Plume, author's interview, Feb. 18, 2003.

11 Debbie White Plume, author's interview, Feb. 18, 2003.

12 Robert Gough, author's interview, Sept. 3, 2002.

13 Natural Resources Defense Council, Coalition for Environmentally Responsible Economies, and Public Service Enterprise Group, "Benchmarking Air Emissions of the 100 Largest Electric Generation Owners in the U.S.—2000," March 2002, p. 18.

14 Norrell.

15 States which have adopted a Renewable Energy Portfolio include Massachusetts, Maine, New Jersey, Colorado, Iowa, Minnesota, and eight others.

16 Fidel Moreno, "In the Arctic, Ice is Life-And it's Disappearing," *Native Americas*, Vol. 16, Nos. 42-45, (Fall/Winter), 1999/2000.

17 "Impacts of Climate Change To Cost The World Over $300 Billion A Year," United Nations Environment Programme press release, Jan. 5, 2001, available at: http://www.un.org/news/press/docs/2001/ENGDEV559.doc.htm.

18 Ross Gelbspan, *Boiling Point* (New York: Basic Books, 2004), p. 112.

19 Dune Lankard, author's interview, Feb. 13, 2003.

20 Scott DeCarlo, "Pay vs. Performance," *Forbes,* May 13, 2002, available at: http://www.forbes.com/finance/lists/12/2002/LIR.jhtml?passListId=12&pa ssYear=2002&passListType=Person&uniqueId=UZ74&datatype=Person.

21 Karen Button, *It's Your Right-to-Know! Your Community's Exposure to Toxics* (Anchorage: Alaska Community Action on Toxics, 2002), p. 39.

22 Violet Yeaton, author's interview, Feb 12, 2003.

23 Robert Thompson, author's interview, Feb. 13, 2003.

24 Clayton Thomas-Muller, author's interview, Feb. 10, 2003.

25 "Here and Now," *The Economist,* Feb. 8, 2001.

26 "The Slumbering Giants Awake."

27 Bob Gough at United Southern and Eastern Tribes meeting, Washington, D.C., Februrary 4, 2003.

28 More information on the "Declaration of Energy Independence," is available from the International Council for Local Environmental Initiatives, http://www.iclei.org/us/ and from Honor the Earth, http://www.honorearth.org/initiatives/energy/independenceday.html.

29 Michigan Interfaith Power and Light web site, http://www.miipl.org.

30 To learn more about what green tags are and how they are retired, go to http://www. ems.org/renewables/green_tags.html.

31 The Institute for America's Future, The Center on Wisconsin Strategy, and The Perryman Group, "The Apollo Jobs Report: For Good Jobs & Energy Independence," The Apollo Alliance, Jan., 2004, p.7, available at: http://www.apolloalliance.org/docUploads/ApolloReport%2Epdf.

32 Oliver Red Cloud, author's interview, Sept. 19 2003.

Index

About the Author

Winona LaDuke became involved with Native American environmental issues after meeting Jimmy Durham, a well-known Cherokee activist, while she was attending Harvard University. At the age of 18, she spoke in front of the United Nations regarding Native American rights and has remained one of the most prominent voices for American Indian economic and environmental concerns. She is an Anishinaabekwe (Ojibwe) enrolled member of the Mississippi Band Anishinaabeg, who lives and works on the White Earth Reservations. LaDuke is the Executive Director of the White Earth Land Recovery Project and Honor the Earth, where she works on a national level to advocate, raise public support, and create funding for frontline native environmental groups. In 1994, Winona was named by *TIME* magazine as one of America's fifty most promising leaders under forty years of age. In both 1996 and 2000 she was Ralph Nader's running mate in his Presidential campaigns, appearing on the Green Party ticket. A graduate of Harvard and Antioch Universities, LaDuke has written extensively on Native American and environmental issues. She is a former board member of Greenpeace USA and serves as co-chair of the Indigenous Women's Network, a North American and Pacific indigenous women's organization. She is the author of six books, including *The Militarization of Indian Country* (2011); *Recovering the Sacred: the Power of Naming and Claiming* (2005), and a novel, *Last Standing Woman* (1997, Voyager Press).

About Haymarket Books

Haymarket Books is a nonprofit, progressive book distributor and publisher, a project of the Center for Economic Research and Social Change. We believe that activists need to take ideas, history, and politics into the many struggles for social justice today. Learning the lessons of past victories, as well as defeats, can arm a new generation of fighters for a better world. As Karl Marx said, "The philosophers have merely interpreted the world; the point, however, is to change it."

We take inspiration and courage from our namesakes, the Haymarket Martyrs, who gave their lives fighting for a better world. Their 1886 struggle for the eight-hour day reminds workers around the world that ordinary people can organize and struggle for their own liberation.

For more information and to shop our complete catalog of titles, visit us online at www.haymarketbooks.org.

Also Available from Haymarket Books

Brazil's Dance with the Devil: The World Cup, the Olympics, and the Struggle for Democracy
Updated Olympics Edition; Dave Zirin

Ecology and Socialism: Solutions to Capitalist Ecological Crisis
Chris Williams

Ecosocialism: A Radical Alternative to Capitalist Catastrophe
Michael Löwy

Floodlines: Community and Resistance from Katrina to the Jena Six
Jordan Flaherty, preface by Tracie Washington, foreword by Amy Goodman

Kivalina: A Climate Change Story
Christine Shearer

Marx and Nature: A Red and Green Perspective
Paul Burkett, foreword by John Bellamy Foster

Myths of Male Dominance: Collected Articles on Women Cross-Culturally
Eleanor Burke Leacock

Recovering the Sacred: The Power of Naming and Claiming
Winona LaDuke

Too Many People?: Population, Immigration, and the Environmental Crisis
Ian Angus and Simon Butler, forewords by Betsy Hartmann and Joel Kovel